Corporate Governance, Ethics and CSR

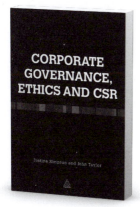

Corporate Governance, Ethics and CSR

Justine Simpson
and John Taylor

KoganPage

LONDON PHILADELPHIA NEW DELHI

First published in Great Britain and the United States in 2013 by Kogan Page Limited

120 Pentonville Road	1518 Walnut Street, Suite 1100	4737/23 Ansari Road
London N1 9JN	Philadelphia PA 19102	Daryaganj
United Kingdom	USA	New Delhi 110002
www.koganpage.com		India

© Justine Simpson and John Taylor, 2013

The right of Justine Simpson and John Taylor to be identified as the authors of this work has been asserted by them in accordance with the Copyright, Designs and Patents Act 1988.

ISBN   978 0 7494 6385 4
E-ISBN   978 0 7494 6386 1

British Library Cataloguing-in-Publication Data

A CIP record for this book is available from the British Library.

Library of Congress Cataloging-in-Publication Data

Simpson, Justine.
    Corporate governance, ethics, and CSR / Justine Simpson and John Taylor.
        p. cm.
    ISBN 978-0-7494-6385-4 – ISBN 978-0-7494-6386-1 (ebk)   1. Corporate governance.
2. Business ethics.   3. Social responsibility of business.   4. Organizational behavior.
I. Taylor, John.   II. Title.
    HD2741.S58 2013
    174'.4–dc23
                                                                    2012029002

Typeset by Graphicraft Limited, Hong Kong
Printed and bound in India by Replika Press Pvt Ltd

CONTENTS

06   Assessing performance and remuneration of directors and senior executives 132

07   The audit function 153

10   Corporate Social Responsibility, its measurement, theories and models 221

11   Small companies, charities and other not-for-profit organizations 241

12   Emerging issues 272

LIST OF FIGURES

LIST OF TABLES

Introduction

The objective of this book is to bring together the three separate strands relevant to the new demands of organizational behaviour and reporting. These are, broadly:

- the principles of good corporate governance, where it came from, what it is and why we need it;
- the ethical framework including reference to personal morality and the dysfunctional organization and how this affects the actual implementation of good corporate governance;
- the links between corporate governance, ethics and Corporate Social Responsibility (CSR), the increased transparency and accountability this brings, why this is a good thing and why companies don't do it.

In short, the book will take an holistic approach to the whole issue of the role of the organization (because it can no longer be confined to companies) in society, its responsibilities to the society within which it operates, its responsibilities to all its stakeholders including its employees and their dependants and the ethical underpinning that has to be in place for any form of honest reporting. It will look not simply at the organization as a reporting entity complying with a set of rules or nebulous concepts but as a functioning part of the business environment.

Most books on corporate governance list, in tedious detail, the principles of good corporate governance, the role of the board, why they need an audit committee etc and, of course this book will have to do that as well, but it will also aim to show:

- how the basic principles of good corporate governance are seen as a good thing by organizations, why they are adopted by most of them but also how they can be abandoned to suit commercial imperatives and how they can be applied selectively to create the illusion of compliance without actually interfering with the power of organizational leaders;

- why companies often acknowledge their commitment to good corporate governance and the principles of Corporate Social Responsibility in their annual financial reports and then go on to do appalling things to the environment or get caught out bribing foreign governments;

- how corrupt practices such as institutional mis-selling of pensions, fraud and low-level theft can become endemic in organizations – and what to do about it;

- how the principles of good reporting can link in with good corporate governance to create an ethical organization.

In short the book aims to look at all the aspects of the functioning organization and internal and external relationships. As stated earlier, the book will include the public sector because it has grown to such a large extent that it is now the major employer in the UK. It will point up the differences and similarities but will also attempt to explain why, despite all the governance, oversight and reporting, many public sector organizations continue to behave dysfunctionally.

Approach

The book will be UK-based because of the legal and regulatory framework in the UK, but many of the principles are universal.

The overall approach will be to make the book as readable as possible with:

- clear demarcation between topics, to facilitate teaching plans, with detailed learning objectives for each chapter;
- diagrammatic representations where possible;
- clear examples of concepts applied in practice;
- case studies.

Justine Simpson and John Taylor

The need for trust

Introduction

In this chapter we start at the very beginning, which, as Julie Andrews observed, is a very good place to start. In order to help us understand the context of the modern corporate structure it is necessary to understand the basic principles it was founded on and which drive it. This will help establish an understanding of the differences between owners and managers and the problems that these differences cause.

If we understand the growth of the modern company we can begin to see what power it has and what influence it can bring to bear on the everyday lives of ordinary people – and just how considerable that influence is.

We can then understand the need for trust and the consequences of violating that trust when:

- owners and others are misled or lied to;
- secrets are concealed not for honourable commercial motives but out of shame or for the personal protection of guilty individuals; and
- companies engage in behaviour that ethical individuals would consider to be unethical or immoral.

We will highlight the need for all of us to trust the individuals who wield real commercial power and to trust what they tell us.

Later in the book we will look at how we can achieve this and why the modern world is beginning to require different forms of corporate behaviour that would have been unrecognizable or, indeed, considered unacceptable less than thirty years ago when corporate titans like Robert Maxwell, 'Tiny' Rowland, Lord Hanson and Asil Nadir bestrode the commercial world like emperors and, like so many before them, faded away, leaving nothing behind but debts or the remnants of once-dominant companies.

Is trade free?

If we are going to explore the ethical questions and the moral dilemmas that organizations may or may not have led us to, let us consider two extreme positions on a global level as this is the context within which modern multinational companies operate.

Proponents of low-level regulation of business and free trade will argue that business, and with it competition, is good, that it brings huge benefits to the world. They will point to scientific discoveries and innumerable products that would not exist without business and competition, everything from computers to chocolate bars, from Valium to the motor car, from electric light and gas central heating to television and newspapers, all of which have been brought about through the desire to create a better product, to compete in the market place, to make or find something that everybody wants – whether they need it or not. Trade, they will argue, has made the world smaller and more accessible. People in the developed West are living longer and have more leisure time and wealth than they have ever had before whilst even in less developed countries individuals formerly doomed to a bleak life of subsistence farming now have the opportunity to work in factories and earn money. They have an opportunity to make a better life for themselves, so the argument goes, as the wealth of those countries grows and more are lifted out of poverty. Proponents of this line of argument point to China and India where economic growth funds welfare and education programmes, where the lot of the average citizen is now considerably better than it was, at least materially, 25 years ago.

Business and trade should therefore be free and unregulated as it is the driver of human progress and betterment. But at what cost? For all the demonstrable improvements to the human condition that trade and business have brought to one part of the world there is an opposing dark side – where there are winners, there are losers. Whilst many in the West may now be living richer, warmer and more fulfilled lives than ever before, in less developed parts of the world people are being exploited to provide that life.

Let us briefly consider precedent. History provides many examples of exploitation of poorer or less developed countries by richer, more advanced ones. Expansion or protection of trade has been one fundamental reason for going to war, not the only one admittedly, but nonetheless one which has had a significant impact. The urge to take from one's neighbour what he or she has and you have not, the drive for possession of desirable goods tempts individuals, be they kings or commoners, into theft – of goods, cities and thrones; possession of raw materials tempts nations into conquest as a way of acquiring those materials and one of the oldest exploitative trades in the world, slavery, has caused misery for millennia. The exploitation of one country by a more powerful one has, for example, led to:

- the depredations wrought by Spain on the kingdoms of Central America for gold and silver;
- the scramble for Africa and the dreadful barbarities perpetrated there by so-called Western civilized nations for land, minerals, diamonds and gold;
- the perceived exploitation of India and its ultimate partition by the British Empire;
- the Chinese incursion into Africa, particularly in oil-rich areas of Angola and Sudan and into the copper mines of Zambia, which some labelled 'neo-colonialism'.

The list appears endless and is all, they say, caused by greed.

Opponents of unfettered capitalism point out that, in the twenty-first century, as global capitalism takes off, the so-called developing countries, particularly Brazil, Russia, India and China (the BRIC nations), are gulping down huge amounts of resources in an effort to catch up with developed

Western nations. The result of this race to riches is an impending unprecedented global catastrophe as the world warms and basic human needs such as water become scarcer in lands that can't keep up or which don't have any natural advantages.

The capitalist trope, partially evidenced it must be said by organizations such as Transparency International, is that greedy individuals, be they entrepreneurs or politicians, will be likely to turn increasingly to fraud and corruption in an attempt to grab wealth for themselves, company managers will pay lip service to their responsibilities to their shareholders and will reward themselves with enormous riches far in excess of what any individual will ever need or realistically may have the right to earn. Opponents of unfettered capitalism claim that, as a result, companies exploit and mislead their customers, selling gimcrack goods as real gold, and, when caught by increasingly powerless regulators, fight attempts to make them pay restitution or even apologize. Transparency International publishes its annual *Corruption Perceptions Index* highlighting countries where, they claim, politicians and business leaders are corrupted by wealth so that, even in the poorest countries, they take from others less able or less fortunate than them. This, it is claimed, is capitalism in all its glory – brutal, unfeeling and corrupt. The price of a good life in the West is paid by the exploited elsewhere.

Of course, nowhere are companies totally free to do what they like, unregulated by government. Regulation may, as some claim, be weak or lacking in scope but it is there and has the potential to become stronger – there is no such thing as unbridled capitalism any more than the communist or socialist states of times past or times present existed in a society where all were equal citizens and were rewarded on merit. There are leanings or tendencies but there are no pure states.

So between these extremes is the terrain occupied by most companies, indeed most organizations. They are neither wholly corrupt nor wholly virtuous – just like the people who control them and the individuals who work for them.

A wider moral imperative?

Let us be clear about one thing from the outset. Company managers can always justify behaviour that some may consider unethical on the grounds that they are fulfilling their duty to shareholders to increase wealth. The first aim of this text is to consider whether management is duty bound to consider a wider moral imperative and to adopt socially responsible attitudes or whether, in the words of Milton Friedman,

> Few trends would so thoroughly undermine the very foundations of our free society as the acceptance by corporate officials of a social responsibility other than to make as much money for their shareholders as they possibly can.
>
> (Friedman, 1962)

Second, if management does accept the need for some social responsibility how far does that responsibility stretch?

Most organizations, if they are being honest, may be forced to admit that their corporate behaviour displays both facets of human behaviour: ethical behaviour most of the time, but engaging in actions that might be unethical but are not actually illegal at other times when it suits them. In one organization it is possible to find a progressive, customer-caring modern business that sources sustainably and looks after its core workers whilst at the same time maximizing results by careful tax planning involving routing profits through tax havens using transfer pricing, quietly suppressing trade union activity and employing lots of sub-contractors and temporary staff who can be ditched when times get tough.

A recent survey by the charity ActionAid reported that 98 of the FTSE top 100 companies had subsidiaries based in tax havens. Directors of these companies will argue that it is their duty to their shareholders to minimize tax; but reducing the tax take for developing countries hampers their efforts to reduce poverty and inequality in those countries as multinationals shovel profits away from them and into low-tax jurisdictions which, incidentally, also tend to have rules that enable those companies to limit the disclosures they have to make regarding those transactions.

Where does the moral imperative lie – do companies have a wider duty of care to the world at large than they do to their own shareholders? Charities such as ActionAid and organizations such as the Organisation for Economic Co-operation and Development claim that the use of tax havens damages developing countries, but do companies that operate in those countries and make profits there have a moral obligation to pay tax there, when they can, through the use of tax havens, preserve value for their shareholders? Is it their responsibility to aid development or to make profits?

There are four issues that we will look at in detail:

1 How the management of companies has become separated from ownership and the implications of that. This is what has become known as 'agency theory' and we look at this in more detail later in this chapter.

2 The influence of corporate culture on the behaviour of individuals and how dysfunctional organizations can, in striving to meet corporate goals, compel individuals to engage in behaviour that outside work they would find reprehensible and unacceptable, such as bullying or corruption.

3 The conflict between the perceived duty of a director to maximize value for the shareholder, and actions that may be ethical but which could be costly and reduce shareholder value. An example of this may be our earlier example of companies reducing tax payments through the use of tax havens that are perfectly legal and which preserve profits in the company, but deprive the home nation of much needed tax revenues that could be used to fund social welfare programmes.

4 How modern companies are coming under pressure to take on some of the responsibilities of ownership and to act like corporate citizens with a moral code. The attitudes espoused by Friedman, above, are, at least publicly, frowned upon by most corporate managers nowadays and most would acknowledge that they owe something to the wider community and have some level of social responsibility that is greater than the compulsion of regulation. Cynics may point out that demonstrated social efforts make good PR and that's why companies do it, but that's not the point – the point is that it is good PR because contemporary Western society has expectations of companies and is pleased to see them met even if the company uses the occasion to boast.

We will consider these themes throughout the book but first we must look at how we got to where we are today – the past informs the present. We will look at the development of corporate governance later; here we will look at the corporate form itself and the intrinsic dilemmas within it.

The history of the company

Throughout most of history trade has been a personal thing – individual merchants or informal caravans traded with their neighbours or across boundaries, often opening up vast trade routes across what were then uncharted lands and seas. As is the nature of such ventures, individuals either made money or suffered loss without any form of protection. Ships sank, pirates and bandits attacked trade routes, agents disappeared with funds, goods turned out to be of worse quality than expected – the risks were endless, but the rewards could be considerable. In renaissance Italy the Medici pioneered new forms of banking, and reputedly invented the bill of exchange to reduce the need for shipments of cash, developments that helped fuel the insatiable desire for trade to meet the increasing demands of populations discovering that there were many interesting and exciting things in the world to eat, wear or smell.

By the middle of the nineteenth century an entrepreneur wishing to risk their capital in a commercial venture had few choices. They could risk their own money and pledge their assets to secure further borrowings, rather like small business people do to this day, or they could go into partnership with other like-minded souls and so spread the risk, assuming they could find enough people to assist in financing the venture, which required a deal of trust and no little faith that all would turn out well.

It was in England in the middle of the nineteenth century that the modern corporate form was invented. A company trades in law as a legal person, a single entity that comprises the investments of its members. The Crown has always had the right to grant charters of incorporation and such companies had, prior to 1844, to be set up either by Act of Parliament or by Royal Charter. The would-be entrepreneur had to have friends in high places and a large amount of capital in order to establish any serious business venture, particularly one involving international trade. Charter companies were not really comparable with the modern corporate form as they had both political and financial considerations affecting their actions; in effect they were often a form of unofficial extension of government or royal policy.

The great advantage of the Charter of Incorporation was that the granting of the charter conferred a legal personality on the company as distinct from the individuals who owned it and thus some measure of protection against debt. Most importantly though it also guaranteed a monopoly of trade, thus creating an opportunity for the members to attain riches if they were prepared to take some, not inconsiderable, risks.

Despite the bureaucratic difficulties many well-known companies were set up in this way. Perhaps the most famous were:

- the Honourable East India Company, granted exclusive trading rights in the East Indies by Royal Charter in 1600 and, arguably, inadvertent founder of the British Empire;
- the Governor and Company of Adventurers of England trading into Hudson's Bay formed by Royal Charter in 1670, later known as the Hudson's Bay Company, famous for opening up Canada and stimulating the market for fur;

- the Company of Merchants of Great Britain trading in the South Seas – or the South Sea Company – formed in 1711, legendary stock operator, creator of the South Sea Bubble, and harbinger of things to come. It is estimated that, at its height, the total value invested in the South Sea Company reached £500m at eighteenth-century prices, twice the value of all the land in England at that time.

Of all of these it was the South Sea Company that had the most profound effect on the corporate governance of the day. There was huge speculation in the affairs of the company, fuelled by claims (which later proved to be fraudulent) that led to a massive investing frenzy, which ended catastrophically. The company crashed and many speculators were ruined. It was the Enron of its day, and just as Enron prompted the Sarbanes–Oxley legislation in the USA in the twenty-first century, so in the eighteenth century the government of the day passed, in 1720, the so-called 'Bubble Act' in order to prevent further fraudulent activity.

This Act provided that all commercial undertakings (both corporations and partnerships) 'tending to the common grievance, prejudice and inconvenience of His Majesty's subjects' would be illegal and void. The Act also banned speculative buying and selling of shares and outlawed stock broking in such shares. Between 1720 and 1825, when the Bubble Act was repealed, shares could only legally be sold to persons genuinely taking over a role in running the corporation or partnership. The problem was that whilst this Act suppressed unincorporated quasi-companies it did nothing to provide any alternative form of legal structure that could be used as a vehicle for trade.

Between 1720 and 1844 new businesses, which might previously have been incorporated, were operated effectively as partnerships based on an elaborate Deed of Settlement. In law these were classed as partnerships and the partners were, accordingly, jointly and severally liable for the debts of the business.

However, as the eighteenth century progressed and the industrial economy grew rapidly, driven by technological advances in textiles and the smelting of iron, there developed a need for expansion of transport links, which took the form of canals and waterways, to move goods and raw materials to the new manufacturing centres and markets of England. The problem was that, because of the Bubble Act, ordinary investors were not readily prepared to put up the money if it meant that they might ultimately be responsible for all debts and liabilities of the business if it failed. The risks were often seen as too high to outweigh the possibility of reward. The governments of the day either could not or would not finance these much-needed developments, so many of these very early transport infrastructure projects were funded by wealthy landowning individuals and banks who often looked at the wealth and reputation of the company's backers before deciding to invest.

An answer was needed and the corporate form appeared ideal. Parliament began to approve specific corporations to be created by Act of Parliament (Statutory Corporations). An Act of Parliament would authorize the creation of a corporation for a specific and narrow purpose and allow it to bring and defend legal actions in its own name, so protecting the financiers from personal responsibility should the corporation fail.

In 1844 Parliament approved the Act for the Registration, Incorporation and Regulation of Joint Stock Companies, which granted legal status to a corporate form that could raise finance through the issue of shares. This form was never considered totally satisfactory as investors still had unlimited liability so, after several enquiries and parliamentary reports, in 1855 the Limited Liability Act established the limit of liability for investors as being confined to the sum invested and no more. In 1856, from which we can really date the modern corporate form, Parliament passed another Joint Stock Companies Act, which allowed any company, with or without limited liability, to be formed by seven or more individuals.

This was effectively superseded by the Companies Act 1862 and, after that, a landmark case, *Salomon v A Salomon Co Ltd (1897) AC22*, firmly established the principle that a limited company has a distinct personality separate from its members.

By the beginning of the twentieth century the legal position was absolutely clear. A company was a distinct legal person, its investors could lose no more than they invested and the managers or directors of the company were trusted to run the business for the benefit of its investors.

Various Companies Acts have followed since then. In turn each one made its mark by:

- tightening the legal restrictions on directors and on the company itself;
- setting rules concerning the issues of shares and the payment of dividends;
- requiring financial statements to undergo an audit by an independent auditor;
- setting the rules for minimum capital requirements for public companies;

- regulating the content of accounts, increasing accounting disclosure, the requirements for accounts preparation and the records to be kept.

The expansion of legislation has increased the level of compliance required and the consequent need for companies to create financial systems to both gather and present the information legally required and to control its internal financial procedures. Legislation has continued to this day, culminating in the mammoth Companies Act 2006, the largest piece of legislation ever passed in the UK.

Limited liability

At this point it is worth looking at some facets of an intense debate that raged in the mid-nineteenth century because elements of it still resound today. The debate centred on the question of limited liability, the principle that an investor loses only their investment should the company fail and consequently the remainder of their worldly goods are safe.

At the time, the arguments for and against limited liability were widely fought and were a serious obstacle to the immediate passing of the 1855 Act limiting liability. The context of this is connected to what has been described as the 'laissez faire' principle. This does not, as some would have it, mean that anything goes or that trade should have an element within it of blind chance. What the Victorians meant by laissez faire was that regulation should be kept to a minimum compatible with the operation of the market. Robert Lowe, Vice President of the Board of Trade, who introduced the 1856 Companies Act, stated:

> When the political economists say 'laissez faire', they do not mean to say
> 'Leave all to blind chance; let everything go on as it may'. What they mean by
> 'laissez faire' is, that we are not to interfere with human laws where other laws,
> so much wiser, already exist.
>
> (Hansard, 1856, vol. 140, col. 136)

In fact, what Lowe believed in was legislation to punish fraudulent companies and legislation to compel publicity about a company's backers so that investors would know who was behind the company – and that was all.

Opponents of limited liability felt that such a thing was a distortion of the free market as it would reduce the penalties for failure, thus encouraging charlatans and fraudsters. J.W. Gilbart of the London & Westminster Bank was firm in his belief:

The righteous Governor of the world must reward the good and punish the wicked whether those actions are performed by public bodies, or private individuals. But the public companies who now perform good or evil actions will not exist in a future world. Therefore public companies must be rewarded or punished in the present world ... it is only in the present world that such collective bodies can in their corporate capacity be either punished or rewarded.

(Gilbart, 1846)

The religious overtones are unmistakably Victorian, but what Gilbart was saying was that the moral or ethical course was that failure or fraud should be punished, not protected. The 'future world' he refers to is a religious expression of Christian salvation, not a prediction about the actions of directors in the twenty-first century!

Proponents believed that granting limited liability status to companies enabled them to work freely in the market, and the protection it afforded would encourage trade and promote growth and wealth. Those who opposed it took the view that the guarantee of a company's probity and moral worth was the personal wealth and reputation of its shareholders, who, in Lord Eldon's frequently quoted formula, were responsible 'to the last shilling and the last acre' for paying its debts. Their view was summed up thus:

For example, under our existing law, if a house [ie a bank] in Glasgow or Belfast, known to have partners of substance, send an order to a London merchant, he executes that order at once on the credit of the wealthy partners ... But he would hesitate to do so, if partners of companies had the power of freeing themselves from liability for the debts of their partnerships.

(Maltby, 1998)

So, providing one knew who the shareholders were, their personal standing, reputation and wealth was the ultimate guarantee of the stability and reputation of the company. What was needed was publicity about who the shareholders or backers of the company were and this was the most important thing potential investors should be informed of. This then rendered any consideration of limited liability irrelevant – or so the argument went. Creditors owed money by the company could rely on men of wealth and reputation to meet the company's liabilities in the event of any failure. Limited liability was also opposed on moral grounds. The argument was that although it may well be a means of sponsoring useful inventions or reducing social conflict by giving workers a stake in their employers' businesses and a valuable outlet for the savings of the middle classes, it was nevertheless a danger to widows, clergymen and other naive investors.

The practical problem, however, with this approach is that there are, fundamentally, only a limited number of wealthy high-principled individuals to go round, and, with the aristocratic preference for land and aversion to trade, there was a severe constraint on the ability of a new venture to raise funds whatever the moral rectitude of unlimited liability may be. There was really no choice. This, coupled with strong arguments in favour of limited liability, principally that it allowed the emerging middle class to buy shares and to partake of the Victorian economic miracle, meant that its ultimate adoption was more or less inevitable.

Investment was expensive, shares were often denominated in large amounts which served to confine investment to the upper levels of society, thus satisfying the Victorian caste system, but the right of an individual to own shares in the company he or she worked for and the social benefits improved trade would bring proved to be sounder arguments than those that the advocates of condign punishment by the market for those who failed could produce.

This idea of laissez faire-style minimal regulation has echoes today in some of the wilder excesses of Republican Party policy in the USA, and, of course, 'light touch' regulation policies in the City of London. The concerns of Gilbart (ironically a banker) have echoes in some of the press comments after the banking collapses of 2007–2008, which were calling for the failed management to be punished financially and for the banks to go to the wall and damn the consequences. Sadly, those commentators failed to appreciate:

- that managers and shareholders are not the same;
- that managers who fail may not lose as much as investors who may have committed a considerable portion of their personal wealth to what they considered to be a safe investment (which proved to be the case); and that
- creditors of banks are often ordinary people who put their money into those institutions trusting that they can get it back.

These arguments have returned in discussions about moral hazard and the adverse effect that limited liability protection may have on the appetite for risk developed by managers.

The case of *Salomon v A Salomon & Co Ltd* in 1897 set out the over-riding principle that a company is a separate legal entity. This principle frees directors from personal accountability for their actions – except in certain specific circumstances – so any attempt to make them 'pay' for the poor performance of a business or loss of shareholder value is doomed to fail. If society wishes to make corporate bodies have a wider moral remit it must encourage non-statutory influences such as Corporate Social Responsibility rather than considering legal remedies.

Ownership and control

In the early years the general view at the time was that corporations should only be created for very specific purposes. Adam Smith (1723–1790), author of the seminal tome *The Wealth of Nations* (1776) and father of much of modern capitalist thinking, believed it was contrary to the public interest for any businesses or trades to be incorporated and that all should be run as partnerships. He believed in the ultimate aspect of laissez faire economics – that all speculators should bear their own risk.

From the end of the eighteenth century to the middle of the nineteenth, Britain transformed itself from a largely agrarian economy to become the world's first industrial nation. Britain embraced capitalism in a way Adam Smith would have been proud of. In his book *The Wealth of Nations* Smith promotes the view that society in general can only be improved through individuals working to benefit themselves – that the creation of wealth through individual effort benefits society as a whole:

> By pursuing his own interest he frequently promotes that of the society more effectually than when he really intends to promote it. I have never known much good done by those who affected to trade for the public good.

Victorian capitalism took this to heart and British industry thrived in a way never before seen. Fuelled by abundant coal, initially supported on a solid agricultural base and inspired by scientific invention turned to practical use, Victorian entrepreneurs straddled the world. Trade blossomed, not only with the Empire but also across Europe and with Britain's former colony, the United States. Britain's industrial capacity meant that it was able to manufacture and sell consumer goods more cheaply than indigenous industries and, by 1860, Great Britain was, by some way, the world's largest trading nation. British banks funded international trade, it was carried in British merchant ships and British engineers helped to industrialize other nations, nations that would ultimately contribute to Britain losing its position as 'top nation' by the time Queen Victoria died in 1901.

Trade costs money and Victorian entrepreneurs needed money to finance factory building, machinery purchase, raw materials and working capital in exactly the same way as industrialists do today. It is arguable that one of the engines of growth, perhaps not as significant as railways or textile machinery but significant nonetheless, was the development of the joint stock company. The use of this as a vehicle for carrying out trading ventures, financing trade and insuring risk created both the modern industrial economy and a host of opportunities for dishonest promoters, mercenary directors and professional fraudsters. With the desire of the public to invest and the growing size and power of commercial organizations, untrammelled by government interference, at least in the early years, the need to trust those who spent the money entrusted to them grew and with it the need for some form of regulation and audit.

As companies grew in size and influence the power of directors grew also, and the influence of the shareholders diminished. Only those who were owner-managers had any real sense of what the company was doing. Investors who simply entrusted their savings to company promoters had no idea what was happening to their money until the law made it mandatory for directors to account to shareholders annually and for those accounts to be audited by a professionally qualified auditor. That didn't fully happen until 1948.

Responding to increasing industrialization and the growth of markets, the ownership and control of companies became increasingly separated. In the UK and USA particularly, with the protection given to minority shareholders, the shareholder base became much more diverse.

This is, incidentally, not necessarily true of companies in countries that do not have the system of common law like that of the UK, which relies on precedent and an independent judiciary. The most common form of company ownership around the world is the family firm or controlling share-holders, but in the UK and USA it is institutional investors who have the biggest influence on corporate behaviour.

Moral hazard

Moral hazard arises when a party that is insulated from risk behaves differently than they would if they had to face the full effect of that risk. As a consequence of the fact that management knows more than the shareholders they may be encouraged into inappropriate courses of action that the shareholders are unable to monitor and which, ultimately, they will have to pay for one way or another. This has echoes of the Victorian limited liability argument outlined above and the view that entrepreneurs should face risks without protection.

Some would have it that the financial collapses of 2007–2008 would not have happened had banks not been willing to take excessive risks with financial instruments, while others attribute that particular collapse to hubris at the heart of the management of major US and British banks. Generally managers escaped the full consequences of their actions in the cases of these banks, except for those who worked for Northern Rock and one particular individual, Sir Fred Goodwin, former CEO of Royal Bank of Scotland, who resigned from his post a month before the bank announced the biggest loss in UK corporate history of £24.1bn. Sir Fred became a focus of much vituperative anti-banking sentiment which reflected much of the feeling of the public at large and served as an indicator of public sentiment towards those who are seen to enjoy the trappings of executive life, make huge blunders and escape with their fortune, if not their reputation, intact.

Shareholder objectives

Before we look at the way that shares are held in companies it may be instructive to consider the objectives of those who own shares in companies.

Shares can be held for more than one reason. Clearly they are all held for investment, but within that broad principle, individual categories of shareholder may have different motivations. Institutional investors contribute by far the bulk of investment funds available to companies and are able to invest large amounts of money in big blocks of shares. Because of this and the effect that their trading activities may have on a company's share price they are courted by large companies and are privy to considerably more information than is the small investor. However, the institutional investor has its own performance targets to meet so will chop and change its portfolio to maximize the return to the institution, often without regard to the company they have invested in; for example, they may sell shares in company A which is a perfectly sound company growing steadily, in order to invest in company B which offers an even better return. There is nothing wrong with company A and, indeed, the institutional investor may return to it at a later date. They owe no loyalty to the firms they invest in – the fund managers owe loyalty only to their employers.

Small investors have a much lower level of information than the institutional investor and react more slowly to changes in the market. They are generally risk-averse, having, proportionally, much more to lose than the institutional investor, so will be looking primarily for security rather than spectacular growth. By small investor we mean an investor who trades in stocks and shares in their own right as opposed to an investor who invests by means of a mutual fund or other form of collective investment vehicle. Such small investors may also be looking for a reasonable dividend return to provide income and steady capital growth.

The speculator may want a rapid increase in the share price so they can buy in and sell out quickly. They may work in concert with other speculators and target specific companies in order to make a short-term gain. For example, in the recent banking crisis it was alleged that speculators targeted shares in banks that were rumoured to be vulnerable. They carried out what are known as 'short selling' operations, which had the effect of driving the share price down.

Short selling involves selling shares you don't own at a fixed price for delivery at a future date. The hope is that at the point you have to deliver the shares you have sold to your buyer the price will have dropped so that you can acquire them at a lower price than the price at which you sold them. Your profit is the difference between the price you agreed to sell them at and the price you are able to buy them at some time later – clearly if you get this wrong and the price goes up you have to stand the losses so there is risk in these operations. Concerted short selling, however, will generally succeed in forcing down the share price, particularly at times when ordinary investors are feeling nervous about corporate performance either generally or in a particular sector.

Loss of confidence can lead to spectacular collapses. For example, the share price of the Royal Bank of Scotland, which was severely weakened by a poorly judged decision to pay far too much to acquire ABN AMRO Bank and was deeply immersed in the sub-prime loans banking, went from £6.03 per share in March 2007 to £0.11 in January 2009 and had struggled back to £0.36 by mid-2011. This formerly blue chip (ie reliable and solid) stock had been ruined by arrogant management; and many small investors who relied on such stocks as the basis of their portfolio were caught out and took heavy losses.

As can be seen in Table 1.1 almost all investors are risk-averse except, of course, for speculators or those looking for short-term gains. Institutional investors spread their risk by diversifying their investment portfolios and wise small investors should limit the level of their investment in any one stock so their losses on one individual investment should be relatively low; however, it should be remembered that losses to a small investor may be a proportionally greater percentage of their total wealth than would be the case with an institutional investor with a balanced portfolio.

Directors and employees of course have their eggs in one basket but are well informed about and willing to commit to the organization. Share option- or savings-type schemes are used to involve employees in the organization. For directors share options are seen as a reward, as a way of ensuring

TABLE 1.1 Shareholder motivations

Shareholder Type	Main Interest	Risk Exposure	Level of Information
Institutional Investor	continued capital growth of fund value demonstrated level of return on funds invested income generation to meet obligations, eg payment of pensions, returns to investors	risk-averse	high
Small Individual Investor	steady growth regular dividend	willing to take small, controlled risks	low
Speculator	rapid share price rise gain due to short selling or other speculative operations	prepared to take risks	high
Employee Shareholder	long-term value maintenance	risk-averse	moderate
Director	increase in share price	risk-averse	high

a certain level of loyalty and as a disincentive to carry out any actions that might jeopardize the share price. This is, effectively, a form of remuneration and so directors may incline towards short-term decision-making, or decision-making designed to protect or increase the share price rather than the more long-term strategic approach required by external investors. We look at this further in Chapter 6.

Research indicates that individual investors (as opposed to speculators or those who see shares as a form of remuneration) tend to view their investment as relatively long term. They require their money to be secure, first of all, and then they will look for steady growth and, possibly, a regular dividend. Research also indicates that investors are generally more influenced by the prospect of capital growth than a regular income. Dividend returns on capital invested tend to be fairly low so many investors could receive a greater level of income from investment in bonds or some other forms of investment such as property; however, they should not achieve the same levels of capital growth.

Part of the investment community is often looking to gain short-term profits from portfolio management investment rather than for strategic approaches centred on strategies that stress the need for survival and long-term growth. In recent years we have seen the rise of private hedge funds that use huge amounts of borrowed money to purchase businesses, which they then 'improve' so as to maximize their return. These businesses are often sold on after a few years, hopefully repaying the borrowed funds and realizing a capital profit. Clearly the return on investment has to be substantial to make the deals attractive so management emphasis is on cost reduction, heavy marketing and operational efficiencies. Hedge funds are about managers, not about owners. What is not at a premium in these companies is research leading to product development or long-term investment in corporate infrastructures.

It is necessary to point out that, since the credit crunch of 2008/2009, many hedge funds relying extensively on borrowed money have suffered badly in the downturn, but recent figures show them rallying strongly and the hedge fund industry appears to be, once again, in rude health.

Institutional investors

The latest figures available from the Office for National Statistics, the *Share Ownership Survey 2008* (published in January 2010), show that:

- Approximately 10 per cent of shares in UK companies were owned by UK individuals and that ownership by UK-based individuals had been on a downward trend since 1963.

- 41.5 per cent of shares were owned by investors from outside the UK, of which 34 per cent were based in Europe and 30 per cent in North America. This percentage has increased dramatically since 1981 when the percentage stood at only 3.6 per cent. This is partly reflective of the growth in international mergers and acquisitions since 1994.

- Insurance companies and pension funds together accounted for approximately 27 per cent of UK shareholdings.

Of course, private investors may hold personal investments through unit trusts and indirectly by being members of pension funds but these, again, are institutions where the voice of the individual shareholder is not heard.

So the accountability of directors to shareholders is not to individuals but to institutions run by, increasingly, non-UK masters. From one corporate governance standpoint this is beneficial. Powerful institutional investors can encourage good corporate governance because their influence on management is considerable and thus will tend to act as a mechanism for aligning the interests of management with those of shareholders, or at least of some shareholders.

Institutional investor organizations

Institutional investors, comprising pension funds and insurance companies, belong to organizations (principally the National Association of Pension Funds (NAPF) and the Association of British Insurers (ABI)) that set out best practice guidelines for corporate governance and monitor compliance. These are powerful bodies that take their responsibilities in promoting the effectiveness of the UK Corporate Governance Code very seriously.

The NAPF, in its introduction to its 'Corporate Governance Policy and Voting Guidelines 2010', quotes the preamble to the *UK Corporate Governance Code*:

> First that much more attention needed to be paid to following the spirit of the Code as well as its letter. Secondly, that the impact of shareholders in monitoring the Code could and should be enhanced by better interaction between the boards of listed companies and their shareholders.
>
> (Financial Reporting Council, 2010)

Both the NAPF and the ABI are members of the Institutional Shareholders Committee (ISC), together with the Association of Investment Companies, representing investment companies and venture capital bodies and the Investment Management Association, representing investment managers. The role of this extremely powerful body is to:

provide a forum through which its member organizations may:

- inform each other about their views on issues of concern to institutional shareholders;
- consider whether there are any such matters on which member organizations should co-ordinate their activities or representations to UK Government and regulators; European institutions; and, any other relevant international legislative, regulatory or standard setting bodies; and
- make joint representations on occasion and by mutual agreement.

The Cadbury Committee considered that institutional investors had a special responsibility to try to ensure that companies adopted its recommendations.

Similar sentiments were expressed in subsequent committees following Cadbury:

- The Greenbury Report (1995) said that 'the investor institutions should use their power and influence to ensure the implementation of best practice as set out in the Code'.
- Similarly the Hampel Report (1998) said, 'it is clear ... that a discussion of the role of shareholders in corporate governance will mainly concern the institutions'.

The Code referred to is the *UK Corporate Governance Code*, of which more in later chapters, which states:

> The board should state in the annual report the steps they have taken to ensure that the members of the board, and, in particular, the non-executive directors, develop an understanding of the views of major shareholders about the company, for example through direct face-to-face contact, analysts' or brokers' briefings and surveys of shareholder opinion.
>
> (Financial Reporting Council, 2010: E1.2)

However, the attention paid by management to the interests of institutional shareholders can lead to information asymmetry. Whilst commenting that all shareholders have a statutory right to be treated equally in access to information, the UK Corporate Governance Code specifically states that '[t]he chairman should discuss governance and strategy with major shareholders' (Financial Reporting Council, 2010: E1.1).

In other words, all shareholders have equal rights to information but some shareholders, to paraphrase Orwell, are more equal than others; for the major shareholders the information comes to them whilst smaller shareholders have to go out and get it! Indeed one of the principal tasks of the chief financial officer is to liaise with institutional investors and to keep them supportive of the company.

Fiduciary capitalism

All of this has led to what has become known as 'fiduciary capitalism'. This is defined as a capitalist model in which corporations are influenced and guided by shareholders, particularly large institutional shareholders – such as pension funds and mutual funds – that act on behalf of many smaller investors through financial intermediaries – insurance companies, pension funds, investment trusts, etc. A very few own a very tiny part of a listed company in their own name but the majority of investors are investors via a third party, an institutional investor, who makes representations on their behalf. In essence most individual investors have no control or influence whatsoever over the company their money might ultimately be invested in because they have, effectively, delegated that responsibility to a financial institution.

Even the small investor, who owns shares in their own name, and who attends the company's annual general meeting, may find their voice subordinated to the need of the board to have their strategies and financial statements approved by the major shareholders, who have been well briefed beforehand and may even not attend, but merely vote by proxy.

The influence of the small investor is thus minimal and only the wishes of major investors are likely to have any impact on board policy. Their only influence can be by mobilizing public opinion and hoping that one of the influential investment bodies mentioned earlier might take up their cause.

So the conventional idea of ownership, where a single individual or group come together to invest in a business, has morphed into something entirely different as the institutional investors, with their own objectives, now influence corporate decision-making. Thus control is exercised by a framework of corporate influences rather than by the moral code of individuals, the framework consisting largely of:

- codes of corporate governance;
- the bodies representing major institutional investors;
- the external auditing profession;
- regulators.

The small investor's choice

Suppose an investor opposes the decision of a company in which they are a small shareholder to trade with a lucrative but morally despicable regime. The investor has two choices – either:

- they can sell their shares and invest their money in a more ethical business; or,
- they can attend the AGM and make their case to the board.

Without the support of the larger institutional investors the small investor's voice is likely to carry little weight, particularly if, as is so often the case, the trade with the despicable regime is profitable. So the determined small investor is forced to seek allies through the press or by lobbying and, if this yields no result, will probably abandon the company for a more morally acceptable one.

Contrast the UK approach with the attitude to investment in the USA. In the United States there has always been a far greater willingness of individuals to invest in the stock market. The culture of share ownership by individuals is much greater in the USA than in the UK, where savers traditionally looked towards financial institutions such as banks, building societies, insurance companies or pension funds to hold their savings and, ultimately, to provide their pension. The performance of the stock market and the share price of companies is thus of huge importance to vast numbers of individual Americans. Because of this business leaders become well known and some almost achieve celebrity status.

In the USA interest in the stock market abounds. For example, in the USA workers can invest in what is commonly known as a 401(k) account. This is a type of savings scheme in which money is deposited tax-free and is invested. Typically employers match workers' contributions and the schemes are administered by employers. The individual can decide how the funds in the 401(k) are invested. Sadly this can often prove to be disadvantageous as in the case of employees of Enron, who were encouraged by the management to invest their 401(k) money in Enron stock and who consequently lost it all when Enron collapsed (McLean and Elkind, 2004).

However, the spectre of Enron brought home to the investing public a stark truth that all investors know but either refuse to acknowledge or become complicit in – that they are surrendering their wealth to other people over which they have absolutely no control. This brings us to the principle of 'agency theory' and the power of modern management.

Agency theory

Imagine the development of a firm from a small family-owned business to a multinational entity. As the business grows in size the capacity of one individual or a small group of individuals to manage it completely declines and they have to take on help to assist them in both the day-to-day tasks and in devising business strategies for the future. They need to import skills of accounting, selling and production, they take on more staff, need supervisors, line managers and ultimately have to share power with a board of directors. As the business grows in size and complexity the role of these managers increases with it to the extent that they are, effectively, running it. When the business raises money by selling shares to outside shareholders the original owner's interest becomes more and more diluted until the business is owned, effectively, by strangers who see it as an investment, not a lifestyle.

Here lies the root of agency theory. The managers or directors are agents for the investors or shareholders, known as principals. The managers or directors of the business are entrusted with the principal's money and their role, it is hoped, is:

- to use that investment to create profits that the principals could receive by way of dividend;
- to expand that initial capital on behalf of the principals, so increasing the value of their investment;
- to preserve the assets of the business;
- to act always in the best interests of their principals.

In return the agents should receive suitable remuneration, concomitant with their status and their level of success in making money for their principals. Thus everybody should get something out of the arrangement – or so it seems. In fact things don't always work out quite as well as might have been anticipated because, as usual, human nature gets in the way. Samuel Smiles (1812–1904) in his book *Self Help* expressed it thus:

> The implicit trust which merchants are accustomed to confide in distant agents, separated from them perhaps by half the globe – often consigning vast wealth to persons, recommended only by their character, whom perhaps they have never seen – is probably the finest homage which men can render to one another.
>
> (Smiles, 1882)

Agency theory holds that agents do not, necessarily, take decisions in the best interests of their principals. It states that the objectives or goals of principals and agents mostly conflict and, where they do, agents will, naturally, make the choice that benefits them the most, choices that may not be the most beneficial decision for the principal. This has been summarized quite simply in Table 1.2.

Agency theory is a relatively simple principle to grasp but its ramifications are extensive and they have important implications for how organizations conduct themselves and on their operational culture. The Institute of Chartered Accountants in England and Wales, in November 2006, expressed it this way:

> In principle the agency model assumes that no agents are trustworthy and if they can make themselves richer at the expense of their principals they will. The poor principal, so the argument goes, has no alternative but to compensate the agent well for their endeavours so that they will not be tempted to go into business for themselves using the principal's assets to do so.
>
> (Audit Quality Forum, 2005)

TABLE 1.2 Agency theory – differing expectations

Party	Objective
Principal	safe investment regular dividends long-term capital growth maintenance of value
Agent	salary and benefits maximum bonus share options personal success of successful business measured by share price

Clearly this is not universally true, but the extent to which principals don't trust their agents tends to:

- govern the level of the monitoring mechanisms principals need to create an overview of their agents' activities; and
- decide the extent to which agents' compensation levels are considered to be acceptable by the agent, even if they are considered to be excessive by the principal.

One of the differences between principals and agents tends to arise because of the different views of the time horizon each party holds. It is not difficult to envisage that agents incline less towards long-term rewards than do owners. Whilst their rewards might, indeed should, be performance-related (see Chapter 6), the period over which performance improvement is measured is often relatively short – often only one financial accounting period, so agents benefit greatly from short-term profitability that may create an illusion of growth rather than real, underlying, organic development.

Agency costs

This separation has also created costs, known as agency costs. These are, broadly, costs that arise because:

- agents and principals may have differing objectives, which have to be aligned to some degree; and

- the agents have vastly more information in their control than do principals.

These costs arise simply from the use of agents such as:

- the risk that they will use the organization's resources for their own benefit so they, effectively, have to be paid not to take actions that might be detrimental to the interests of the shareholders; and

- the costs arising from monitoring the agents' activities (eg by producing audited financial statements) and the costs of incentives such as share options designed to align the objectives of principals and agents to some degree.

Stakeholder theory

Stakeholder theory is wrapped up in a general theory of the company as having a wider range of responsibilities to a broad range of stakeholders rather than simply exercising its duty to its shareholders. This is linked to the wider ideas of Corporate Social Responsibility, which we cover elsewhere in this book and which is becoming a major issue for companies in the current social climate.

However, there are two other considerations that need to be reconciled. First, the legal obligation on directors, based on the Companies Act 2005, is, broadly, to act in the best interests of shareholders, that is to maximize shareholder value. The Act makes no provision for other stakeholders such as employees, suppliers or lenders. There is therefore a conflict between the idealism of some of the objectives of Corporate Social Responsibility and the blunt legal requirements. The best directors can do in this situation is to make the business case for Corporate Social Responsibility – which, as we will see, is becoming increasingly strong.

Second, there is the conflict between stakeholder theory and the principles of agency theory. The conflict is this – directors, in theory, should take into consideration the interests of a wide range of stakeholders, but their inclination, in practice, will be towards benefiting only one stakeholder group, ie themselves. Superficially it may seem difficult to reconcile these two paradigms; however, closer examination reveals that there is common ground. If ethically sound policies and following the principles of good Corporate Social Responsibility improves corporate performance, and there is evidence that it does (cited in *Pensions Week*, 2003), then this will benefit directors as well as other stakeholders. Conversely, following socially irresponsible or unethical policies may be highly detrimental to company results that will, again, reflect badly on the directors.

Consequently, agency theory, which after all is perhaps only a narrow form of stakeholder theory, can be reconciled with ethical performance and Corporate Social Responsibility if only out of narrow self-interest.

The power of modern management

As we have seen, the increasing size of corporations has resulted in the fragmentation of share ownership. In many cases large investors are not individual shareholders but are themselves institutions that are looking for a commercial return on their investment. The private individual shareholder prepared to hold their investment in a single company, as opposed to some sort of composite investment fund, over the longer term and to accept moderate levels of growth in return for security of their investment is now very much a minority. It can thus be argued that today it is largely managers who now control shares in companies run by other managers.

All of these factors have combined to give managers of big companies extraordinary power to the extent that major multinationals are bigger than some countries and decisions made in their boardrooms can have an effect on national economies. The recent banking crisis created by the decisions of major international banks to abandon risk management in favour of huge but illusory gains is a striking example of this. It took the combined economies of most of the developed countries of the world to avoid a global collapse of the entire banking system – such is the power, or destructive potential, of company managers.

The separation of ownership from control and the increasing power of company managers in large corporations encourages them to do two things:

- Take risks in order to maximize short-term advantage. This might mean, say, an aggressive acquisition programme funded by short-term borrowing, overseas expansion into foreign markets, or aggressive marketing of products to drive up market share in the short term.

- Adopt aggressive accounting practices that may, in extreme cases, amount to fraudulent manipulation of the figures. The classic cases in recent years of this are those of Enron and WorldCom (Jeter, 2003) in the USA, where managers actively colluded in misleading investors in order to maintain an otherwise unsustainable share price, enriching themselves in the process.

As we will see in later chapters it can be argued that workplace malfeasance, involving employees at all levels in the organization, starts from this divorcing of ownership from control and the consequent need for strong corporate governance. As we will see, where corporate governance is weak that weakness forms the context for much of the bad behaviour of managers within organizations and, consequently, following their lead, also by their staff.

In 1932 Adolf Berle and Gardiner Means published *The Modern Corporation and Private Property*. In it they said:

> The property owner who invests in a modern corporation so far surrenders his wealth to those in control of the corporation that he has exchanged the position of independent owner for one in which he may become merely recipient of the wages of capital ... [Such owners] have surrendered the right that the corporation should be operated in their sole interest.
>
> (Berle and Means, 1932)

They pointed out that, even if the directors have an interest (ie a shareholding) in the business, the size of their investment will be dwarfed by the overall size of the holdings of other shareholders with the result that their pecuniary interest is not in the growth in value of those shares, or the dividends that they could earn, but is rather from their earnings as directors.

Berle and Means went on to say that the growth of the modern corporation had taken the property of the many and concentrated it in the hands of the few. The millions of small investors who fund huge enterprises have granted enormous power to the small groups of individuals who control those businesses on a day-to-day basis. The individual owner of shares has no influence over the activities of those who run the company in which they are a shareholder; instead, the company has grown to such a size that it can dominate aspects of society. As Berle and Means saw it:

> The economic power in the hands of the few persons who control a giant corporation is a tremendous force which can harm or benefit a multitude of individuals, affect whole districts, shift the currents of trade, bring ruin to one community and prosperity to another. The organizations which they control have passed far beyond the realm of private enterprise – they have become more nearly social institutions.
>
> (Berle and Means, 1932)

Those who doubt this should consider:

- the effect on the high street of a new out-of-town hypermarket;
- the influence of Starbucks on coffee consumption;
- the influence of McDonald's and Burger King on the nation's eating habits and the behaviour of its children;
- the economic power of oil companies.

In short, the activities of very large corporations have a significant effect on everyday life and these corporations are controlled by small groups of individuals, most of whom are unknown to the public and who are never, unless something disastrous happens, held accountable.

Berle and Means were the first to articulate as agency theory, although they never used that term:

> [H]ave we any justification for the assumption that those in control of a modern corporation will also choose to operate it in the interests of the owners? The answer to this question will depend on the degree to which the self-interest of those in control may run parallel to the interests of ownership and, insofar as they differ, on the checks on the use of power which may be established by political, economic, or social conditions ... If we are to assume that the desire for personal profit is the prime force motivating control, we must conclude that the interests of control are different from and often radically opposed to those of ownership; that the owners most emphatically will not be served by a profit-seeking controlling group.
>
> (Berle and Means, 1932)

The interests of the controlling group – the directors – may be opposed to the interests of the majority – the shareholders. The owners, they say surprisingly, will not have their interests served by a profit-seeking controlling group. Why is this? Because in the pursuit of profit only short-term advantage is sought – the approach taken is the approach that will bring the most profit immediately. However, this is somewhat simplistic as both groups, the directors and the institutional investors, have a common goal, which is the maintenance of the share price. This can be achieved by:

- building a solid, reliable business that takes few risks, grows steadily and delivers value for money to its customers, and there are companies that do this; or,
- by constant activity, by acquisitions and mergers in order to reach a dominant market position, through trumpeting the launch of new products and through, fundamentally, creating a smokescreen or illusion of success and hiding the bad news – and there are companies like this too.

The public sector

In the UK as a whole the public sector accounts for some 20 per cent of all jobs. In some regions that percentage is even higher – in Scotland, for example, the public sector accounts for 23 per cent of all jobs. Public expenditure was forecast to be 47 per cent of GDP in 2011; it is, consequently, of enormous importance to the UK economy and is an area that has not been well served by researchers in the past. To ignore the size of organizations within the public sector is to ignore a major aspect of UK economic life. Some of the organizations are vast:

- the NHS employs almost 1.2 million full-time equivalent staff and the government spends about £100bn per year on it;
- Manchester City Council spends £1.6bn per year;
- the Department for Work and Pensions makes payments of some form of benefit to over 9 million people of working age and to over 13 million pensioners;
- the Metropolitan Police in London dealt with over 820,000 crimes in 2010.

In other words, the number and diversity of public service transactions across the UK economy is vast.

In 1994 the then Prime Minister, John Major, set up the Committee on Standards in Public Life, presided over by the Law Lord Rt Hon Lord Nolan. The committee was tasked with raising standards of behaviour by individuals in public life following the sleazy 'cash for questions' scandal involving two Tory MPs. The Committee produced various reports over the next three years and included in their reports were the seven principles by which all those involved in serving the public, not simply MPs, were to abide. These are shown in the box on p32.

The Committee carries out public attitude surveys every two years – the last one available being for 2011. This showed, generally, a decline, between 2004 and 2010, in the perception of the public towards standards of behaviour of those in public life. This, of course, was just before the MPs' expenses scandal was broken by the *Daily Telegraph* on 8 May 2009, when dozens of MPs were found to have breached parliamentary rules on claiming expenses. Four MPs and one Lord were imprisoned and some cases were still ongoing in 2011. The perception of widespread abuse of the expenses system had a profound effect on public perception of the probity, at least, of members of parliament and there has been much talk of tough new expenses regimes and 'this must never happen again.'

Whether this perception of widespread dishonesty has tainted public perceptions of local politicians or of senior civil servants and officers of public bodies is harder to say without evidence. The 2011 public attitude survey by the Committee on Standards in Public Life revealed that almost half of respondents thought that standards of conduct amongst public office holders had deteriorated and that the 'bounce back' effect of the 2010 election may be masking an even steeper decline in the public opinion of politicians. However, one thing is quite clear and has been reinforced by past surveys, both those carried out by the Committee on Standards in Public Life and in a survey carried out in 2010 by academics at Essex University (Birch and Allen, 2010). This is that the public prize honesty over competence. They feel that the most important attribute anyone in public life should have, and MPs in particular, is to be honest. Research shows that the public do take notice of scandals and deplore the actions of those in public life who are seen to be less than straightforward in their dealings – it is all about trust.

Seven principles of public life set out by the Committee on Standards in Public Life

Selflessness: Holders of public office should act solely in terms of the public interest. They should not do so in order to gain financial or other material benefits for themselves, their family, or their friends.

Integrity: Holders of public office should not place themselves under any financial or other obligation to outside individuals or organizations that might seek to influence them in the performance of their official duties.

Objectivity: In carrying out public business, including making public appointments, awarding contracts, or recommending individuals for rewards and benefits, holders of public office should make choices on merit.

Accountability: Holders of public office are accountable for their decisions and actions to the public and must submit themselves to whatever scrutiny is appropriate to their office.

Openness: Holders of public office should be as open as possible about all the decisions and actions that they take. They should give reasons for their decisions and restrict information only when the wider public interest clearly demands they do so.

Honesty: Holders of public office have a duty to declare any private interests relating to their public duties and to take steps to resolve any conflicts arising in a way that protects the public interest.

Leadership: Holders of public office should promote and support these principles by leadership and example.

These principles apply to all aspects of public life. The Committee has set them out for the benefit of all who serve the public in any way.

(Nolan, 1995)

Because it is funded through public money, the emphasis in the public sector is very much on accountability. A vast array of statistics is produced to tell the public where the money has gone. The accountancy body for the public sector, the Chartered Institute of Public Finance and Accountancy (CIPFA), produces several Statements of Professional Practice regulating ethical behaviour by accountants within the public sector and these are seen as a benchmark for all employees. We look at this in more detail in Chapter 7 where we review the audit function.

In terms of ethics and Corporate Social Responsibility, it can be argued that the whole purpose of large parts of the public sector is founded on ethical principles and its very purpose has a social responsibility. The NHS for example has a responsibility for the nation's health, different government departments have responsibilities for payment of pensions to the elderly, benefits to the disabled or unemployed; they are involved in administering much of the infrastructure and they employ 6.2 million people, so the impact of the public sector in the UK is immense.

But the objectives of a public sector organization do not make it a fully socially responsible one in our terms and, as we will see as we progress, there are situations where the public sector leads the way and there are areas where public sector practice lags behind its commercial cousins. We will look at the difference between the public and private sectors in terms of ethics and accountability and this will, undoubtedly, throw up some interesting and challenging issues that may be of value to both sectors.

CASE STUDY

Megatron plc is a multinational company with extensive manufacturing and distribution facilities in the UK, France and the USA. Its head office is in London and it sells its products worldwide under a range of popular brand names. Those same brand names are used to sponsor major sporting events and art exhibitions. Megatron, using its 'Lifesaver' medical products brand name, recently funded the 'Lifesaver' laboratories that specialize in finding cures for tropical diseases.

Under its 'New Learner' brand name it funds several schools in sub-Saharan Africa where the children use the 'New Learner' educational books and resources. The CEO of Megatron, Sir 'Billy' Bustler, is a well-known media figure and appears frequently on TV debates or radio phone-ins as 'the voice of British business'. He is seen as a cheerful, avuncular figure who has a ready wit and a charming manner. However, in the USA investigative journalists have revealed that:

- Megatron has 32 subsidiaries based in tax havens.
- Analysis of its recent accounts revealed that Megatron reported a group profit of £2.4bn but paid only £1.2m in tax. It paid no tax at all in any of the countries where several of its manufacturing units were sited.
- Authorities in China recently closed down four suppliers to Megatron for using under-age or illegal labour.
- One of the Megatron subsidiaries has been the subject of violent protests in India from farmers. They were accused of diverting local watercourses to a newly constructed bottle-washing plant. Local management denied the accusation and claimed that the reason the crops all died was bad farming practice, not loss of water.
- In Canada the CEO of another Megatron subsidiary that assembles and sells computer equipment has pleaded guilty in court to five charges of bribing public officials in order to obtain computer supply contracts. She claimed that this was accepted practice in Megatron and that 'everybody did it'.

Discuss

- Which, if any, of these actions by Megatron might be considered acceptable business practice?
- Which, if any, of these actions by Megatron might be considered acceptable business practice if they were never revealed to the outside world, ie if Megatron was never caught?
- What do these events reveal about the corporate culture within Megatron?
- When is it acceptable for any company to maximize profits without considering external factors that might affect people not directly connected with the company?
- How can Megatron defend itself against the accusations of the US journalists, should it defend itself and what actions should it take to correct any unethical practice?

Bibliography

ActionAid (2011) *Addicted to Tax Havens: The secret life of the FTSE top 100*, ActionAid UK, London

Audit Quality Forum (2005) *Agency Theory and the Role of Audit*, ICAEW, London

Berle, A and Means, G (1932) *The Modern Corporation and Private Property*, revised edition 1991, Transaction Publishers, Piscataway, NJ

Birch, S and Allen, N (2010) How honest do politicians need to be? *The Political Quarterly* **81** (1), pp 49–56

Bubble Act 1720 (6 Geo 1, c 18)

Cadbury, Sir A (1992) *Financial Aspects of Corporate Governance*, Gee & Co, London

Caldwell, Christopher (2007) Putin's colonial exploitation, *Financial Times*, 28 July

Committee on Standards in Public Life (2011) *Survey of public attitudes towards conduct in public life 2010*, Committee on Standards in Public Life, London

Companies Act, 1862 (25 & 26 Vict c 89)

Department for Work and Pensions (2011) *Statistical Quarterly*, 16 March 2011, DWP, London

Financial Reporting Council (2010) *UK Corporate Governance Code*, FRC, London

Friedman, M (1962) *Capitalism and Freedom*, University of Chicago Press, Chicago

Gilbart, JW (1846) *Moral and Religious Duties of Public Companies*, Waterlow & Sons, London

Greenbury, Sir R (1995) *Directors' Remuneration: Report of a study group chaired by Sir Richard Greenbury*, Gee & Co, London

Griseri, P and Seppala, N (2010) *Business Ethics and Social Responsibility*, Cengage, Andover

Gurria, A (Secretary General of the OECD)(2008) The global dodgers, *Guardian*, 27 November

Hampel, R (1998) *Hampel Committee Final Report*, Gee & Co, London

HMSO (2005) *Companies Act 2005*, HMSO, London

HM Treasury (2011) *Public Expenditure Statistical Analysis 2010*, HM Treasury, London

Jensen, M and Meckling, WH (1976) Theory of the firm: Managerial behaviour, agency costs and ownership structure, *Journal of Financial Economics*, **3** (4), pp 305–360

Jeter, L (2003) *Disconnected Deceit and Betrayal at World Com*, John Wiley & Sons Inc, Hoboken, NJ

Joint Stock Companies Act 1844 (7 & 8 Vict c 110)

Limited Liability Act 1855 (18 & 19 Vict c 133)

Maltby, J (1998) UK joint stock companies legislation 1844–1900: accounting publicity and mercantile caution, *Accounting History*, **3** (9)

McLean, B and Elkind, P (2004) *The Smartest Guys in the Room*, Penguin, London

Nolan, Lord (1995) *First Report of the Committee on Standards in Public Life*, TSO, London, Cm2850-I

Office for National Statistics (2009) Regional analysis of public sector employment, *Economic and Labour Market Review*, **3** (9), September

Office for National Statistics (2010) *Share Ownership Survey 2008*, ONS, London

Parl. Debs. (series 3), vol. 140, col. 136 (1856)

Pensions Week (2003) Green firms perform better than their peers: Pensions week 28.07.03, *Financial Times*, p 7

Salomon v A Salomon Co Ltd (1897) AC22

Smith, A (1977) [1776] *Wealth of Nations*, selected edition 2008, Oxford Paperbacks, Oxford

Smiles, S (1882) *Self Help*, John Murray, London

Solomon, J (2010) *Corporate Governance and Accountability*, John Wiley, Chichester

The Law Times (1851) *Law of Partnership*, 17, p 154

Transparency International (2011) *Corruption Perceptions Index, 2011*, Transparency International, Berlin

Winnett, R (2009) MPs expenses: how Brown and his cabinet exploit expenses system, *Daily Telegraph*, 8 May

Websites

http://nla.gov.au/nla-nla.gen-vn4739379

www.abi.org.uk

www.dwp.gov.uk

www.ft.com

www.ic.nhs.uk/statistics

www.institutionalshareholderscommittee.org.uk

www.met.police.uk/crimefigures

www.napf.org.uk

www.public-standards.gov.uk

www.transparency.org

Corporate culture

Introduction

We saw in Chapter 1 that companies have grown in size and influence to the extent that they have, effectively, passed out of direct control of their owners. Owners of large, influential companies are themselves often huge institutions that prioritize financial returns over ethical or moral behaviour. These huge multinational companies are controlled by directors who, agency theory tells us, incline towards maximizing short-term rewards rather than long-term gain as this will be more likely to bring immediate and direct benefit to them.

We have seen how multinational and national corporations have an influence on the everyday lives of billions of people and that, consequently, the power vested in a small number of individuals within these corporations is considerable and, to a large extent, may be unable to be controlled by either regulators or even market forces because they straddle many jurisdictions and operate in many markets. As a result, the ethics of management, and thus the morality of the organization, is of considerable interest.

During the early part of this century the drive towards increased transparency and accountability of action, together with an increasing awareness of environment-related issues, has accelerated from its beginnings in the early 1990s following the publication of the Cadbury Report (1992) and its adoption as mandatory by the London Stock Exchange. This code was followed by other, similar codes around the world such as the Sarbanes–Oxley legislation in the USA after the corporate scandals of the early part of this millennium. We will look at the mechanics of these rules in later chapters but for now will examine the more general principles of moral and ethical behaviour in the workplace.

Not all organizations are the same; even organizations of comparable size have different cultures and values, for an organization is not a machine, nor is it a passive vehicle for carrying out tasks, it is an entity that embodies the collective values and efforts of the people who inhabit and control it.

Common sense might say that the culture of the organization is principally determined by those who are in a position to set the rules and to enforce compliance but this is too simplistic and undervalues the individual employee and the collective will. The people who inhabit the organization cannot, ultimately, be bullied into compliance with a set of values and mores with which they disagree; management who adopt a bullying culture will tend to find that the staff counteract this by avoidant behaviour and the growth of sub-cultures that adopt their own sets of values and approaches to corporate behaviour. In effect, whilst paying lip service to management, staff institute practices that may seek to undermine unpopular managers or to damage the institution in some way without overtly seeming to do so.

Research carried out in Australia, which we look at later in this chapter, indicates that the values of the organization will tend to reflect the values of the society from which the employees are drawn (Farrell, Cobbin and Farrell, 2002), so if employees are drawn from a society that sees painting yourself purple as a perfectly acceptable social activity then there will be a lot of purple employees around the water cooler, despite management's best efforts to promote another colour!

So in understanding organizations we must also take into consideration the prevailing views, customs and values of the society within which the organization operates and within which the employees live; thus meetings in multinational companies may be conducted very differently in their Tokyo office than in their meeting room in Stuttgart.

What is 'corporate culture'?

Academics have come up with various definitions of corporate culture over the years, some of them involving concepts more suited to the anthropological study of lost tribes! According to academic researchers corporate culture is:

> Shared meanings, values, attitudes and beliefs that are created and communicated within an organisation
>
> (Ashkenasy, Widerson and Peterson, 2000)

or:

> The set of shared taken for granted implicit assumptions that members of an organisation hold and that determine how they perceive, think about and react to their various environments
>
> (Schein, 1992)

or, more pragmatically:

> Culture is the best way we do things around here.
>
> (Bowers and Seashore, 1966)

Indeed 'the way we do things around here' could be adopted as a simplistic shorthand definition but there is more to culture than might be apparent.

Corporate culture is more than simply a set of company rules, the mission statement and corporate objectives, or even a set of common values; it is a more complex mix of factors that combine together to form the prevailing culture of the organization. Some of these attributes of culture are visible but one key aspect of corporate culture is not.

'Culture' incorporates:

- unwritten rules;
- assumptions about expected behaviour;
- styles and attitudes formed from national culture; and
- prevailing orthodoxies or moralities in the society and environment that surrounds the organization and from which most of the employees come.

Figure 2.1 shows the combination of factors that one commentator described as being similar to the iceberg insofar as only a portion of it is visible and a large proportion isn't. Clearly this is not a representation of proportions, it is a picture of the construct of a corporate culture, but it makes the point.

FIGURE 2.1 Components of corporate culture

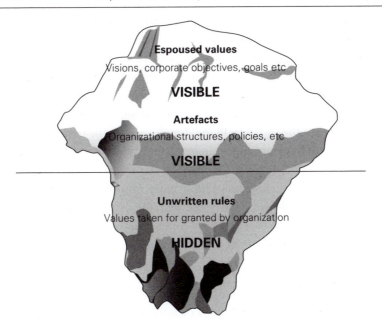

Visible aspects of culture

The visible aspects of culture are what you see when you walk in the door. They include the attitude of the staff, the expression of common corporate objectives, the staff handbook containing all the policies, the management style and how this affects the employees of the organization.

Espoused values

These are the overt values of the organization, the ones they make public. They are the mission statement, the corporate objectives and goals, in other words they are the stated aims and aspirations of the organization that someone new to it is told about and which existing staff have been made familiar with through training and management reminders. These are not financial goals but the commitments the organization makes to its stakeholders and towards which corporate effort is directed. Financial strategies may be subordinated, in some cases, to these goals; for example the organization may eschew employing part-time, contract workers in favour of full-time employees because of a commitment to creating jobs and developing individuals, even though this is a much more expensive staffing option.

Artefacts

This is a slightly peculiar word that has its derivation from the period when studies of organizations were a branch of social anthropology. Artefacts to an archaeologist or an anthropologist could be cooking pots or knives but to an organization they are the visible manifestation of the espoused values that are comprised, for example, in the hierarchical structure of the organization, its arrangements for management and supervision and the policies and procedures in the staff handbook. Employees will be familiar with these. The management structure can be an indicator of the style of organization – is it bureaucratic and controlled with many layers of management or is it a flatter, less rigid organization with a more informal style? Policies, procedures and protocols are part of the way the organization carries on its activities and the extent to which they control the activities of the employees is, again, an integral part of the prevailing culture.

Unwritten rules

What is not apparent are the hidden or unwritten rules of the organization that can derive from the prevailing national culture or be unwritten rules of the business. For example, it may be a cliché but the attitude of the Greeks and the Spanish towards time could perhaps be described as somewhat more flexible than that of, say, the Germans or the Swiss. In Greece or Spain arriving on time for a meeting might well be construed as unnecessarily punctual whilst in Switzerland or Germany meetings are expected to start on time with everybody present. The UK falls somewhere in between these two positions with most people arriving more or less on time, and one or two arriving late with some excuse.

Other unwritten rules may be more sinister, such as 'you never argue with the Chief Executive'. This kind of implicit or unspoken understanding is part of corporate culture and is the part that new employees take time to understand. This is not to say that they are necessarily wrong, bad or in any way detrimental; they simply represent a kind of unspoken consensus within the workforce that everyone understands and they are part of the way things are done. Of course they could be disguising some appalling management practices or institutionalized racism or sexism. For example, the UK police force has been criticized for allegedly having an overly macho 'canteen culture' and a culture of institutionalized racism, which senior managers are trying to eradicate; and several merchant banks and large corporate legal firms have been sued for sex discrimination either arising from pay differentials or from inbuilt sex discrimination derived from a testosterone-fuelled culture.

Hypocrisy is never far from the surface. An example of this is quoted in Michael Lewis's book *Liar's Poker* (1999). Lewis was advised by a friend who had been through the interview process at merchant bank Salomon Brothers not to mention money when he was being interviewed:

> When they ask you why you want to be an investment banker you're supposed to talk about the challenges and the thrill of the deal ... that money wasn't the binding force was, of course, complete and utter bullshit.

Lewis conformed to get the job, but inwardly his view was, '[l]earning a new lie was easy ... believing it was another matter'. Thus the illusion was preserved that employees were motivated by abstract concepts such as a challenging environment, the thrill of competition and the satisfaction of making a good deal but the unwritten rules were that each trader was fiercely competitive, that making money was all that mattered and your success or failure was measured by the profits you made, not by how hard you tried.

Unwritten rules can be used to resist management pressure for change where the workforce do not accept changes and will effectively sabotage management's efforts without any of it being overt simply because the workforce is reluctant to alter its shared hidden values. This is one of the reasons why institutionalized attitudes, towards race and gender in particular, are very difficult to change.

To illustrate the complex nature of corporate culture let us adapt a technique that was originally developed in the USA by two cognitive psychologists, Joseph Luft and Harry Ingham, in 1955. They designed the Johari Window tool to help people understand their interpersonal communication and relationships. The original idea is that the subject picks half a dozen adjectives from a list, and their peers do the same. These are then mapped on a grid.

Management guru Charles Handy calls this concept the Johari House, with four rooms. Room 1 is the part of ourselves that we see and others see. Room 2 is the aspects that others see but we are not aware of. Room 3 is the most mysterious room in that the unconscious or subconscious part of us is seen by neither ourselves nor others. Room 4 is our private space, which we know but keep from others. Figure 2.2 illustrates the different aspects of corporate culture using a Johari Window.

FIGURE 2.2 Johari Window – complexities of corporate culture

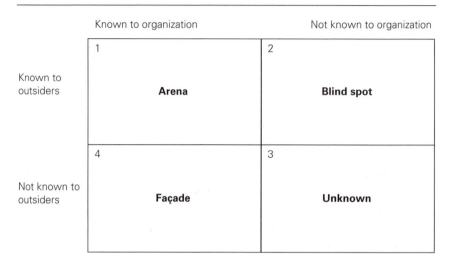

Anyone who wants to play the game can review an organization in depth from all sources including some of the wilder shores of the blogosphere if necessary and allocate descriptions of the organization into each area – Area 3 clearly being the most difficult and needing the participation of employees. Table 2.1 illustrates the format.

Clearly all organizations have aspects that are apparent both to them and to the outside world but there are substantial elements of every organization that are:

- known only to the organization or to parts of it;
- not known properly at all;
- not known to the organization but known by those outside it.

Tools such as the Johari Window are used by consultants in such tasks as improving communications and change management, but here we use it simply to illustrate the complexity of the organization. An organization is not simply an amalgam of managers and employees, of products and services, of policies, procedures and objectives, but the view of the organization also encompasses the perception of it by outsiders and the image that it presents to the outside world that may hide somewhat darker activities.

TABLE 2.1 Johari Window – analyzing the complexities of the organization and its culture

Area	Description	Examples
Area 1	**Arena** **Known to organization and known to outsiders** The aspects of the organization that it is aware of and makes known to outsiders	Public documents, eg financial statements, marketing literature, details of products, services, website and press
Area 2	**Blind spot** **Not known to organization but known to outsiders** Aspects of the organization that outsiders are aware of but which the organization appears not to recognize	Weaknesses and vulnerabilities identified by competitors or as a possible takeover target, perceptions of the organization as an employer – eg 'ruthless', 'uncaring', 'wonderful'; reputation for reliability of products (as opposed to claims made by company)
Area 3	**Unknown** **Not known to organization and not known to outsiders** Aspects of the organization of which neither the organization itself nor the outside world is aware	Untapped potential in staff due to poor staff development or training, missed opportunities for product development or marketing due to weak or incompetent staff or management repression of initiative
Area 4	**Façade** **Known to organization but not known to outsiders** This is an area of activity known to the organization but not known to the outside world. Areas here can contradict the image of the organization that the management prefer to disseminate	Extensive use of offshore banking, special purpose vehicles or transfer pricing to earn profits in countries with low tax regimes or limited corporate disclosure, aggressive legal response to public criticism, production or trading activities that breach environmental rules or human rights in countries with weak enforcement regimes

Sociability versus solidarity

These aspects of corporate culture may be the visible or invisible components but how do these components manifest themselves in terms of how the organization presents itself to the outside world? As an illustration we will look at two aspects of the visible part of organizational culture, broadly divided by organizational psychologists into two characteristics – sociability and solidarity.

Sociability is, effectively, what it sounds like – a synonym for friendliness, affability, an open approach to strangers, in other words the organization's emphasis is on social relations rather than achieving tasks and goals. There is a basis of consensus and objectives take into account the needs of employees as much as financial objectives. Often such organizations are not commercially as successful as they might be and many of these types of organization are not commercial at all as the shared values of the employees take the organization away from a task-focused, rather aggressive commercial culture.

An organization that prizes solidarity, on the other hand, is very task-oriented. It values achievement of goals, getting a result, achieving the objective over social interaction and the emphasis in the organization is on results. These organizations can be very focused and usually have a very strong supervision and review culture such that employees who don't fit in or who consistently fail are removed from the organization. The most notorious instance of this is the 'rank and yank', or 'vitality curve', system where everyone is reviewed annually and their performance appraised and scored.

'Rank and yank' is based on the somewhat dubious principle that about 70 per cent of employees will be performing moderately well and are neither failures or high flyers, about 20 per cent are high flyers that need to be fostered and encouraged and the bottom 10 per cent are underperforming and can be fired. Thus about 10 per cent of the workforce is replaced every year and the theory is that this system fosters a culture that encourages performance and raises the standard of the firm. However, this can also foster a climate of fear in the organization and be abused by managers who can play favourites as they do the appraisals, to keep employees they like and get rid of employees they don't like or who threaten their position. Experience shows that employees become obsessed by their ranking in the company and behave in a way that will improve their personal ranking rather than for the benefit of the organization generally. Figure 2.3 is a simple matrix showing how sociability and solidarity combine in different organizational forms.

FIGURE 2.3 Sociability and solidarity

Solidarity

	Low	High
High ***Sociability***	**High sociability/low solidarity** • Networked organization. • Emphasis on social relations, less on performance. • Informal knowledge sharing, innovation. • Good social relations. • Tolerance of under-performance. **Example: family firm**	**High sociability/high solidarity** • Communal organization. • Emphasis on social relations and performance. • Emphasis on communal culture may hamper change. • May be tension between two opposing elements. **Example: large aid agency**
Low	**Low sociability/low solidarity** • Fragmented organization. • No commitment to performance or maintaining good social relations. • Individuals may be task-oriented – little or no team working. • Goals may not be accepted by all employees. **Example: university department**	**Low sociability/high solidarity** • Mercenary organization. • Task-oriented, emphasis on performance. • Little concern over quality of social relations. • Shared purpose links employees. **Example: professional services – accountants/lawyers**

SOURCE: Goffee and Jones, 1998

How the organization combines sociability and solidarity depends on:

• the nature of its activities;
• the availability of skilled labour.

Clearly a very task-oriented organization, such as a large firm of chartered accountants, may fundamentally not have a tremendous interest, from a management perspective, in the social relations of its employees or even their happiness and contentment at work. Managerial emphasis is on getting the job done and any staff social relations are usually staff-initiated activities rather than managerial initiatives. However, where there is a shortage of skilled staff the emphasis on solidarity may be modified to encourage a more social organization, and formality and rigidity may be reduced in an attempt to encourage skilled workers to join the organization.

Conversely, management may feel that the organization has become a little too social and solidarity is being lost. In these cases solidarity may be increased by reminding workers about the need for quality, the problems with competitors and they may create a sense of urgency among employees in order to boost performance and reduce sociability.

Note that it is not a matter of management somehow balancing these two factors in order to create a 'perfect' working environment – this is how organizations have evolved and the level of solidarity vs sociability that has evolved over time in each one individually is what works for them – it may just be a question of management 'tweaking' it from time to time.

Factors such as equal opportunities legislation have changed the internal demographics of companies and compelled management to reflect the ethnic and gender mix of the population from which they draw their employees. For example, research indicates that the increased employment of women in the workforce may have an influence on the sociability/solidarity tendencies in an organization as those features that women bring to the workplace, such as better communication skills and willingness to negotiate, may dilute the more task-focused, aggressive male tendencies that have previously dominated the workplace.

Sub-cultures and counter-cultures

Within every organization there will exist various sub-groups and alliances which create networks and links through the organization and across organizational boundaries. These sub-cultures share patterns of behaviour and philosophies that arise from their backgrounds, training, social class, education or any other affiliations that create stronger bonds than merely working for the same employer. For example, accountants share a common bond derived from training, background and skills that will link all accountants in an organization together no matter where they are located or to whom they report. The bonds that hold members of a sub-culture together are stronger than simply having a common area of mutual interest. The members of the company angling club may all be anglers but share no other values; similarly all the Chelsea supporters in the organization may support the same team but have no other common bond outside football.

Members of sub-cultures tend to have common values and ethical standards that may not be influenced by managerial initiatives or management fads. Indeed any managerial initiative that contradicts the values of any powerful sub-culture will be difficult to implement, as it will be covertly opposed for long enough for it to fall into abeyance.

Management itself is likely to be a form of sub-culture and it must be aware of not isolating itself from the rest of the organization. This was a common feature of management in the mid-twentieth century where an 'us and them' divide within companies led to huge amounts of conflict, industrial unrest and poor working practices, which had catastrophic effects on large sections of British industry. Today the need to form effective working relationships at all levels within the organization and the increasing informality of society in general has, hopefully, led to more harmonious relationships within organizations.

In some organizations, particularly after a merger or takeover, a counter-culture develops. This is a grouping of individuals who are not in agreement with the prevailing orthodoxies of the new organization and who bond together, united in a common bond of dissatisfaction. This may manifest itself at one level in grumbling, high levels of staff turnover, increased sickness and absenteeism but at a more serious level it can result in increased levels of theft and active sabotage such as arson and damage to machinery and equipment as a way of protesting against the organization.

Organizational climate

Organizational culture and organizational climate are not the same thing. Fundamentally the climate of an organization is defined as the day-to-day experience of the employee. It comprises the experiences and perceptions of the organization, for example:

- Are the people friendly or are they 'heads-down', involved in their own work and barely speak?
- Is it authoritarian – is everyone scared of the boss?
- Are the offices cold and impersonal or covered in plants, posters and fluffy toys?
- If the employee has a problem or doesn't understand something do they feel they can approach co-workers without feeling disparaged?
- Do management encourage initiative and innovation or is communication only one-way?

The corporate climate is the responsibility of management and represents, perhaps, the most visible aspect of the day-to-day experience of management in action experienced by the employee. The way this is done includes:

- Setting standards and incorporating them in policies employees can follow. This includes ethics policies, the staff manual and procedures.
- Following their own policies and leading from the front.
- Encouraging initiative and co-operation.
- Encouraging two-way communication so employees feel valued and listened to and avoiding management by exhortation.

These and many other issues are part of the employees' daily experience, particularly when new to an organization. The climate of the organization is set by senior management and derives from its culture; however, day-to-day experiences are important in shaping attitudes to employment that affect both the performance and stability of the workforce.

Remember that individual employees differ and many people, for example, are themselves task-oriented and would prefer to work in a high-solidarity environment where employees are very task-focused and the emphasis is on delivering the product or service. Conversely, others thrive in a highly social climate where there is a more collaborative approach to tasks. Management has the unenviable job of satisfying the majority – it will never please everyone.

Corporate morality

In the absence of clear, unequivocal academic research in the UK it is not certain whether any attempt by an employer to impose a greater set of moral values on employees than those required of them by the kind of society in which they live is doomed to failure. Researchers in Australia discovered that the effect on employee behaviour of ethical codes was minimal and what influenced them the most, in practice, was the prevailing morality of society rather than of their workplace (Farrell, Cobbin and Farrell, 2002).

Does this mean that ethical codes are doomed to failure? Possibly. It may mean that people who live in a society that emphasizes the cult of the individual at the expense of a collective morality have a weaker commitment to ethical behaviour than individuals who have been brought up to believe in the collective good.

As we will see, there is evidence to indicate that, in the absence of clear, strong leadership, codes of corporate ethics or values are seen by employees as nothing more than PR waffle or something for the HR department to disseminate and pontificate upon rather than as a practical, everyday code to operate by.

Do codes of ethics work? Research in Australia

Research carried out in Australia (Farrell, Cobbin and Farrell, 2002) revealed that there was no discernable association between the patterns of behaviour of employees and the approach of the organization towards its ethical culture. It did not seem to matter whether the organization had a strong ethical policy or not. Instead, researchers determined that the strongest ethical culture affecting employee behaviour, in the organizations surveyed, came from an external shared source.

The researchers were not able to identify this external shared source but suggested it may range anywhere from the culture of office workers in large Australian corporations via the common culture of the Australian community to a generalized contemporary worldview. What this means is that societal norms may have a greater influence on behaviour in the workplace than some form of 'company code'.

Whether or not this is an exclusively Australian phenomenon is unknown but that possibility should not be excluded given the known Australian predilection for individual behaviour and resistance to imposed regulations.

If the employees of the company have no functioning moral code of behaviour other than that set out by society as a whole, they will never adopt any of management's exhortations about 'doing the right thing', whatever that may be. They will tend to see themselves as separate from the organization, owing no loyalty to it other than that which can be bought by a monthly salary.

Following this logic results in the conclusion that only the fear of being caught, or their own personal morality, will prevent employees from committing dysfunctional acts against the company such as:

- disloyalty – talking the company and its products down, discouraging prospective employees;
- inertia – moving at their own pace to process information or conduct business;
- betrayal – disclosing confidential information about the company and its products;
- corruption – accepting bribes or undue hospitality to favour particular suppliers or customers at the expense of others;
- theft – of company assets;
- fraud – theft covered up by deliberate manipulation of company records.

This, clearly, is not the case. Modern companies do not, or at least should not, operate in a climate of fear where 'ethical police' study every action. Most companies accept that societal norms should not be the only measure of business morality; instead they take the view that they have a responsibility to their employees and part of that responsibility is the elimination, wherever possible, of dysfunctional behaviour by establishing and disseminating a code of ethics and encouraging compliance with it.

There is some evidence to indicate that a degree of cynicism is present in employees that is directed towards statements of ethical values expressed by their employers which are at variance with the actual behaviour of those organizations. Clearly organizations that claim to have an idealistic set of moral values and then act inconsistently with them, or where those who purport to lead contravene their own code of ethics, will be unlikely to carry the workforce with them in a quest for moral correctness.

For example, an organization may set great importance, in its ethical code and related employee rules and instructions, by what it calls 'ethical behaviour'. It may claim that the company will not tolerate examples of unethical behaviour including bribery, fraud or misrepresentation. All this is fine and to be expected. If the company is then caught out:

- paying backhanders to agents to obtain contracts; or
- tolerating the use of child labour in a supplier in a developing country; or
- breaching environmental regulations; or
- misrepresenting or mis-selling its products to the public,

particularly where such actions were carried out by or condoned by directors or senior management, it is likely that employees of such a company would treat the ethical code with some indifference. Clearly, in that case, it would be the employee's inherent personal morality that would be the determining factor in behaviour, not the rules set by the company.

The ethical or moral culture of an organization, what we might describe as its value system or moral code, is set by those at its pinnacle, namely the senior, most influential, even the most inspiring directors. This has been called 'tone at the top' and we will examine this in more detail later. What is of interest, when examining any particular organization, is the reality behind the façade, or Area 4 in the Johari Window (page 42). This is the dichotomy of behaviour or the internal conflict in the organization in situations where the actual behaviour of managers and employees differs from the organization's published expressed values, and what the effect of that is on individual employees.

Tone at the top

Tone at the top refers to how an organization's leadership creates an ethical (or unethical) atmosphere in the workplace. The management's attitudes and actions will set the tone or culture of the organization. If the senior management demonstrate a commitment to ethical values and observe their own control policies and procedures this will influence behaviour throughout the organization, but if upper management appear unconcerned with ethics and, for example, condone unethical behaviour in order to boost profits, employees will be more prone to commit fraud and feel that ethical conduct isn't a priority.

Tone at the top is about creating a culture where everyone has ownership and responsibility for doing the right thing, because it is the right thing to do. A report prepared by PricewaterhouseCoopers in 2010 identified an approach that set out the following principles as key to establishing and sustaining an ethical culture:

- Consistent and visible executive sponsorship for ethics and compliance-related issues is not just key, it is mandatory.

- Managers must understanding what the prevailing culture is first, before attempting to make any wide-sweeping changes.

- Leaders must consistently 'do as they say', not 'do as they want to do', in a way that is aligned with and enforces the values and ethical standards of the business.

- Good behaviours must be rewarded and recognized, poor behaviours must be acted upon and necessary action undertaken, openly and transparently.

- Embedding systems and processes to support the tone at the top as 'business as usual' will help shape the organizational culture and measure the effectiveness of leadership actions and behaviours over a period of time. These include statements of values and ethical policies as well as procedures designed to reinforce ethical behaviour such as training initiatives, a whistleblowing hotline and inclusion of ethical and anti-fraud policies in staff handbooks etc.

Ethics in the workplace

In 2010 the Institute of Business Ethics (IBE) carried out a survey entitled *Corporate Ethics Policies and Programmes: UK and continental Europe survey 2010*. This was the latest in a series of triennial surveys carried out by the Institute and, they report, it shows some significant changes from their previous survey in 2007.

The survey was sent to 295 companies listed in the FTSE 350. The usable response rate was 16 per cent or 47 companies and from this the IBE claimed they had sufficient data to be able to draw conclusions and evaluate trends. The summary of results revealed the following:

- 98 per cent of the companies responding gave the main reason for having a code as guidance to staff as to what to do in situations giving rise to an ethical conflict.

- The IBE estimated that at least 80 per cent of FTSE 350 companies had an explicit ethics policy or code of ethics.

- Only 8 per cent (2007: 27 per cent) of companies stated that the board of directors were taking direct responsibility for the ethical programme, which reflects a growing tendency to delegate the function to a compliance function, often a board sub-committee. In 41 per cent of companies the company secretary or the legal department was responsible for ethical policy and codes of business ethics.

- In 2010, 85 per cent of companies saw the use of a code of ethics as an aid to creating a shared and consistent company culture.

- 83 per cent of companies screened suppliers for ethical standards.

- Companies also saw codes as aids to safeguarding the company's reputation (92 per cent) and as a public statement of their ethical commitment (83 per cent). 81 per cent of the responses (as part of multiple answers) stated that companies saw ethical codes as a component of reducing operational risk.

- 66 per cent of companies gave ethics training to staff on the meaning and use of their ethical code. This is down from 74 per cent in 2007. In-house seminars were the most popular method, followed by e-learning, which was not a feature in 2007.

- Electronic copies of codes were the preferred method of communication to staff, generally through use of the company intranet. Only half of the companies included the code in their staff handbook compared with 70 per cent in 2007. This may indicate either less reliance on the printed word or a feeling that electronic media is more accessible. A feature of a number of recently issued codes is the provision of a simple guide to its content that can be easily understood and carried in a purse or wallet. It normally includes help as to how to raise a matter involving ethics, and clear instructions of what to do when staff encounter an ethical dilemma.

- 81 per cent of companies mentioned their code in their annual report and 72 per cent in their corporate responsibilities or similar statement.

- 69 per cent (in 2007 the figure was 72 per cent) required compliance as part of the contract of employment and 50 per cent (in 2007 it was 52 per cent) of companies had used the code in disciplinary proceedings. 41 per cent included ethics as part of the performance appraisal for managers and half the companies responding required managers to sign a copy of the ethics policy.

- 76 per cent took active steps to monitor the effectiveness of codes, down from 82 per cent in 2007.

- The most important ethical issue overall was bribery and corruption and discrimination policies and whistleblowing were seen as the key issues. In 2007 safety and security was the key issue with concerns about the environment second.

What does this, admittedly limited, survey tell us about attitudes to ethics in UK business?

In her introduction to the report, Director Philippa Foster Back says:

> I am glad to note the growing evidence that boards of directors are taking the effectiveness of their ethics policies and programmes seriously. It is a bit of a cliché now to talk of the importance of 'tone at the top' but it is true! If the standard is not set by senior management in the way they behave, then it is likely to be only a question of time before reputation and other integrity problems appear.
>
> (Institute of Business Ethics, 2010)

This is borne out by the survey finding that there was consistent use of codes as an aid to creating an appropriate company culture and in screening suppliers, but there was a decrease in the direct involvement of the board of directors and the use of codes was almost universally seen as being primarily for staff training, even if they had additional uses such as part of risk management.

There is a greater awareness of the need for these codes and companies do tend to broadcast their ethical credentials. The codes are disseminated to staff, although worryingly through less reliance on printed media, and ethics is becoming an issue for line management. In short companies have recognized the practical and business values of ethical codes and appear to value them as an aid to creating a business climate with a strong ethical component.

How much of this has been stimulated by the passing of the Bribery Act 2010 is not known. Certainly corruption now features strongly as a concern in the responses to the survey, much more so than in 2007, so it may be that a strong commitment to ethical values is a response to the requirement in the Act that companies have proper procedures in place to prevent bribery and corruption taking place. Certainly ethical policies would feature strongly as part of these, so one would expect to see:

- a renewed emphasis on existing ethics policies being brought to the attention of staff;
- new policies being written particularly relevant to bribery issues;
- an increase in staff training and dissemination of advice about 'what to do';
- introduction or emphasis on whistleblowing arrangements.

Whatever the reason, the increased emphasis on ethical and moral values and an increased commitment to ethical practice by companies, whether stimulated by fear of the penalties under the Bribery Act or not, can be no bad thing.

In 2008 the Institute of Business Ethics carried out a survey into *Employee Views of Ethics at Work*. It was conducted through MORI so had some credibility as a statistically valid survey. The first survey was in 2005 and there are some interesting changes since that first survey was carried out.

- Compared to 2005, British full-time workers are generally less tolerant of unethical practices in the workplace.
- Employees feel less pressured to compromise ethical standards in their place of work than in 2005.
- Staff perceived their organizations as more ethical than three years previously.
- There is evidence in this survey that the existence of formal ethics programmes and a positive ethical climate are linked to higher standards of ethical behaviour in the workplace.
- In terms of which employees are likely to have higher ethical standards, the survey data shows that:
  - female employees are generally stricter in their ethical standards than male employees;

– employees aged 16–34 are significantly more likely to be tolerant of unethical workplace practices, which is similar to the 2005 findings so may be a consistent facet of employee behaviour.

There are, however, some concerns revealed by the survey:

● Around a quarter of British employees are aware of misconduct in their organizations but of these only three out of five are reporting it.

● Attitudes of indifference ('none of my business') and the belief that no corrective action would be taken deter employees who are aware of misconduct from reporting it to management.

● The provision of formal assistance to employees on ethical matters is still relatively low in private sector organizations compared to that provided for those working in the public sector.

● Of note is that minor 'fiddling' is still considered to be inevitable in a modern organization by three in ten of those in managerial or supervisory roles.

The survey brings heartening news that matters do appear to have improved between 2005 and 2008 that may be as a result of the generally increased emphasis on Corporate Social Responsibility. The survey generally reinforces the effectiveness of ethics policies and training. However, the survey also tells us that it is one thing to have a policy; it is entirely another to expect it to act as a mechanism of social control within an organization. There is still an expectation that minor theft or fraud is a fact of business life. More worryingly there is an expectation in many areas that nothing will be done where ethical misconduct is reported so employees either don't bother or are afraid to do so. The expression 'none of my business' appears to be a simple rationalization for not reporting unethical behaviour for fear of adverse consequences and there is still a significant element of unethical behaviour in UK companies.

Corporate culture

The culture of an organization exerts a strong but subtle pressure on an individual employee. Human beings generally feel the need to fit in with group norms, they tend to go along with 'the way we do things around here' because not doing so can lead to unpleasant personal consequences such as:

- social ostracism;
- disfavour from more senior colleagues;
- reduced promotion prospects; and
- gentle (or indeed not so gentle) pressure to leave both from colleagues and superiors.

Individual employees tend to identify most closely with colleagues in their immediate working environment. The larger the organization the more distant other parts of it become one to another and, despite management's best endeavours to create corporate harmony and engender a feeling of oneness throughout the organization, individual employees will naturally gravitate towards those they feel most secure and comfortable with – which will primarily be colleagues carrying out similar roles to themselves or working in the same sub-group.

It is a mistake to assume that organizations only have one style or culture. Different parts of an organization, subsidiaries, divisions or departments can have their own cultures within the overall tone of the organization, established by local management.

Table 2.2 is a synthesis of several attempts to categorise cultural styles and is not based on any particular piece of research. It serves as an example of the variations it is possible to find either at an organizational level or at a sub-level within an individual entity. For the purpose of this exercise organizational cultures have been sub-divided into four broad categories. Organizational psychologists and researchers will probably frown at the simplicity of these sub-divisions but this is not a book on organizational theory so these are merely illustrations. It would be invidious or misleading to try to provide examples of each type of organization so students should attempt to identify their own; however, a suggestion is made of the type of organization purely by way of illustration.

Following on from this broad sub-division, relating cultural styles to the control environment very rapidly indicates where problem areas arise. Table 2.3 sets out four possible cultural approaches, the management style most associated with that type of culture and the consequential risk factors that arise. The culture of the organization clearly influences the behaviour of individuals and research shows that this can result in individual dysfunctional behaviour or can reinforce patterns of behaviour among groups that may seem acceptable within the bounds of the organization but are, in fact, inappropriate in wider society. The organization is the context for individual actions and we will return to this analysis in Chapter 3.

TABLE 2.2 Examples of corporate culture

Cultural Approach	Symptoms
Anarchic (eg dot.com, design-led organization, financial traders and speculators)	• informal • risk-taking • individualistic – individuals held responsible for own actions • charismatic leadership • constant upheaval • high levels of drinking/socialization • consider themselves outside the norm/special cases • rewards can be very high but also very volatile – emphasis on performance-based rewards systems • anti-bureaucratic • high level of commitment to work • organization is outward-looking and aggressive
Dictatorial (eg large family-owned company)	• culture reflects values of dominant individual or group • formalized structures with power in the hands of an individual or small group • promotion difficult if not impossible but constant turnover of staff • blame culture – tendency to allocate blame for failures and mistakes to lowest-ranking employees • limited amount of delegation – power remains in hands of dominant group so all decisions must be referred to the next level upward • cautious and unwilling to take risks – the price of failure is high • sub-culture of gossip and plotting – organization is inward-looking and defensive • high levels of reward for employees with favoured status – rigid pay structures for others • action outside group norms severely punished • rejection of criticism originated from outside ruling group • reluctance to change • approach to risk erratic dependent on views of controlling individual/group • can make erratic/illogical decisions

TABLE 2.2 *continued*

Cultural Approach	Symptoms
Bureaucratic (eg public sector body)	• rules-based • rigid hierarchical structures • delegated powers strictly determined – decisions outside delegated powers referred upwards and discussed with key decision-makers • rewards are time-based – pay rises determined by length of service rather than ability • formal processes and procedures • blame culture – tendency to allocate blame for failures and to hide mistakes • often high levels of individual skills confined in specific areas • employees tend to be conformist and not totally financially motivated • objective and impersonal – very senior management often faceless • extremely risk-averse
Democratic (eg plc with strong corporate governance)	• culture consensual – management attempt to persuade workforce of value of initiatives • high levels of explanation and transparency • high levels of delegation and individual initiative within overarching framework – powers fairly widely drawn • high levels of accountability – managers making serious errors expected to fall on their swords • senior management hold themselves accountable to stakeholders • high levels of loyalty to organization • some element of 'benevolent paternalism' – efforts by management to ensure workers feel valued • co-operative ways of working • blurring of boundaries in approaches to tasks • rewards based on abilities and achievements • risk-averse – high levels of planning and consideration

TABLE 2.3 Corporate culture and risk factors

Cultural Approach	Management Style	Risk Factors
Anarchic	<ul><li>incompetent</li><li>confused and contradictory</li><li>constant change for no obvious reason</li><li>high levels of individualistic behaviour</li><li>blame culture</li><li>flexible ethics driven by necessity rather than principle</li></ul>	<ul><li>low levels of control</li><li>high possibility of errors or mistakes going undetected</li><li>low levels of consideration towards organizational assets</li><li>attempts to cover mistakes through additional risk-taking, which may make them even larger</li></ul>
Dictatorial	<ul><li>domineering</li><li>one-way communication</li><li>employees undervalued</li><li>imbalance of reward structures</li><li>rewards not related to performance but to relationships</li><li>perceived unfairness</li><li>cultural values those of senior management</li></ul>	<ul><li>attitudes coloured by resentment – dysfunctional behaviour may arise through employees wishing to challenge or 'get back' at the organization</li><li>overt observance of rules but possible covert behaviour</li><li>rigid demarcation of management territories may give rise to avoidance of decision-making where 'boundaries' have been crossed</li><li>blame culture encourages the hiding of mistakes</li></ul>

TABLE 2.3 *continued*

Cultural Approach	Management Style	Risk Factors
Bureaucratic	• slow • conformist • emphasis on collective decision-making • blame culture • rigid conformance to plans and strategies • discourages individual initiative • homogenous employees with similar cultural values • rewards not linked to performance but to length of service	• high levels of conformism • rules tend to be obeyed and rule-breakers informed on • security valued as key aspect of job role so risk is not considered acceptable • highly bureaucratic systems make fraud difficult • employees in remote locations may exploit rigidity of structures once removed from immediate supervision
Democratic	• accountable • decisions await consensus so can be slow to respond • initiative fostered if of demonstrable benefit • low level of risk taking • rewards linked to performance • culture geared around job satisfaction • high level of ethical values	• high levels of trust within organization • unscrupulous employees can exploit tendency to emphasize individual initiative and delegated responsibility • high levels of accountability reinforce tendency to hide mistakes and errors • rewards based on performance encourage aggressive accounting practices to 'improve' results or hide losses

The public sector

It is important to understand that organizations in the public sector are conceptually different from those in the private sector. Their raison d'être, their ethos, even their accounting is completely different from comparably sized commercial organizations.

Public sector organizations are much more accountable than their commercial cousins. What might be considered to be mild profligacy or bending of rules in the private sector can become a huge scandal when it involves public money – witness the furore in 2009 over MPs' expenses, which, though egregious in some cases, provoked a massive media storm resulting in many MPs either deciding not to stand or being prevented from standing at the election of May 2010, effectively losing their jobs.

Public service organizations don't have shareholders but they do have governing bodies that are, effectively, non-executives. These can be, for example, elected councillors in a local authority, or members of a board of trustees in a local health authority. These boards are responsible for accountability to stakeholders as well as dealing with strategic and political issues affecting the organization.

In order to carry out these functions effectively, governing bodies of public service organizations need:

- effective risk management approaches;
- oversight and supervision of functions;
- internal audit.

Such organizations tend therefore to be:

- hierarchical with many levels of management;
- committee-driven with accountability vested in various committees staffed by a mixture of executives and non-executives.

Public sector bodies will have, as a minimum, a finance committee, a remuneration committee that decides the pay of executives, and an audit committee (see Chapter 4) in addition to the governing body. Frequently seats on these committees can be seen as political prizes.

Good governance suggests that members of oversight committees should challenge the executive and ask searching questions of management, not desisting until they have the answers, but experience shows that, in practice, many organizations avoid such individuals because of the 'trouble' they cause by asking questions and the organization relies on the following as key planks of good governance:

- its policies and procedures;
- its manuals and internal control structures;
- internal audit; and
- supervision and oversight functions.

The committee structures are there to enhance reporting and accountability. It is not the role of a powerful committee chairman to usurp the chief executive or vice versa. Consequently the boundaries of each role must be clearly understood.

Ethics in the public sector

The public sector has some features which make it distinctly different from commercial organizations and that will affect the motivation and behaviour of individuals working within it:

- Many public sector bodies have no clear goals – they have more generalized aims and ambitions but these are not necessarily spelled out in terms of clear, measurable objectives. Note that an objective is different from a target – cutting waiting times by 50 per cent is a target, making sure all benefit claimants receive the benefits they are entitled to is an objective. Objectives tend to be fairly generalized or expressed in terms of a mission that may have no impact on the daily working lives of employees.

- Many public sector employees are decision-makers, eg social workers, benefit claims assessors, police officers, so the effect of their processes has an impact on the daily lives of other people, often in a most direct way. Many public sector employees are not divorced from the public they serve and are in contact with them on a daily basis. This is a reminder of their role and responsibility and they have to behave in an ethical and fair manner wherever possible as the mechanisms of control are such that they are accountable for their actions.

- In many cases employees function under more than one form of control. For example, they will be under the day-to-day control of line management – and in some cases, for example in social services, this may be more than one manager where employees are involved in dealing with cases. In addition there may be legal requirements to be adhered to, budgetary constraints or higher-level policy decisions that influence the thrust of day-to-day behaviour.

- Employees in the public sector display high levels of intrinsic motivation, known by researchers in this field as public sector motivation. Research indicates that employees feel that the service delivered to the end user must be delivered properly and fully to benefit them and if it is not, the level of service will fall and the individuals served by the organization will suffer. The end user of the service is, in most cases, indifferent to the individuals or even the organization that provides the service; they are interested only in the outcome, ie the effect on them as an individual. Consequently there is little incentive for the employee to promote the interests of the organization as such; they are promoting the efficacy of the outcome.

As expected, the research also revealed that individuals working in the public sector had a much greater awareness of ethical issues and received more support than their colleagues in the private sector. The reason for this is likely to be cultural. The organizations in the public sector, eg local authorities, the National Health Service (NHS), suppliers of social housing etc are non-profit making and are concerned primarily with service delivery, ie with outcomes. They also have limited control over their income as they are funded through the public revenue. There is no incentive for senior managers to distort results for personal gain and the prevailing ethical climate within the organization serves to discourage individuals from committing fraud without a strong motive other than personal financial enrichment.

In addition, control systems, particularly financial controls, are generally fairly strong and there is a high level of supervision and authorization in such bodies. This may act as a deterrent although there have been some spectacular frauds in the public sector, mostly committed by finance managers with a degree of autonomy.

However, in the public sector there have been instances where, despite the overt commitment to good corporate governance, management has displayed an adverse reaction to criticism or claims of unfair or discriminatory practice. The National Health Service (NHS), for example, has displayed extreme behaviour in treating whistleblowers extremely badly and there are several instances where employees reporting malpractice have been hounded out of employment and denied future work prospects as NHS management and senior staff backtrack to cover up the offences. Several local authorities have had to pay compensation for unfair treatment of or unfair discrimination between workers; Wakefield City Council, for example, responded to whistle-blowing by six care workers concerning management failures in local authority homes by sacking them. This cost the council an estimated £1m in an out-of-court settlement by the time the employment tribunal had finished with it (Waugh, 2007).

These cases may serve to weaken public sector motivation and encourage employees to leave the public sector. This may serve to restrict improvements and to foster a climate of blame and cover-up which, as we have seen, if perpetuated by higher management fosters dysfunctional behaviour among lower level employees. This may manifest itself not in fraud, theft or damage, but in:

● extreme risk aversion;

● unwillingness to assume responsibility and make decisions;

● lack of motivation resulting in inertia and laziness;

● bullying and abuse of power;

● increased use of lower grade staff with less inclination to challenge management behaviour.

The consequence is that inefficiency and unethical behaviour becomes institutionalized and, because abuses are not reported, the service provided by the organization declines even if additional financial resources are provided for it. This may breed a fear of speaking out, thus creating the illusion that all is well in the public sector and that instances of unethical behaviour are much lower than in the private sector when the reverse may be true; the root of the problems of organizations, in such cases, are not financial but ethical.

CASE STUDY

Susan Chumley applied for a job at Suspenders plc, a subsidiary of the giant Megatron organization. She was successful and was pleased to accept the job as her friend Maureen also worked there.

On her first day Susan was given an induction by her line manager Dave Sparkel, who also introduced her to the rest of the team. Susan noticed that the offices were very spartan and there were no personal items on desks or pinned to the walls – she was told that this was company policy. At lunchtime the other workers left the offices and returned ten minutes later with sandwiches that they ate at their desks while continuing to work. No one showed Susan where the sandwich shop was.

After several weeks her colleagues became more approachable and she was invited to join a few of them for a drink after work. There she learned that their line manager Dave Sparkel was rumoured to be having an affair with the purchasing manager of their biggest customer, Lofticel, and that he had negotiated some private commission for himself in return for cutting prices to Lofticel.

Susan also spoke to her friend Maureen who worked in a different department. Maureen told her that a supervisor had recently been fired for sending an e-mail critical of management policy. She also learned that, before she joined, seven members of the finance team had been made redundant and had been replaced with casual workers. The remainder of the finance team was hostile to the company and in order to revenge themselves on the company carried out small acts of sabotage such as deliberately delaying payments to suppliers thus causing supply problems to manufacturing units, and failing to claim discounts, thereby increasing costs.

The staff handbook claimed there was a whistleblowing hotline that was totally confidential but the only person known to have used it was marched off company premises by security and never returned.

Discuss

- What are the main features of the corporate culture at Suspenders plc?
- What impact does this culture have on employees like Susan and Maureen?
- Does the culture and climate of the company need to be changed and if so how could this be achieved?
- What benefit might any changes bring to the company?

Bibliography

Ashkenasy, N, Widerson, C and Peterson, M (2000) *The Handbook of Organisational Culture and Climate*, Sage, London

Barratt, M and Davidson, M (2006) *Gender and Communication at Work*, Ashgate Publishing Ltd, Farnham

Bowers, D and Seashore, S (1966) Predicting organisational effectiveness with a four factor theory of leadership, *Administrative Science Quarterly*, **11**: 238–263

Cadbury, Sir Peter (1992) *Financial Aspects of Corporate Governance*, Gee & Co, London

Drummond, H (2000) *Introduction to Organizational Behaviour*, Oxford University Press, Oxford

Farrell, B, Cobbin, D and Farrell, H (2002) Can codes of ethics really produce consistent behaviours? *Journal of Managerial Psychology*, **17**, 6

Francois, P (2000) 'Public service motivation' as an argument for government provision, *Journal of Public Economics*, **78**: 275–299

French, R, Rayner, C, Rees, G and Rumbles, S (2008) *Organisational Behaviour*, John Wiley, Chichester

Furnham, A (2006) *The Psychology of Behaviour at Work*, Psychology Press, Hove

Goffee, R and Jones, G (1998) *The Character of a Corporation: How your company's culture can make or break your business*, Collins, London

Handy, Charles (2000) *21 Ideas for Managers*, Jossey-Bass, San Francisco

HMSO (2010) *Bribery Act 2010*, HMSO, London

Institute of Business Ethics (2008) *Employee Views of Ethics at Work*, Institute of Business Ethics, London

Institute of Business Ethics (2010) *Corporate Ethics Policies and Programmes: UK and continental Europe survey 2010*, IBE, London

Lewis, M (1999) *Liar's Poker: Playing the money markets*, Coronet Books, Philadelphia, PA

Luft, J (1961) The Johari Window: A graphic model of awareness in interpersonal relations, *Human Relations Training News*, NTL, Arlington, VA

PricewaterhouseCoopers (2010) *Tone from the Top: Transforming words into action*, PwC, London

Sarbanes–Oxley Act (2002) H.R.Rep 107-610 25 July 2002. US Government Printing Office, Washington DC

Schein (1992) *Organisational Culture and Leadership*, Jossey-Bass, San Francisco

Waugh, R (2007) Sacked whistleblowers win £1m payout from council, *Yorkshire Past News*, 14 August

Woods, S and West, M (2010) *The Psychology of Work and Organisations*, Cengage, Andover

Wulfson, M (1998) Rules of the game: Do corporate codes of ethics work? *Review of Business*, **20**

Ethical behaviour

LEARNING OBJECTIVES

This chapter will enable you to:

- understand the principles of ethical theory and the motivations for ethical behaviour;
- understand the socialization of individuals into unethical behaviour towards customers and towards the organization;
- learn how to combat dysfunctional behaviour in the workplace;
- understand the role of the human resources department and the design and content of ethical policies including ethics and whistleblowing policies.

Introduction

In Chapter 2 we looked at some organizational theory and we identified what we mean by corporate culture and how corporate morality and ethics at the level of the organization develops and is fostered by the organization. We also looked at some of the effects the organization can experience when corporate ethics are subverted or the culture is corrupted to the extent that the expressed values conflict with actual behaviour.

Now we need to drill down a little and look at the effects of corporate culture on the individual. After all, ethics and Corporate Social Responsibility do not exist in a vacuum, nor are they simply theoretical concepts, so we must place them in the context of employees and the organizations they work for so we can consider how one affects the other.

It is a consistent theme of this book that corporate governance and Corporate Social Responsibility, in the end, are about people. It should be remembered that Enron had lots of corporate governance, an audit committee, non-executive directors, separate chairman and CEO, all the classic requirements, but, because the senior management were corrupt from the very top down, the whole organization's values were skewed to such an extent that, for example, causing rolling electricity blackouts to homes, factories and hospitals in California was seen as acceptable because it enabled the electricity traders to make money (McLean and Elkind, 2004).

Lying to regulators and deceiving each other became the norm to such an extent that the chief financial officer (CFO), Andrew Fastow, even used the financial devices that Enron was using to manipulate its accounts to cheat the company he was paid to lie for and make money for himself and his wife.

When good people go bad no amount of policies and procedures will protect the organization from whatever the employees want to do to it. So what we must consider in this chapter is the question of ethics. In particular we need answers to questions such as:

- What do we mean by ethics?
- How do individuals respond to ethical initiatives?
- How can they be corrupted in a dysfunctional organization?
- What can be done to prevent this happening?

This topic is far from easy. Ethics is a matter of philosophy and ethical conflicts and philosophical conundrums abound. We will look briefly at these without, hopefully, getting too bogged down in philosophical speculation, just to set the scene from a theoretical perspective, then we will deal with the real world as it is and the actions of individuals and the organizations they create.

Ethical theories

There are, basically, three principal ethical theories that are relevant to what we are trying to consider here. In summary the three theories we are going to consider are:

- **Consequentialism:** The end justifies the means – so if the outcome of actions is moral or ethical then the steps taken to achieve it are moral or ethical, whatever they may be. This derives some of its beginnings from utilitarianism propounded by, among others, John Stuart Mill (1806–1873), which held that the moral worth of an action was derived from the amount of good it did to society or for the benefit of individuals – the greatest good of the greatest number.

- **Deontology:** This theory was largely based on the writings of Immanuel Kant (1724–1804) who held that there were moral absolutes and that, for an outcome to be moral or ethical, all the actions leading up to it must be moral or ethical. We should behave in a moral or ethical way based upon universal principles of morality and ethics.

- **Contractualism:** This theory is based on the notion that individuals can agree what is moral and what is not in a form of social contract; so an immoral act is one that is wrong by any set of social principles that no one would reasonably reject. In this case there are no moral absolutes, but also the end does not necessarily justify the means so, broadly, this sits somewhere in the middle.

Apologies to any moral philosophers reading this who may well be offended by the necessary simplicity of these definitions but we must, essentially, get to the point.

Take for example a classic moral dilemma. Mr A's son is ill and needs an operation that can only be performed in the United States. Despite his best efforts he can only raise half the money by fundraising and his own resources and needs another £25,000 for his son. If he does not raise the money his son will die. He is presented with an opportunity to steal £25,000 from his employer. If he is clever the fraud may not be detected but if he is not he will be caught and may face jail and his son will be put into care. He steals the money and the fraud goes undetected, he takes his son to America and his son is cured. Is what he did ethical or moral in any way?

- Consequentialist theory might hold that it is of greater moral good for the father to act to save his son's life than to stand by and do nothing. To watch his son die would be an immoral act when he could do something to save him. The end justified the means so the act could be construed as a moral or ethical one.

- Deontologists would, however, say that stealing is, of itself, an immoral act. No one could argue that theft of another person's goods is a moral act of itself. Accordingly what he did is not moral or ethical.

- Constructivists might say that to act to save his son's life was a humanitarian act and other individuals in society would do the same thing given a similar dilemma. This stance depends on the moral viewpoint of the society – for example, Jehovah's Witnesses will deny themselves medical treatment, even if this leads to death, because they believe that certain treatments are morally wrong. Certain sections of society believe it is alright to kill in the name of *jihad*, others that all life, even that of the tiniest insect or worm, is sacred and should not be taken.

Moral dilemmas are just that – dilemmas – and we must be aware that before we judge others or make decisions about what is ethical and what is not we should evaluate our own moral standpoint.

Aspirations and attitudes

In 1965 Jane Deverson and Charles Hamblett produced a book they called *Generation X*. Jane Deverson had originally been commissioned by middle-of-the-road magazine *Woman's Own* to interview teenagers and find out what the youth of 1965 were thinking. The outcome of those interviews was deemed to be so shocking to *Woman's Own* readers that the magazine refused to publish it so the research was eventually turned into a book. The interviews revealed a teenage culture that:

- formed itself into 'tribal' groups – in those days Mods and Rockers;
- took purple hearts (a mixture of amphetamine and barbiturates);
- had sex before marriage;
- wore outlandish fashions; and
- didn't respect the Queen very much.

This shocked the older, more traditional public still conscious of wartime austerity and imbued with patriotic values and a trust in politicians that was to be rudely shattered some years later by John Profumo and Christine Keeler.

What the survey revealed was a widespread youth culture that made up its own rules, had its own values and even its own language and, far from being confined to smaller groups such as jazz-loving students or disaffected working-class teenage boys, appeared to cross every demographic and to involve both men and women.

Generation X, growing up in the 1960s and 1970s, did not display the same loyalties to Queen and country that their parents did, and challenged the political status quo. This, many have argued, was the beginning of the 'me' generation symbolized by the L'Oréal advertising slogan 'Because you're worth it'. Social commentators argued that this generation, reinforced by the principles of the Thatcher government in the 1980s, sacrificed the old ideals of duty and service on the altar of greed and consumerism, so that greed became good and taking advantage of your opportunities, even at the expense of others, was acceptable providing you were a winner and stayed a winner. They have gone on to argue that the next generation, the one born in the 1970s and 1980s, has taken this to extremes, resulting in the celebrity-obsessed, culturally vacant society of the new millennium.

This is an oversimplification but it serves to illustrate the point that the expectations of people born in 1981 are very different from those born in 1931 – the world changed beyond all recognition and personal morality changed with it. What is considered acceptable or even normal behaviour now would have shocked the pre-war society to its core.

In her book *Trust and Honesty* (2006) Professor Tamar Frankel claims that deception has spread across the entire population and now affects not only corporate life but suppliers of healthcare, shoppers, applicants for jobs, students in examinations, journalists in their publications, competing athletes, scientists in research materials, politicians and even government employees. She claims that this is not confined to the USA but that deception and abuse of trust is a worldwide phenomenon. She claims that, increasingly, individual personal morality is declining and that this is what underpins much of the deception and abuse of trust encountered in daily life. When such crimes are committed by significant figures in society such as high profile businessmen, rock stars, film actors etc, they somehow validate the actions of lesser mortals like you and me. If this decline in personal morality is coupled with a failure of regulators to regulate and enforcers to enforce, the epidemic spreads. Professor Frankel argues that it is against what she sees as this international decline in moral standards that the efforts of companies to create a corporate morality must be placed.

Clearly there is a general social disapproval of stealing and lying – these are not seen as desirable socially – for good reasons, and yet it transpires that, for example, employees who intellectually accept that it is wrong to take home company stationery, to surf the net on company time or to ring their relatives using the company phone nevertheless still do so. Thus the absolute morality that would prevent an individual from stealing someone's wallet containing £20 wouldn't stop them taking £20 worth of stationery home.

One survey, carried out by online recruiter Fish4jobs, estimated that small-scale pilfering and office fraud cost UK business over £800m per year (www.thisiswiltshire.co.uk, 2004). Whilst this may not be the most statistically valid survey carried out it does have similarities with some of the findings of the surveys carried out by the Institute of Business Ethics, referred to in Chapter 2, and is a good indicator of the scale of the problem. According to the Fish4jobs survey:

- 78 per cent of office workers had taken home stationery during the last year;
- 59 per cent put personal mail through the company post;
- 20 per cent added £10 or more to expenses claims;
- 15 per cent inflated travel claims;
- 2 per cent took a friend out for a meal and charged it to the company;
- 3 per cent said they had falsely claimed £50 or more back on an expenses claim.

Workers offered reasons for this behaviour:

- 80 per cent of workers thought their bosses regularly charged personal items to the company;
- 20 per cent thought that small 'fiddles' were an accepted part of company life – as long as they stayed small;
- 29 per cent felt that getting a little back on expenses was acceptable because bosses often asked them for extras such as working late without pay;
- 67 per cent said taking home stationery was justified due to them having to make work calls from their personal mobile phone.

Here we can see examples of:

- The perception that the boss doesn't abide by the same rules that workers are expected to insofar as they are able to override procedures and controls. Note this may not be actually the case but the workers questioned perceived it to be, so the effect is the same.
- Workers 'getting their own back'. They had to work late so they're getting a little unofficial 'reward'.
- A part of corporate culture that believes that it is acceptable to use stationery and office equipment for personal gain, because the boss does it or because the amounts involved are small.

These statistics illustrate the scale of the problem. Individuals distance themselves from the organization and justify, to themselves, actions that, if carried out in another context, they might simply abhor. We assume that most individuals would not:

- steal £5 from a colleague or friend;
- take a charity collection box;
- shoplift from a department store.

However, they are prepared to justify to themselves such 'small' things as minor pilfering of company stationery or use of computers and telephones for private purposes.

Individuals in organizations

Dysfunctional behaviour is a personal thing – organizations don't commit frauds or corrupt people – people within organizations do. What we have to look at now is, given both the organizational context and the prevailing moral climate in society, how does individual motivation fit in?

Work plays a significant part in most people's lives and consequently social scientists have, unsurprisingly, discovered a plethora of feelings, attitudes, responses and behaviours in the workplace. There are innumerable scholarly works of door-stopping size on the motivations and rationales for people's behaviour at work. In addition there are stunning numbers of 'how to' management books that provide instant, guaranteed solutions to managing those pesky workers and even peskier managers.

Because we are all human and so exhibit the full array of human frailties under stress and because of our propensity for irrational behaviour and our often emotional and irrational reaction to events, it is horribly difficult for anyone to come up with a checklist of actions or signs that will:

- guarantee ethical behaviour;
- stop dysfunctional behaviour by employees or managers; or
- manage workplace change.

To understand the actions of individuals we need to consider the effect that the organizational climate, the prevailing culture and values of the organization have on the individual employee. Note that here we are referring to the real culture that operates within the entity, not the expressed hopes of policies and procedures.

Let us begin at the beginning. Organizations employ people and people have to be managed; no one is born with a full array of management skills. Good managers may have personal qualities such as:

- good communication skills;
- empathy;
- the ability to motivate;
- patience.

These qualities distinguish them from bad or ineffective managers, but it can be argued that the approach they take or the organizational culture within which they operate is one that, consciously or unconsciously, is largely following precepts laid down by one or other of the leading management thinkers of the last 40 years.

Management thinkers such as W. Edwards Deming, Peter Drucker, Tom Peters and Charles Handy became stars of what has become an industry producing a veritable avalanche of management theory and motivational tomes all designed to get the best out of the workforce and increase wealth and happiness for everyone. In following the precepts of these management thinkers, managers with influence can create an environment where the individual employee can be left behind. All too often the euphemisms used by higher-level management are perceived by those lower down the organization as something completely different, as Table 3.1 illustrates. Whilst this might be slightly tongue-in-cheek it serves to illustrate that the message transmitted by management may not be the one received by employees. Situations where individual employees feel that the latest management initiative doesn't take into account their needs, where they feel imposed upon or ignored, can be fertile breeding grounds for a rather different form of entrepreneurial behaviour.

TABLE 3.1 Management speak – what we say is not what we mean

Management Concept	Perceived Meaning
self-actualization	being left to battle on by yourself
empowered	expected to carry out an unfeasibly large workload without resources
lean management	had their resources cut
horizontal organization	not knowing who to report to
sweating the assets	working with outdated, unreliable equipment

Motivation and the role of corporate culture

The prevailing ethical climate of an organization, its mores and values, have a great effect on the employee. Whilst an ethical climate may not, by itself, stop the dysfunctional employee, the prevailing ethos in the organization may serve to blunt the self-rationalizations they must engage in to justify their actions to themselves.

Similarly, an organization that couples a strong set of ethical values with a successful HR policy towards its employees, successful in the sense that they feel valued and rewarded by the organization, has created a strong deterrent to dysfunctional behaviour. This may also serve to isolate the dysfunctional individual and reveal them as a person who stands out from the crowd for the wrong reasons.

Individuals in organizations often have less time to consider the ethics of any course of action than might be supposed. Within organizations there is a conflicting mass of:

● targets;
● instructions;
● routines;
● timetables;
● precedents;
● pressures.

This can result in individuals making instant, expedient decisions that may not be particularly ethical or moral but that 'get the job done'. Once this behaviour becomes acceptable it becomes institutionalized and the consequent rationalizations overwhelm the moral high ground.

Where unethical practice is accepted in organizations or, worse still, rewarded, the temptation to help oneself is reinforced. Thus a corporate culture that values 'winning' at any price may well, for example, encourage deviant behaviour in executives by rewarding them by results irrespective of how those results were achieved. For example, this can create a climate where, say, bribery and corruption to obtain contracts is considered acceptable and normal. A corollary to such behaviour may be that, in such an organization executives might think it perfectly acceptable to inflate their expenses or even to invent fictitious officials to bribe whilst, in reality, transferring the money to themselves.

Forms of deviant behaviour can come to be seen as normal because, within the organization, this type of behaviour is seen as acceptable, or even praiseworthy. This might include:

- misrepresentations to customers;
- mis-selling of financial products;
- petty pilfering;
- price fixing;
- exploitation of staff – eg use of part-time immigrant workers on low wages;
- breaches of health and safety legislation;
- excessive remuneration packages for senior executives;
- bribery and corruption;
- abusing expense accounts;
- abuse of product labelling rules.

The employees who do this are otherwise quite normal, reasonable moral citizens who simply rationalize their unethical behaviour as being 'part of the game'.

For example, management in many organizations is often fully aware that the use of company resources for private purposes is generally officially frowned on but unofficially tolerated so, in practice, organizations turn a blind eye to:

- employees making personal phone calls;
- photocopying personal documents;
- using the internet for private purposes during working hours;
- taking company equipment such as laptops home in contravention of security policies;
- submitting expenses claims not fully evidenced by documentation;
- encouraging close friendships with suppliers or customers in the interest of 'good business relations'.

The reason is that, first, such relatively small amounts of 'unofficial' activity would doubtless cost more to police than the activity costs the organization and, second, no organization would want to lose the goodwill of its employees by engendering a culture based on the fear of reprisals or punishment for taking home an office pencil.

However, consider the following:

- Public sector bodies such as local authorities, hospitals, NHS trusts, housing associations etc are funded by public money, which has to be accounted for.

- If it is acceptable to surf the internet, where is the line drawn as to what it is acceptable to access – online holiday companies or shopping websites might be acceptable but what about employees using social networking sites like Facebook or MySpace, online gaming or Ebay?

- If an organization has 50 employees and each one steals as little as £10 worth of goods each week for 48 weeks, this results in a loss of profit of £24,000 per year.

As we will see later, when we look at socialization, those employees who are determined to cling to some form of higher moral values may not be accepted as part of the team and can thus be isolated or even forced out. They feel uncomfortable with the prevailing ethos and, consequently, leave.

In some situations, where employees feel the level of dysfunctionality is actually harmful, they may become whistleblowers and inform on colleagues or the organization in the interests of maintaining a level of ethical standards. In some notable cases involving the NHS, employees finally reported dysfunctional behaviour by other employees, which appeared to be tolerated both by them and by their immediate managers as routine, which, in reality, had turned into actual physical and mental abuse of vulnerable individuals.

Socialization

New individuals learn about the organization they have joined and its culture through a number of socialization processes. Clearly there are often formal induction procedures involving the dissemination of corporate literature, including all the policies and mission statements. In ethical organizations subsequent socialization processes reinforce the messages of ethical activity and the individual accepts the group norms of moral behaviour.

The employee receives the corporate message and will respond in their individual way. As we saw in Chapter 2 the most receptive employees will be those where the values and ethics of the organization fit most closely with the values and ethics of the individual, which may be wholly or partially determined by the values of the society in which they live. Thus employees who might come from a society that values personal benefit above all else may have a more negotiable sense of ethics than one that comes from a society with a stern set of moral principles. Here, when we refer to 'society', we are referring to the immediate society within which the individual spends their time, ie their friends and colleagues, and their influences such as the TV they watch and the papers they read – we are not referring to 'society' in the abstract.

Good socialization processes will help the employee fit in and will inculcate them with the values and prevailing climate of the organization such that an organization which has a strong drive towards ethical and moral behaviour spearheaded by the directors and senior managers will be able to pass those values down to employees at all levels in the organization.

However, in dysfunctional organizations the same is true of immoral behaviour – socialization processes can perpetuate unethical or corrupt behaviour as much as ethical and moral behaviour. In these cases the processes act subtly to convince the individual that what they are doing is somehow ethical and right. The sense of values becomes distorted through processes of rationalization, described later, reinforced by social interactions. One of the key considerations in the socialization process involves the effect of working in groups or teams.

Let us consider not the good and worthy employee who takes on board the ethical message and conforms to corporate standards of morality and Corporate Social Responsibility, but look instead at the employees who do not, those who perpetuate dysfunctional behaviour – defined here as behaviour that an ethical organization would consider unacceptable – as it is from them that we can learn. We will begin by looking at how individuals become subsumed into teams and the effects this can have on them.

Group attractiveness

Researchers have identified that dysfunctional behaviour can exist among sub-groups of employees, such as teams or work groups, rather than being confined solely to certain individuals although these individuals might set the 'tone'. Clearly some of what follows depends on the size of the organization. The larger the organization the more likely it is to contain groups or sub-cultures comprising employees who see themselves as part of, but at the same time separate from, the organization as a whole.

On occasion these sub-cultures establish a clear identity for themselves and create barriers between themselves and the rest of the organization.

This strengthens loyalty to the group within the framework of the organization, or a part of the organization, and creates barriers to entry into the group so that a new employee is only admitted gradually and is accepted only when the other members of the group are satisfied that they will abide by the group norms.

This can happen in divisions or subsidiaries that are remote from the centre and which have a degree of local autonomy. Managers of remote divisions or subsidiaries strive to build a clear identity, maybe in the interests of 'team building', which can serve to increase group cohesion, the desired outcome, but which may also serve to set them apart from the rest of the organization if they don't feel part of the mainstream. For example, management frauds in large organizations have frequently been found in remote divisions or subsidiaries that operate in this way as local management either strive to achieve unrealistic goals imposed upon them or decide to benefit themselves at the expense of what they perceive to be a rather faceless and indifferent organization.

The processes of rationalization and socialization begin to work on the new individual who makes the effort to join the group. The alternative, for the new employee, can be isolation or even hostility as the group consciously or unconsciously seeks to expel the member who doesn't fit. Research has shown that individuals are more likely to be loyal to their immediate colleagues rather than to some concept of corporate identity promoted by remote management.

These sub-cultures can start to develop solutions to perceived or actual problems that are outside the codes of behaviour of the organization as a whole. The more desirable a group is to join, the more readily individuals will be to surrender their moral consciousness and accept rationalizations for actions which, outside work, they would see as being unacceptable.

Socialization at Arthur Andersen

Former Andersen employees Barbara Ley Toffler and Jennifer Reingold looked at the fall of Arthur Andersen, the huge accounting firm that collapsed when their role in the Enron scandal was revealed, shortly to be followed by a similar problem at WorldCom. They said:

New recruits were socialized into believing that Arthur Andersen was a special and exclusive organization. Arthur Andersen offered something special: a way of life ... getting a job there meant making it. They all knew that their chances of making partner were slim, and that they were in for a rigorous, exhausting few years as the grunts. But there was a big fat brass ring at the end.

> In this way new recruits – or even more established employees – were less inclined to ask difficult questions or question dubious practices as this would undoubtedly nullify their chances of winning the brass ring.
>
> (Toffler and Reingold, 2003)

Ironically the emphasis on team building and similar practices designed to create coherent identities can serve to emphasize these practices, which is not to say that they should not be carried out, but that managers should be aware that, if the group norms become corrupted, such practices will tend to facilitate acceptance of them rather than to counteract them.

Once the group norms are corrupted the process of socialization works insidiously:

- Veterans act as role models for the dysfunctional behaviour and demonstrate acceptance of it.

- Newcomers are encouraged to affiliate with the veterans and develop behaviours that fit in with and please them.

- Newcomers have the rationalizations of dysfunctional behaviour reinforced by the group so that they begin to justify it to themselves and even to see it as being positive.

- Newcomers are encouraged to attribute any doubts they have to their own shortcomings, particularly naivety, so they are more susceptible to accepting dysfunctional behaviour as the norm.

Clearly the more senior the management demonstrating unethical or corrupt behaviour, the greater the example shown to subordinates and the more readily it is seen as being acceptable. Thus at Enron the roles of Geoffrey Skilling (CEO) and Kenneth Lay (Chairman) were seen as critical factors in developing the dysfunctional culture that flourished there. Students are encouraged to read one or more of the many books written, both by ex-employees of Enron and by former bankers and currency traders, which described their acceptance of practices which, once they had left the fevered world of the office or trading desk, they wondered how they had ever accepted as being in any way normal.

The discontinuity between acceptable or encouraged behaviour at work and social norms and ethics outside work is rationalized by individuals by compartmentalizing their lives – they become one person at work and another at home. In order to do this they frequently seek support by socializing with work colleagues outside work or with those in a similar situation. This reinforces the group norms and provides rationalization and self-justification for their actions; Enron employees socialized extensively with each other, bank traders related to other bank traders, all of which provided a framework for them to rationalize their actions which was often, however, at the expense of personal relationships with individuals outside the group.

Socialization techniques

Patterns of unethical behaviour can develop inside an organization gradually and insidiously to such an extent that normal standards of ethics become distorted. The distortions then become rationalized to the extent that employees feel that what they do is entirely justifiable. However, newcomers to the organization have to be inducted into accepting these patterns of behaviour and this is done through processes of socialization.

Newcomers into organizations have to be socialized into the prevailing ethos or behaviour patterns of the entity they have just become part of. If they are not they will remain outsiders and may leave the organization quite quickly if they find themselves, for whatever reason, unable to fit in with the prevailing ethos and are thereby excluded. They may even become a danger to existing employees who are engaging in dysfunctional behaviour by reporting to a third party, ie higher management, the auditors or a regulator, so it is important that they be socialized into the prevailing ethos as early as possible.

This may not be a conscious process. New employees are simply shown the processes and procedures and these are described as 'the way things are done around here' by an existing employee who is convinced that what they are doing is acceptable. Readers who wish to question these statements are referred to the books written by individuals who have worked for merchant banks, or even as a chef in a busy restaurant kitchen where violence and abuse of low-level workers was endemic.

When they first become exposed to corrupt practices new employees often feel some sense of apprehension because of what psychologists call 'cognitive dissonance'. In a dysfunctional entity the culture of the organization, ie what are seen to be its behavioural norms, are at odds with the incoming individual's personal internal moral code and, perhaps, their experiences in other non-dysfunctional organizations. This creates an internal conflict between how they are expected to behave and what they instinctively feel is right.

Where the internal conflict is unsustainable the individual tends to leave the organization, or seek relocation away from the dysfunctional area. Ironically this may serve to help perpetuate corrupt practices by weeding out those employees who might object to them or 'betray' them.

Research has uncovered some very powerful techniques whereby new individuals become socialized into tolerating dysfunctional or unethical behaviour. Three socialization techniques have been identified by researchers Vikas Anand, Blake Ashforth and Mahendra Joshi (2005). These are:

- **Co-optation:** In co-optation rewards are used to induce an attitude change towards dysfunctional behaviour. This sort of behaviour has been seen in the financial services industry where pension or savings policies from companies paying the highest commission were pushed at clients irrespective of whether or not they were suitable for their circumstances. In extreme cases normal standards of business behaviour would be suspended simply because of the sheer size of fees available for co-operating in a dubious venture. The prospect of reward in these situations often encourages individuals to resolve moral ambiguities in a way that benefits them in some way either financially or through enhanced prestige.

- **Incrementalism:** In some organizations individuals are introduced gradually to corrupt acts. As already stated, when the individual first meets instances of dysfunctional behaviour this creates a level of dissonance as a consequence of which they tend to grasp at any rationalizations offered by their colleagues. Individuals gradually become immersed in corrupt behaviour to an extent that they would never have imagined themselves doing. When the scale and extent of their behaviour is revealed or becomes apparent to them the individuals are often shocked and amazed that they could have engaged in such behaviour.

- **Compromise:** Sometimes corrupt acts are carried out because individuals are seeking a solution to some problem or dilemma.

The box on page 83 gives an example of such a practice to illustrate the point that the individuals concerned could rationalize an immoral act as being the solution to a problem that, in a way, actually benefited their employer. In the example it could be argued that the used car dealership benefited through the payment of bribes as, otherwise, they wouldn't get the quality vehicles. In such cases corruption becomes institutionalized as business practice. This type of behaviour is frequently advanced as an excuse for the payment of bribes to secure contracts, ie that without such payments the work would not be forthcoming – 'that's just the way you do business here'.

Spreading corruption: used car dealerships

One study of used car dealerships in the USA discovered that used car dealers were paying bribes to sales staff in new car dealerships so they would get the best trade-in vehicles. If the used car dealers didn't get the good trade-in vehicles these would be sold on by the new car dealerships to other purchasers, resulting in the used car dealers being cut off from the supply of these quality used cars unless they paid the bribes.

In order to free up cash to pay these bribes the used car dealers then often resorted to selling cars at an apparent undervalue – for example, a £5,000 car would be invoiced and 'sold' officially at £4,500 with £500 being paid in cash by the purchaser which could be used by the managers of the used car dealerships to pay the bribes. Thus the corruption spread.

(Anand, Ashforth and Joshi, 2005)

Of course these methodologies are not mutually exclusive; indeed they may happen simultaneously and reinforce each other. New employees may be co-opted gently into the system through the identification of rewards; co-optation is encouraged as new employees are drawn in by tiny steps until finally employees are fully involved in the corrupt methods of working and either they have abandoned most moral principles in the work environment or they consciously choose the unethical way over the other.

The point is that it is a matter of perceived choice. Unethical acts are more likely to be seen as justifiable if the individuals perceive themselves to have a choice – the problem is that these are socialization practices that often give only the *illusion* of choice. The changes from moral to immoral behaviour are subtle and appear to be not unreasonable.

Groupthink

It is instructive to consider groupthink, an extreme aspect of organizational culture and its interaction with small groups of individuals. This

Orwellian-sounding phenomenon has been described as a contributory factor to the *Challenger* shuttle disaster in 1986 and may well have influenced political decision-making more often than may be admitted.

Groupthink was a term coined by sociologist and journalist William H. Whyte in *Fortune* magazine in 1952. Whyte defined it as:

> Groupthink being a coinage – and, admittedly, a loaded one – a working definition is in order. We are not talking about mere instinctive conformity – it is, after all, a perennial failing of mankind. What we are talking about is a rationalized conformity – an open, articulate philosophy which holds that group values are not only expedient but right and good as well.

It was, however, the work of psychologist Irving Janis in the 1970s that brought the concept to popular attention. Janis defined it as:

> a mode of thinking that people engage in when they are deeply involved in a cohesive in-group, when the members' strivings for unanimity override their motivation to realistically appraise alternative courses of action.
>
> (Janis 1972)

Janis looked at collective decision-making in the context of group dynamics whereby a dominant leader influences the decision-making of others, not in a hectoring or domineering way but in often inadvertent ways. In these cases subordinates are not afraid to speak their minds, nor is the leader averse to hearing what they have to say, but subtle constraints may prevent a member of the group from openly expressing doubt or criticism or even of thinking consistently in an independent way. So they are free to speak their minds, as long as doing so doesn't ripple the calm surface of the group's collective pond.

Janis predicated that groupthink is most likely to be present under two basic situations:

1 Where there are:
   - structural faults in the organization leading to insulation of the decision-making group;
   - a lack of a tradition of impartial leadership;
   - a lack of norms requiring method in decision-making and, perhaps most importantly, homogeneity of members' social background/ attitudes/ideology.

   This is the so-called 'golf club syndrome' where members of the group share similar social attitudes, come from similar backgrounds and have similar lifestyles. Behaviour considered to be outside group norms threatens to punish the perpetrator with the ultimate sanction –

expulsion or rejection by the group. Part of the shock felt by many victims of Ponzi scheme fraudster Bernard Madoff was not simply that he had stolen their money but that he had defrauded fellow members of the exclusive Palm Beach Country Club who thought he was one of them.

2 Where the group is under actual or perceived pressure, ie where:

- there is high stress from external threats with a low hope of any better solution than the leader's;
- there is low self-esteem temporarily induced by a history of recent failures that make members' inadequacies relevant;
- there are excessive difficulties in the decision-making process that lowers each member's sense of self-efficacy;
- the group is faced with moral dilemmas involving an apparent lack of feasible alternatives except ones that violate ethical standards.

Identifying groupthink

Janis identified symptoms that are indicative of groupthink and they are divided into three main types that are familiar features of many, but not all, cohesive groups:

1 Overestimation of the group:

- Illusions of invulnerability: the illusion of the group somehow being invulnerable to dangers and risks that affect other people. This tends to encourage over-optimism and risk-taking.
- A belief in the inherent morality of the group. This results in members failing to acknowledge the consequences of their actions.

2 Closed mindedness:

- Collective rationalization: concurrence among group members which assists in discounting warnings or other information that might cause members to reconsider their assumptions before recommitting to past policy decisions.
- Stereotyped views of outsiders: defining them as ignorant, stupid, ill informed, evil etc, which again aids in reinforcing group cohesion and assists in the process of collective rationalization.

This serves to demean outsiders so their views can be safely ignored or the effects of the group's actions on them minimized.

3 Pressures towards uniformity:

- Self-censorship of deviations from the apparent group consensus. Each member tends to minimize the importance of their own doubts and counterarguments.

- A shared illusion of unanimity concerning judgements conforming to the majority view. This partly results from self-censorship of doubts and the false assumption that silence means consent.

- Direct pressure on any member who expresses strong arguments against any of the group's stereotypes, illusions or commitments, making clear that this type of dissent is contrary to what is expected of all loyal members. Members become reluctant to break group cohesion for fear of expulsion.

- The emergence of self-appointed 'mind guards' or 'gatekeepers' who protect the group from dissenting information that might shatter their shared complacency about the effectiveness and morality of their decisions. Thus the fearsome PA or assistant who supports the group and reinforces it without ever really being part of it.

When a group, such as a board of directors, displays these sorts of symptoms their decision-making process becomes ineffective and the group may begin to take decisions that may steer them away from an ethical course and, at an extreme level, lead to distortions of financial statements and even to corruption and plundering of the organization.

But be careful! These situations are difficult to spot. Not every cohesive group is subject to groupthink, and circumstances may change over time as individuals within the group part company with it. It is more likely to exist where:

- there is a strong or inspiring, but not overly dominant leader. An overtly dominant leader would tend to act dictatorially and would not act within the context of a group, except perhaps nominally. An ostensibly inspiring or strong leader, particularly in the absence of equally strong or effective subordinates, may create a situation where a small group of decision-makers, headed by the leader, feels itself to be in charge and invulnerable

- in the absence of effective externalities such as strong non-executive directors and where there are weak communication lines to and from the group, ineffective finance functions and compliant external auditors. In these cases the decisions of the group go unchallenged and, particularly if their initial decisions bring success, the group may start to become self-reinforcing and feel itself to be all-knowing and all-powerful.

It is now considered that symptoms of groupthink manifest themselves more frequently than was originally postulated by Janis. Indeed part of the Enron collapse can be attributed to a groupthink-style culture, inspired by Geoffrey Skilling, which set the tone and style of the business in the early years of its meteoric growth and which fostered a culture of constant success, at any price, no bad news and no excuses for failure.

Rationalizing unethical behaviour

As we have seen, employees can be seduced into unethical or dysfunctional behaviour despite their internal moral code. The dysfunctional employee recognizes that the actions they are carrying out, in order to retain presence in their group, may not be socially acceptable outside work so must rationalize their actions to themselves in some way if they are to avoid cognitive dissonance.

It is important to understand that corrupt individuals often do not see themselves as corrupt. Research into white-collar crime, which encompasses a rather wider spectrum of unethical behaviour than simple fraud, shows that individuals who are convicted of these crimes acknowledge the offence but go on to deny any criminal intent. They use a number of rationalizing techniques that enable them to look at their unethical behaviour and justify it as normal business practice.

Gresham Sykes and David Matza, sociologists working on juvenile delinquency in the 1950s and 1960s, established several forms of rationalization that cropped up time and time again in their research. Their theory, which they called 'neutralization', held that:

- people are always aware of their moral obligation to abide by the law; and

- they have the same moral obligation within themselves to avoid illegitimate acts.

Thus, they reasoned, when a person did commit illegitimate acts, they must employ some sort of mechanism to silence the urge to follow these moral obligations. The theory was built upon four observations:

- Delinquents expressed guilt over their illegal acts.
- Delinquents frequently respected and admired honest, law-abiding individuals.
- A line was drawn between those whom they could victimize and those they could not.
- Delinquents were not immune to the demands of conformity.

This explained why individuals, other than those who might be described as full-time professional criminals, can drift between legitimate and illegitimate behaviours. As their own moral and ethical belief systems have not been replaced by a new, less stringent code, they simply find a way of justifying dysfunctional behaviour so that it fits in with their personal standards of what they consider to be right or wrong.

These types of rationalization are used again and again by everyone from politicians to football hooligans but inside an organization they can be clues to the mindset of an individual and the culture within which they function. Perpetrators of crimes often adopted various distancing techniques such as:

- claiming their actions were caused by forces beyond the perpetrator's control – eg some sort of need, real or perceived – 'I really needed the money';
- stating that anyone condemning the actions of the perpetrator was doing so out of spite as it was really not their fault – 'I don't know what came over me';
- the victim is demeaned or seen as stupid – 'serves them right';
- the victim is seen as somehow culpable – 'it's their own fault';
- any loss or damage to the victim is minimized – 'well they're insured'.

Rationalizations in this way would serve to justify or explain the actions of individuals to themselves and to assist them in coming to terms with their actions and to reconcile their at-work behaviour with their personal moral code or upbringing, thus reducing cognitive dissonance (Table 3.2). They seek to alleviate the pressure this places on their inner set of moral values by finding some form of rationale or justification for their actions. Over time commission of dysfunctional acts becomes easier to live with and may even become almost routine.

TABLE 3.2 Rationalizing unethical behaviour

Strategy	Manifestation	Example
Denial of Responsibility	individuals claim they have little choice but to act unethically	'What could I do? I'm only a cog in the machine.' 'It's not my responsibility what they get up to in that department.'
Denial of Injury	claims that what they did was a 'victimless crime', that no one was harmed so that actions are not corrupt	'It could have been worse.' 'Nobody died.'
Acceptable	individuals claim that unethical behaviour is normal in their particular industry	'Everybody does it.' 'You wouldn't get very far in this business if you weren't prepared to cut a few corners.'
Denial of Victim	the effect of the corrupt actions is seen as being the fault of the victim, not caused by the dysfunctional behaviour	'It's their own fault.' 'They chose to get involved.' 'They should have checked it out.'
Appeal to Higher Loyalty	the actions are justified as they are part of a process with a much higher order value	'I did what I did to help the company.' 'I did not report it because I am loyal to my boss and my colleagues.'
Entitlement	individuals justify immoral or illegal acts as being justified because they have 'earned' it due to unrewarded effort	'I'm entitled to this because of all the unpaid overtime I put in for this organization.' 'They owe me a few perks – I work hard enough without anyone noticing.'
Invidious Comparison	the individuals compare themselves with others or attempt to rebut their accuser	'Others are worse than we are.' 'You don't have the right to criticize me.'

Dysfunctional acts by individuals

One study of workplace pilfering believed that at least some of it was 'hitting out at the boss, the company, the system or the state' and this may be true in some cases. Other researchers have identified it as a reaction to feelings of alienation at work, feelings that neither the company nor the boss actually cares about you as an individual. In most cases though experienced investigators say that the most common reason why people do this is because they can, because it's easy.

Research has shown that most small-scale theft occurred because it was simple to do and there appeared to be no prohibition against doing it – even where the individual's own internal moral code told them it was wrong. This had nothing to do with need and everything to do with succumbing to temptation. It is interesting to note that one of the most common defences in cases of white-collar crime is the claim that upper management condoned it or that there was no clear policy in the organization to distinguish right from wrong.

Of course there is a big difference at the individual level between minor pilfering and systematic embezzlement and, clearly, most individuals who 'acquire' things from their employer would never contemplate larger-scale theft. However, the ease with which an individual under pressure, given the right opportunity, can turn small-scale pilfering into large-scale fraud is something all managers should consider.

Clearly, as we have seen above, corporate culture has a large part to play in determining the actions of employees. Research by Hollinger and Clark (1983) and Geis, Meir and Salinger (1994) indicates that it is the interaction between these factors that determines whether or not individuals will engage in unethical or immoral acts, which can range from theft or arson to deliberate misrepresentation of a product to a customer motivated by the commission payable on the sale:

- corporate culture;
- personal feelings;
- the level of corporate internal controls.

Researchers are mostly of a consensus that most dysfunctional acts, described broadly as 'white-collar crime', take place as:

- a form of rebellion – as a way of hitting out at the boss, the company, the system or the state; and/or

- as a challenge – to see if the individual can overcome the controls and restrictions placed upon them by the system; and/or
- where the culture of the organization encourages such behaviour or has socialized employees into believing it is acceptable (see page 81).

Where there is a dysfunction between a person's job and their ideas, attitudes and values they will adopt one of these strategies:

- leave – resign or depart, effectively withdrawing from the conflict;
- break down – not resolve the conflict but struggle on in an increasingly dysfunctional way, subsequently becoming long-term sick or otherwise ineffective;
- become alienated – this manifests itself in increased absenteeism, sabotage and 'fiddling'.

The commission of a successful fraud or theft represents a triumph of the individual over the organization. What the individual achieves by doing this is a demonstration of their creativity, a reassertion of their individualism in a conformist organization. Consequently in organizations where:

- the individual feels or is actively undervalued;
- individuals feel or are isolated and unsupported;
- relationships between parts of the organization or between levels of management are dysfunctional;
- individuals are engaged in monotonous, routine tasks with little opportunity to exercise some level of control or to assert their own individualism,

they may well, if they don't leave or break down in some way, begin to act negatively and, if the opportunity arises, they are highly likely to collude or instigate dysfunctional acts even if their personal morality would, in other social situations, prevent them from acting in that way.

When asked why they started to commit fraud, for example, many individuals, apart from those who blatantly carried out their frauds for gain, were at a loss to come up with a convincing explanation – the problem was that, once they started, they couldn't stop.

Preventing unethical behaviour and the role of management

Clearly the prevention of unethical or dysfunctional behaviour is part of the remit of management. In Chapter 2 we looked at organizational culture and climate and the role management plays in creating and nurturing an organizational climate where ethical behaviour is the norm and employees who engage in unethical behaviour are exposed and seen to be outside the norms of the organization.

Thus the first consideration, and one which goes to the heart of this book, is for the directors to establish a strong corporate governance structure (Chapter 4). This requires a lead from the directors who will set both the organization's tone and its attitude towards specific instances of what is considered unacceptable and what is considered acceptable moral and ethical behaviour by *all* employees of the business, including its directors and senior managers.

Consequently, the first aspect of prevention of dysfunctional behaviour is the stated position of the organization led by the directors and senior management and these are embodied in the statements made and the policies written by the directors and disseminated to all employees. The organization should make it certain, beyond doubt, where it stands with regard to unethical acts by its employees including senior staff and directors. It has been advocated by some authorities (mostly those based in the USA) that the organization's ethical stance should be included in any mission statement used by the organization to state its objectives, approach and values. In the UK mission statements have often been derided as being rather vain posturing, usually incorporating unfortunate clichés such as 'world class', 'delighting the customer' and offering 'solutions' but, properly written, they can be a clear statement of intentions and values.

A mission statement that clearly states the organization's commitment to ethical principles and an intolerance of dysfunctional behaviour does make its case from the outset and inclusion of a declaration of corporate values in a mission statement should be seriously considered.

If dysfunctional behaviour becomes embedded in the organization the effect can be catastrophic. Because the rationalization and socialization processes described above are mutually reinforcing, the effect of them can become entrenched and spread throughout the organization. As a consequence the organization can lose the awareness of some of its practices being unethical and its internal checks and balances will fail to identify the dysfunctional behaviour that has now become accepted as normal.

If and when this is pointed out to them by a third party the first response is likely to be denial. Frequently organizations will continue to carry on the dysfunctional behaviour or other behaviours that reinforce the original opinion. This can lead to loss of reputation or financial penalties or criminal prosecutions where the offences contravene the law. Managers must be aware of the propensity for such behaviours to become embodied in the organization and should actively work to prevent it.

How can this be achieved if the behaviour is embedded in the very culture of the organization? There are several key aspects that are crucial to this process:

- Lead from the front – senior management should set an example of honesty and openness.
- Train employees to:
  - question their actions – use examples such as the 'headline test', ie would they be happy if their actions became public knowledge?
  - recognize the use of euphemisms such as those quoted in Table 3.2 as part of the rationalization process.
- Require an internal audit or HR review of ethical policies and compliance with them as part of control procedures. Employees could be asked to certify annually that they have not been engaged in unethical or corrupt behaviour.
- Use performance evaluations to look at behaviour rather than simply outcomes. Many forms of performance evaluations are outcome-based – looking at the employees' ability to hit predetermined targets. The reliance on outcome-based performance appraisals is more likely to encourage unethical behaviour. This is true particularly where conditions are challenging and penalties for not hitting targets are severe. In such cases, if employees hit their targets the evaluator is often not tempted to question how the success has been achieved.
- Nurture an ethical environment within the organization. This can require the establishment of ethical codes or practices and reinforcement of them by severely punishing breaches of the code. The code must not simply become a fig leaf sheltering bad practice – it must be real. The organization must facilitate communication within the organization, including whistleblowing, and make it

acceptable to question bad practice or unethical behaviour. Punishing whistleblowers provides a rationalization for not disclosing unethical practices and reinforces the group norms in situations where such behaviour flourishes.

- Review practices to ensure that dysfunctional behaviour has not been institutionalized. In large organizations, including those involved in the public sector where resources may be short, unethical practices may become the norm simply because they become the easy or most convenient way of achieving the desired outcome. Thus, for example, tendering procedures are by-passed or only paid lip service to, safety concerns are ignored or rationalized away and accounts and budgets are manipulated to achieve desired or acceptable results.

- Introduce change agents or external reviewers. One of the ways of breaking down group bonds is to introduce change in such a way that it reformats ways of working and mixes up previously individual departments or sub-groups. This often requires external input as insiders tend to be wedded to existing modes of operation. This must be handled carefully as change can produce uncertainty and is unsettling. Constant change can create resentment and barriers that are contrary to what management is trying to achieve and may, in fact, encourage the development of dysfunctional behaviour.

Ethics and the HR department

The role of the HR department here is crucial simply because they have the responsibility for three aspects of corporate life relating to employees which include:

- recruitment;
- training;
- policies.

This book is not about deterring fraud or investigating employees so on the first two points suffice to say that HR policies should, wherever possible:

- strive to recruit only employees who are likely to abide by ethical principles;
- reinforce ethical and other policies through training and repeated dissemination of content.

There are many and various recommendations as to what sort of policies organizations should institute. Clearly providing detailed sample policies for all aspects of the organization are well outside the scope of this book but, for example, the Institute of Business Ethics publishes several good practice and advisory guides on developing such a code. Any code of ethics must deal with situations where there is a high risk of unethical behaviour taking place, such as business gifts and bribery and corruption.

The company's policy towards business entertaining and bribery is one that every employee should have as part of their staff handbook. Not only should staff have this as part of their contract of employment but they should also be reminded about the policy on a regular basis.

A key part of reinforcing commitment to the policy is an annual reminder. All new staff should be given and acknowledge receipt of a copy of the ethics policy on commencing work. Existing staff should be sent it both on paper, by e-mail and through any corporate reporting mechanisms such as a company newspaper or bulletin.

However the policy is written, it should be brief and easy to understand so that staff of all levels of competence can appreciate its contents. Staff who are blind, for example, should be provided with the policy in an acceptable format, either Braille or audio. The policy may well be backed up by standing orders, instructions and disciplinary procedures. Employees throughout the organization should be in no doubt that the policy is going to be enforced and that it is not simply there as an appendix to the staff handbook for everyone to ignore. The ethics policy will form part of a suite of policies that will include such matters as health and safety, code of conduct for suppliers, fraud and bribery policy, whistleblowing policy and environmental policy.

The HR department plays a key role in disseminating the facts about corporate governance and ethics but it can also aid the organization in another way – by organizing the whistleblower hotline.

Whistleblowing

We mentioned earlier the problems in certain public sector organizations where employees who reported dysfunctional behaviour were persecuted or dismissed by management. This has led to massive compensation payouts for some workers but for others it has led to unofficial blacklisting and – effectively – the end of a career. This does seem particularly brutal behaviour against individuals who were ostensibly acting in the best interests of the people the organization is there to serve but it is indicative of what might best be described as a rather paranoid management determined not to reveal any hint of failure or admit to any fault.

This type of action by management does nothing to aid the organization and simply allows bad practice to flourish with the inevitable result that it spreads through the organization and corrupts it on a large enough scale that the truth, when it is finally revealed, is more damaging to the organization than the initial whistleblowing incidents would have been had they been properly dealt with.

Whistleblowing and internal tip-offs are a major source of information about dysfunctional behaviour in the organization and it should introduce processes to facilitate these and to make the process as non-threatening and straightforward as possible. The organization should set up and communicate to employees a whistleblowing policy to encourage the flow of information. Clearly care has to be taken that this does not encourage malicious reporting but any protections against this must not be so draconian that they discourage speculative reports that may lead to the exposure of dysfunctional behaviour. The policy should contain statements to the effect that:

- Whistleblowing is not a grievance – the aim of whistleblowing is to report wrongdoing, not to air workplace grievances.
- Arrangements can be made that by-pass line management.
- An employee has a right to confidentiality if required.
- There is a confidential helpline. One good way of doing this is for it to be operated by a third party which then reports concerns to the appropriate level of management.
- The policy should explain under what circumstances concerns can be raised with an external body such as a regulator, eg where the unethical behaviour is being carried out by the directors or senior management and either there is no alternative reporting line such as an audit committee (Chapter 4) or it is not perceived to be trustworthy.
- Persecution or exposure of a whistleblower or malicious reporting should be a disciplinary offence – possibly classed as gross misconduct.

The practical arrangements made should reflect the policy.

Organizations must be aware of and comply with the provisions of the Public Interest Disclosure Act, 1998 (PIDA). Note that under PIDA there is no statutory requirement for organizations to introduce a whistleblowing policy, although good practice in corporate governance does require that, if possible, a whistleblowing policy should be instituted.

There are some specific instances where whistleblowing policies are required:

- Listed companies subject to the UK Code of Corporate Governance are obliged to have whistleblowing arrangements or explain why they do not.

- Public bodies are expected to have a policy in place that is assessed regularly as part of the external audit and review of local authorities and NHS bodies.

- Companies subject to the Sarbanes–Oxley legislation ('Sarbox') – basically UK subsidiaries of US companies – are also required to have whistleblowing arrangements.

The nature of the whistleblowing arrangements will be determined by an organization's size, structure, culture, nature of the risks that it faces and the legal framework in which it operates.

One of the best methods for reporting fraud is a confidential 24/7 hotline whether internal or operated by an external provider. However, this will not work unless management creates the appropriate environment of honesty and trust to encourage individuals to come forward without fear. Clear channels of communication from employees to management are essential in creating an environment that encourages fraud prevention and detection of dysfunctional behaviour.

The challenge for management is to encourage these 'innocent' people to speak out and to demonstrate that it is very much in their own interest to do so. As we saw in Chapter 2 a survey by the Institute of Business Ethics indicated that although some 25 per cent of employees were aware of mal-practice in the workplace only 60 per cent of them were reporting it for various reasons, but mainly a mixture of fear and loyalty. These include:

- loyalty to working groups or family;
- the concept of not 'grassing' on colleagues;
- disinterest – the concept that it is the organization's problem;
- unacknowledged admiration for someone 'getting away with it';
- fear of persecution by the organization;

- fear of being shunned by colleagues if the individual's role is revealed;
- suspicion rather than proof.

The organization's ethical culture and reporting processes can be a major influence on the whistleblower, as fear of reprisals often has a major effect on them and results in them remaining silent.

Where the malpractice is being committed by senior managers this worsens the situation for the whistleblower. Management's challenge is to convince staff that:

- combating dysfunctional behaviour is the responsibility of everyone;
- no one, no matter how senior, is exempt from exposure and its consequences;
- the future health of the organization, and clearly potentially their future employment, could be at risk.

Some organizations dislike the term whistleblowing and prefer to use euphemisms such as 'speaking out' or 'raising concerns' – it matters not.

Whilst confidentiality should be guaranteed, anonymity is a different issue. Anonymous reports over an internal hotline can make allegations difficult to substantiate and investigate so individuals making a report should be encouraged to give their name. This, of course, will require a leap of faith by them so internal hotlines and designated officers may not be enough to convince employees that they will be safeguarded. Legal advice should be sought when setting up a 'hotline' as, in some circumstances there are technical issues involving EU data protection rules and the Sarbox legislation with anonymous reporting, which there is no need to expand on here.

Bribery Act 2010

Ethical or moral behaviour is rarely if ever specifically reinforced by statute. Crimes such as murder, theft, fraud and arson are, of course, statutorily forbidden but the Bribery Act goes a step further insofar as it seeks to punish organizations for taking insufficient precautions against it happening.

The Act contains two general offences covering the offering, promising or giving of a bribe (active bribery) and the requesting, agreeing to receive or accepting of a bribe (passive bribery) at sections 1 and 2 respectively. It also sets out two further offences that specifically address commercial bribery. Bribery in this context also covers what are euphemistically known as 'facilitation payments' or 'grease to oil the wheels'. These are payments made to contractors or agents where the work has already been obtained and matters simply need speeding up or blockages cleared. Interestingly, the US version of this Act, the Foreign and Corrupt Practices Act 1977, allows such payments as legitimate but the UK has taken a hard line and banned them.

Section 6 of the UK Bribery Act creates an offence relating to bribery of a foreign public official in order to obtain or retain business or an advantage in the conduct of business, and Section 7 creates a new form of corporate liability for failing to prevent bribery on behalf of a commercial organization. The Act covers offences committed anywhere in the world by commercial organizations or persons associated with them, such as individuals, partners, agents, contractors or joint ventures within the jurisdiction of the UK. There is no size limit for organizations so even the smallest may be caught.

Of course what constitutes a bribe may be open to interpretation where it consists of, say, hospitality – what is an appropriate and reasonable level of corporate hospitality in a given set of circumstances has to be tested in the courts. For example, if the individual concerned is an oil billionaire simply putting them up in a Travelodge may not be appropriate so a suite at Claridges and all bills paid would be normal for them – but it would be abnormal to do the same for, say, a contracts manager from a construction company in Rotherham – that could be a bribe on the grounds it was excessive.

It is Section 7 we are particularly interested in. A commercial organization will have a full defence if it can show that despite a particular case of bribery it nevertheless had adequate procedures in place to prevent persons associated with it from bribing. In accordance with established case law, the standard of proof that the commercial organization would need to discharge in order to prove the defence, in the event it was prosecuted, is the balance of probabilities. The Act requires commercial organizations to adopt a risk-based approach to managing bribery risks.

Procedures should be proportionate to the risks faced by an organization. No policies or procedures are capable of detecting and preventing all bribery. A risk-based approach will, however, serve to focus the effort where it is needed and will have most impact. A risk-based approach recognizes that the bribery threat to organizations varies across jurisdictions, business sectors, business partners and transactions.

Guidance to the Act sets out six principles for the Section 7 defence. These are:

- proportionate procedures – based on the risk evaluation;
- top-level commitment;
- risk assessment;
- due diligence – investigating agents, partners or associated bodies for bribery risk;
- communication and training – about the risks and the provisions of the Act;
- monitoring and review.

In short it behoves the management of every commercial organization or organization acting in a commercial way to carry out a risk evaluation and to ensure that all their staff are aware of the provisions of the Act and the penalties under it – which are personal liabilities, not totally corporate ones.

Thus ethical behaviour is now subject to legislation and we await with interest the Court's interpretation of the provisions of the Act and its effect on UK business.

CASE STUDY

Susan Chumley has worked at Suspenders Ltd for six months and has been appointed a team leader. In the time she has been there, out of the eight members of her team who were there when she joined three have left and one is on long-term sick after having a breakdown.

She has to attend meetings of other team leaders and supervisors. At one of the meetings she was told that certain suppliers were to be given 'special payments' providing certain delivery and quality targets were met. These were to be paid directly to named individuals and arrangements would be made to pay them in cash. In the records these were to be described as 'advisory fees'. Susan and her colleagues were told only to deal with these named individuals and no one else.

After work her friend Maureen asked Susan if she would like some electrical goods that had been 'damaged' in the stores. Maureen revealed that stores staff regularly siphoned off consumer electrical goods and sold them cheaply to staff – suppliers simply replaced any damaged goods and didn't ask for them to be returned so this practice was simple and effective. Maureen had bought a 42 inch plasma television for £100 from one of the stores staff. Susan declined.

At home Susan's daughter asked her if she could have some paper and pens for school. Susan said she would bring home a packet of paper and a box of pens the next day from the stationery store. Next day Susan finished her work, messaged a friend in Cyprus on Facebook and bought some new outfits for work from some online shopping websites. She then went home, remembering to take with her the pens and paper her daughter wanted.

Discuss

- How has the behaviour of the staff been influenced by the ethical behaviour of the company?

- Is Susan's behaviour acceptable or excusable in any way?

- How should management deal with incidences of such behaviour by staff?

- What processes and procedures could be put in place to reduce incidences of this type of behaviour by staff and what should management do to make them effective?

Bibliography

Anand, V, Ashforth, B and Joshi, M (2005) *Business as Usual: The acceptance and perpetuation of corruption in organisations*, Academy of Management Executive, 19.4

Ashkenasy, Widerson and Peterson (2000) *Handbook of Organisational Culture and Climate*, Sage, London

Bentham, J (1789) *An Introduction to the Principles of Morals and Legislation*, Dover Publications, Minneola, NY

Bourdain, A (2000) *Kitchen Confidential: Adventures in the culinary underbelly*, Bloomsbury, London

British Government (1998) The Public Disclosure Act, TSO, London

Chartered Institute of Management Accountants (CIMA) (2008) *Fraud Risk Management: A guide to good practice*, CIMA, London

Deverson, J and Hamblett, C (1965) *Generation X*, Tandem Books, London

Drummond, H (2000) *Introduction to Organizational Behaviour*, Oxford University Press, Oxford

Editorial, [accessed 20 September 2012] Good day stealing at the office dear? 8 January 2004 [online] www.thisiswiltshire.co.uk

Farrell, BJ, Cobbin, DM and Farrell, HM (2002) Can codes of ethics really produce consistent behaviour? *Journal of Managerial Psychology*, **17** (6), pp 468–490

Foreign and Corrupt Practices Act 1977, Department of Justice, Washington, DC

Frankel, T (2006) *Trust and Honesty: America's Business Culture at a Crossroad*, Oxford University Press, Oxford

French, R, Rayner, C, Rees, G and Rumbles, S (2008) *Organisational Behaviour*, John Wiley, Chichester

Furnham, A (2006) *The Psychology of Behaviour at Work*, Psychology Press, Hove

Geis, RF, Meir, R and Salinger, LM (eds) (1994) *White Collar Crime: Classic and contemporary views*, Free Press, New York

Griseri, P and Seppala, N (2010) *Business Ethics and Corporate Social Responsibility*, Cengage, Andover

Guyer, P (1998, 2004) Immanuel Kant. In E Craig (ed.), *Routledge Encyclopaedia of Philosophy*, Routledge, London

Hollinger, RC and Clark, JP (1983) *Theft by Employees*, Lexington Books, Lexington, KT

Janis, I (1972) *Groupthink*, 2nd edition, Houghton Miflin, Boston, MA

HMSO (2000) *Regulation of Investigatory Powers Act, 2000*, HMSO, London

HMSO (2010) *Bribery Act 2010*, HMSO, London

Institute of Business Ethics (2010) *Corporate Ethics Policies and Programmes: UK and continental Europe Survey 2010*, IBE, London

McLean, B and Elkind, P (2004) *The Smartest Guys in the Room*, Penguin, London

Mars, G (1994) *Cheats at Work: An anthropology of workplace crime*, Allen & Unwin, London

Ministry of Justice (2011) *Bribery Act 2010 Guidance*, Ministry of Justice, London

Sarbanes–Oxley Act (2002) H.R.Rep 107-610 25 July 2002. US Government Printing Office, Washington DC

Scanlon, TM (1982) Contractualism and utilitarianism', in *Utilitarianism and Beyond*, ed A Sen and B Williams, Cambridge University Press, Cambridge

Sen, A and Williams, B, eds (1982) *Utilitarianism and Beyond*, Cambridge University Press, Cambridge

Sykes, GM and Matza, D (1957) Techniques of neutralisation: A theory of delinquency, *American sociological review*, **22**: 664–670

Taylor, J (2011) *Forensic Accounting*, Pearson, Harlow

Toffler, BL and Reingold, J (2003) *Final Accounting: Ambition, greed and the fall of Arthur Andersen*, Crown Publishing, New York

Waugh, R (2007) Sacked whistleblowers win £1m pay out from council, *Yorkshire Post News*, 14 August

Whyte, W (1952) Groupthink, *Fortune*, March

Woods, SA and West, MA (2010) *The Psychology of Work and Organizations*, Cengage, Andover

Zalta, EN (ed.) [accessed 20 September 2012] *Stanford Encyclopedia of Philosophy* [Online] http://plato.stanford.edu

Websites

www.cimaglobal.org
www.ethics.iit.edu
www.ibe.org.uk
www.justice.gov.uk
www.lexisnexis.co/uk/legal
www.psychnet–uk.com
www.rep.routledge.com

Principles of corporate governance

Introduction

The previous chapter introduced the subject of ethical behaviour and its implications for a business. The subject of ethics is a key one in terms of the development of corporate governance principles and the success of a business in achieving them. Therefore the previous chapter provided underpinning knowledge of where the terms and concepts have come from and why.

History and background of corporate governance

The development of the limited company in 1856 split the roles of ownership and control for the first time and created the need for corporate governance. Limited liability alongside the separation of ownership and control introduced the risk of financial irregularity arising from dishonest or incompetent managers.

Corporate governance is the system by which organizations are directed and controlled. Cadbury defined corporate governance as 'the direction, management and control of an organisation' (1992). It relates to the way in which companies are governed, with a particular emphasis on the relationship between shareholders and directors. Corporate governance looks at how an organization is managed in order to achieve its objectives. A company should be managed in the best interests of its stakeholders, with a particular emphasis on its shareholders. Consideration should be given to all stakeholders in relation to the activities a business undertakes, for example employees, the general public, lenders, suppliers should all be considered and all factors affecting them covered, not just financial issues. For example, any social and environmental issues connected with activities should realistically be thought through. In the United Kingdom, company law protects shareholders but it does not protect other stakeholders affected by a company's decisions.

The link between corporate governance and ethics

The day-to-day understanding of the term 'ethics' brings to mind acting in a way that considers what is right and wrong. What is right and wrong in society can vary over time and between different cultures but generally gives rise to practices that are acceptable and those that are not.

Businesses also need to have ethical values with regard to their activities. Some of their activities are controlled by legal requirements such as health and safety legislation but some are not. This gives rise to the concept of corporate ethics that aims to apply ethical values to the way businesses conduct themselves. As corporate governance is concerned with how businesses operate and aims for consideration to be given to all stakeholders when carrying out its activities, it has underlying issues of the need for concern for good corporate ethics to value what is right in society with how it conducts itself.

Definition of corporate governance

Corporate governance covers a number of key areas but is generally summarized as stated above as the way in which organizations are directed and controlled. The latest UK Corporate Governance Code (June 2010) states that 'the purpose of corporate governance is to facilitate effective, entrepreneurial and prudent management that can deliver the long-term success of the company'. In order to achieve good corporate governance a company must have regard to the following:

- It must act in the best interest of its owners (shareholders).
- Consideration should be given to all stakeholders.
- It must comply with relevant codes.
- Consideration should be given to the balance of power within the board of directors.
- Fair remuneration should be exhibited.
- Risk must be monitored and managed.
- Good ethics must be observed and Corporate Social Responsibility must be considered.
- It should employ independent auditors.

The first version of the UK Corporate Governance Code (the Code) was produced in 1992 by the Cadbury Committee. Its paragraph 2.5 is still the classic definition of the context of the Code, which covers the following points:

- Corporate governance is the system by which companies are directed and controlled.
- Governance of companies is the responsibility of the board of directors.
- The appointment of directors and auditors is the shareholders' role in governance.
- Shareholders also need to satisfy themselves that an appropriate governance structure is in place.

- The board is responsible for setting the company's strategic aims and providing the leadership to put them into effect.

- The role of the board is to supervise the management of the business and report to shareholders on their stewardship.

- The board's actions are subject to laws, regulations and the approval of shareholders in general meeting.

Therefore corporate governance is largely concerned with what the board of a company does and in particular how it sets the values of the company. It is separate from the day-to-day operational management of the company by full-time executives.

In the UK the Code is a guide to a number of key components of effective board practice. Underpinning it are underlying principles of all good governance, which are accountability, transparency, probity and the focus on the sustainable success of an entity over the longer term.

The basic principles of the Code based on the work of Cadbury have stood the test of time well. However, the economic and social business environment companies operate in changes constantly and therefore the Code requires review at appropriate intervals. Reviews have taken place in 2005, 2007 and most recently 2010.

Reports that have been produced in relation to corporate governance issues

In the UK, despite the development of the limited company giving rise to the need for corporate governance issues to be considered as long ago as the nineteenth century, it was not really until the 1990s that the issue was given thorough consideration. The collapse of a number of large corporations through fraudulent and unethical behaviour was really when the definition and control of corporate governance started to be taken seriously as worried investors and regulators through the media started to demand action. Below is a summary of some of the key company collapses that gave rise to the foundations of corporate governance:

- Coloroll (1990);
- Asil Nadir's Polly Peck (1990);
- Robert Maxwell's Maxwell Communications Corporation (1991);
- Bank of Credit and Commerce International (1991).

Coloroll collapsed due to an acquisitions programme that gave rise to £400m in debts, which was missed by investors in the accounts. Once it became public knowledge the company collapsed.

Polly Peck collapsed due to Asil Nadir committing fraud and theft to the tune of £28m.

Maxwell committed one of the greatest frauds of the twentieth century. He tried to build his empire up over time but took on too much debt and then carried out fraudulent activities to survive. He stole over £700m from pension funds to try to finance other activities. This was due to a lack of separation of positions of power.

The Bank of Credit and Commerce was also a big scandal in financial history involving money laundering, bribery and support for terrorism with a total of £13bn unaccounted for.

Investors started to lose confidence in businesses and so the City of London, predicting that government regulation would soon be introduced, commissioned Sir Adrian Cadbury to review the reasons behind the collapses and develop proposals to introduce good practice. A number of problems were identified that gave rise to the collapse of these organizations and underpinned the proposals that Cadbury came up with in terms of best practice. Problems identified included:

- dominant individual;
- inexperienced or limited board;
- companies run in the interests of executive directors – high remuneration packages and share options;
- unreliable financial reporting;
- auditors not sufficiently independent of the company, misled or incompetent;
- ineffective internal controls;
- inadequate risk management;
- non-involvement by institutional shareholders.

Following on from the problems identified, the 1992 Cadbury Report came up with good practice proposals that would:

- reinforce the responsibilities of executive directors;
- strengthen the role of the non-executive director;
- make the case for audit committees of the board;
- restate the principal responsibilities of auditors;
- reinforce the links between shareholders, boards and auditors.

A voluntary code was introduced in 1992 following publication of the Cadbury Report.

A number of reports followed the initial work of Cadbury that have further refined and enhanced the definitions of what corporate governance is:

- Greenbury (1995) reviewed directors' pay. This was partly in response to the 'Cedric the Pig' campaign at the 1994 AGM for newly privatized British Gas when the then chairman, Cedric Brown, was looking for a 75 per cent pay rise.

- Hampel (1998) reinforced points made in the original Cadbury Report, in particular the separation of the roles of chairman and managing director and the balance of the composition of the board between executive and non-executive directors.

- Turnbull (1999) examined the role of internal audit.

- Higgs (2003) looked at reinforcing the role of non-executive directors.

- Tyson (2003) provided guidance on the recruitment and training of non-executive directors.

- Smith (2003) focused on the role of the audit committee and the relationship between auditors and the audit committee.

Following on from Hampel's work in 1998 the Financial Reporting Council (FRC) has issued several editions of the Combined Code to incorporate the findings from subsequent reports and reviews. The latest edition was issued in 2010 and covers the following main principles:

- leadership;
- effectiveness;
- accountability;
- remuneration;
- relations with shareholders.

Each area has a definition of what the principle means in terms of good governance followed by a series of provisions that illustrate how the principle may be achieved, which are explained below.

Key concepts and principles

The 1992 Cadbury Report provided a Code of Best Practice for companies. This code was built around key principles of accountability, probity and

FIGURE 4.1 The Code of Best Practice

Definitions: Oxford English Dictionary

SOURCE: Chartered Institute of Internal Auditors

transparency. These principles, together with the concept of equity, became the benchmark for good corporate governance (see Figure 4.1). These principles were further reinforced by the 1995 Nolan Committee, which produced the public sector equivalent – a report on required standards in public life (Nolan, 1995).

From these beginnings other organizations have produced their own ideas of what good corporate governance looks like. The Organisation for Economic Co-operation and Development (OECD) has produced principles of corporate governance that have gained worldwide recognition as an international benchmark for good corporate governance. The UK Independent Commission for Good Governance in Public Services published a Governance Standard in 2005 that sets out its core principles of good corporate governance. The document provides a list of supporting principles and a number of practical applications. Both these documents are summarized in Table 4.1.

These documents, and others such as the FRC's Combined Code, show how corporate governance has gradually changed and evolved. From characteristics from the private and public sectors the Chartered Institute of Internal Auditors has created a generic list of bullet points that describe good corporate governance. They stress that governance is about direction,

TABLE 4.1 Principles of corporate governance

The OECD Principles of Corporate Governance	Good Governance Standards for Public Services 6: Core Principles of Good Governance	Generic Principles of Good Governance
protect and facilitate the exercise of shareholders' rights	promote values for the whole organization and demonstrate good governance through behaviour	develop the capacity and effectiveness of the governing body
		agree and promote values
ensure strategic guidance of the company, the effective monitoring of management by the board	focus on the organization's purpose and on outcomes for citizens and service users	engage with shareholders and stakeholders
		be fair and impartial
		protect people's rights
		behave ethically
make timely and accurate disclosure on all material matters	take informed transparent decisions and manage risks	set strategic purpose and outcomes
		identify and manage risk
recognize the rights of stakeholders and encourage active co-operation	engage with stakeholders and make accountability real	make informed and transparent decisions
		monitor performance
ensure equitable treatment of all shareholders	develop the capacity and capability of the governing body to be effective	disclose everything so that accountability is effective
		comply with the law
promote transparent and efficient markets, be consistent with the rule of law	perform effectively in clearly defined roles	define roles and responsibilities

SOURCE: Chartered Institute of Internal Auditors

structure, process and control and also about the behaviour of the people who own and represent the organization, and the relationship that the organization has with society. As with this and other models, key elements of good corporate governance come to light, namely, honesty and integrity, transparency and openness, responsibility and accountability, which are discussed in the next section.

In order to adhere to good corporate governance a company needs to be accountable, transparent, ethical and responsible. To be accountable is about being answerable to another party for actions or activities. To be transparent, a business needs to adhere to the full, accurate and timely disclosure of information. Underpinning these concepts ethical principles must be followed, which means that the business must focus on doing 'what is right' and what is expected from society compared with what is expected from them from an economic and legal viewpoint. These definitions imply that Corporate Social Responsibility has a direct linkage to a company having good corporate governance procedures and is therefore an important part of how a company operates if it is to adhere to suitable corporate governance policies. However, these are guidelines and are not compulsory, so this begs the question that unless a legal framework is produced to force companies to behave in a way which adheres to good corporate governance, how can shareholder and other stakeholder needs be safely protected and considered when a business undertakes its activities? This is something that will be considered in a later section in this chapter.

The UK Corporate Governance Code

The latest UK Corporate Governance Code (2010) is underpinned by the following main principles:

Leadership

- Companies need to be headed by an effective board.
- The board is collectively responsible for the long-term success of the company.
- The role of the head of the company running the board and the executive running the company's business should be carried out by more than one individual.
- The chairman leads the board and is responsible for its effectiveness.
- Non-executive directors should challenge and develop proposals on strategy.

Effectiveness

- The board and its committees should consist of members with appropriate skills, experience, independence and knowledge to enable them to carry out their duties and responsibilities effectively.

- Formal, rigorous and transparent procedures for the appointment of new directors to the board should exist.

- Directors need to devote sufficient time to the company to enable them to carry out their responsibilities effectively.

- Directors should receive an induction when they join the board.

- Directors need to update and refresh their skills and knowledge regularly.

- Information needs to be provided to the board in a timely manner and of appropriate quality to enable it to carry out its duties.

- The board needs to have a formal and rigorous policy that annually evaluates its own performance and that of its committees and individual directors.

- All directors need to be submitted for re-election at regular intervals, provided they have continued satisfactory performance.

Accountability

- It is the responsibility of the board to produce an understandable and balanced assessment of the company's prospects and position.

- The board needs to maintain a suitable relationship with the company's auditor.

- Corporate reporting, risk management and internal control principles need established formal and transparent arrangements determined by the board.

- The board needs to establish the level of risk it is willing to take to achieve the company's strategic objectives.

- It is the board's responsibility to maintain sound risk management and internal control systems.

Remuneration

- No director should be in a position where they are involved in deciding their own remuneration.

- Remuneration packages need to be sufficient to attract, retain and motivate directors of the right quality to run the company successfully.

- A company should not pay more than is necessary for the services of directors.

- A significant proportion of executive directors' remuneration needs to be linked to corporate and individual performance.

- A formal and transparent policy needs to exist to develop executive remuneration and fix the remuneration packages of individual directors.

Relations with shareholders

- The board has a responsibility to ensure that satisfactory dialogue with shareholders takes place.

- This dialogue should ensure that shareholders have a mutual understanding of company objectives.

- The AGM is a suitable mechanism to communicate with investors and encourage their participation.

The relative merits of a framework approach to corporate governance versus a regulatory approach

There are essentially two main approaches to corporate governance: a framework, principles-based approach as in the United Kingdom; or a regulatory, rules-based approach as in the United States. Most developed countries follow one of these two systems, which are usually supported by the relevant stock exchanges that exist in a country. Whichever system is used, there is an element of required conformance. In the UK this is through corporate governance codes developed from the initial work of Cadbury. In the US the required corporate governance principles have been covered by legislation introduced by the Sarbanes–Oxley Act of 2002.

The 'comply or explain' concept is the trademark of corporate governance in the UK. This approach has been in operation since the Code's beginnings and is at the core of its flexibility. Both companies and shareholders support this approach and it has been widely respected and copied around the world. The Code is not an inflexible set of rules. It comprises principles (main and supporting) and provisions. The Stock Exchange Listing Rules require companies to apply the main principles and provide a report to shareholders as to how they have done this. Table 4.2 compares and summarizes the general requirements of the regulatory approach to corporate governance and the principles-based approach.

TABLE 4.2 The requirements of the regulatory approach and the principles-based approach to corporate governance

Regulatory Approach	Principles-Based Approach
given set of corporate governance requirements to be adhered to	key principles need to be complied with or explained
limited discretion on application and interpretation	different organizations may interpret and apply principles differently
may not be flexible enough to deal with new and changing circumstances and business environments	flexibility to handle changing circumstances and business environments
narrower definition of 'rules'	broader definition of 'rules'
more of a tick-box exercise	less of a tick-box activity, more a set of guiding practices
clear guidance on what is appropriate and what isn't	behaviour is more open to interpretation

The role of the audit function

In terms of the role of the audit function in helping a company achieve good corporate governance, the Combined Code provides a main principle with provisions. The key way in which a company can achieve good corporate governance via its audit function is through the duties and responsibilities of an audit committee.

The main principle stated in the June 2010 Corporate Governance Code states:

> The board should establish formal and transparent arrangements for considering how they should apply the corporate reporting and risk management and internal control principles and for maintaining an appropriate relationship with the company's auditor.

The Code provisions then go on to clarify what this involves, which covers the format and role of the audit committee.

The provisions recommend that the board should establish an audit committee of at least three, or in the case of smaller companies two, independent non-executive directors. Within this committee, the board should ensure that at least one member of the audit committee has recent and relevant financial experience.

The audit committee should have written terms of reference that set out its main role and responsibilities, which should include the following:

- The integrity of the financial statements of the company should be monitored including any formal announcements relating to the company's financial performance, reviewing significant financial reporting judgements contained in them.

- The company's internal financial controls and risk management systems need to be reviewed (sometimes this can be addressed by a separate board risk committee composed of independent directors, or by the board itself as an alternative).

- The effectiveness of the company's internal audit function needs to be reviewed and monitored.

- Recommendations need to be made to the board in relation to the appointment, re-appointment and removal of the external auditor and to approve the remuneration and terms of engagement of the external auditor. The board then needs to put these recommendations forward to the shareholders for their approval in general meeting.

- The external auditor's independence and objectivity needs to be reviewed and monitored alongside the effectiveness of the audit process. As part of this, consideration needs to be given to relevant UK professional and regulatory requirements.

- Policy on the engagement of the external auditor to supply non-audit services needs to be developed and implemented. This policy needs to take into account relevant ethical guidance regarding the provision of non-audit services by the external audit firm, and to report to the board, identifying any matters in respect of which it considers that action or improvement is needed and making recommendations as to the steps to be taken.

The terms of reference of the audit committee that cover its role and authority, as delegated to it by the board, should be made available to anyone who wants to review it. In a separate section of the annual report a description of the work of the committee in discharging those responsibilities should be provided.

Another function of the audit committee is to review the arrangements by which staff of the company may, in confidence, raise concerns about possible improprieties in matters of financial reporting or other matters. As part of this function, the audit committee's objective should be to ensure that arrangements are in place for the proportionate and independent investigation of such matters and for appropriate follow-up action.

The audit committee also has a responsibility to monitor and review the effectiveness of internal audit activities. Where there is no internal audit function, the audit committee should consider annually whether there is a need for one and make suitable recommendations to the board. Any reasons for the absence of such a function should also be explained in the relevant section of the annual report.

A key part of the audit committee's role is the recommendation on the appointment, re-appointment and removal of the external auditor. If the main board does not accept the audit committee's recommendation, the reasons for this should be included in the annual report, and in any papers recommending appointment or re-appointment, a statement from the audit committee explaining the recommendation should set out reasons why the board has taken a different position.

The annual report should also explain to shareholders how, if the auditor provides non-audit services, auditor objectivity and independence is safeguarded.

A key aspect of a business achieving good corporate governance is through the development of a good internal audit function that adheres to the standards set out for it both via the audit committee it reports into and international standards setting out their expectations of the internal audit function. The Definition of Internal Auditing and International Standards identifies that internal audit has an important role to play in providing assurance upon and evaluating and helping to improve the organization's governance processes. The International Standards make specific reference to internal audit, making recommendations on:

- improving the promotion of appropriate ethics and values within the organization;
- ensuring effective organizational performance management and accountability;
- communicating risk and control information to appropriate areas of the organization; and

- coordinating the activities of and communicating information to the board, external and internal auditors and management.

Therefore the audit committee and audit functions help to underpin the activities of a business and reinforce and check that it is doing all it can to carry out good corporate governance practices by introducing appropriate mechanisms to deliver and control good practice in its activities.

CASE STUDY

You are an audit manager for a firm of accountants and you have been put in charge of the audit of Expansive Industries plc.

You have been given the background briefing note so are aware of broadly what the company does, its directors and board structure and a summary of its financial performance. You are just beginning to understand and document audit matters and as part of your review you have been speaking to Financial Director Georgia Tickett and Head of Legal Mike Wong.

Mike Wong is worried about compliance with the UK Corporate Governance Code and the possible effect of any non-compliance on the auditors' report and possibly the share price. Georgia Tickett is of the view that whilst there may be some what she calls 'technical infringements' of the Code, these are easily explained as being for commercial reasons. She says she feels that a streamlined board makes it more responsive and 'hands on' and less of a discussion forum. She explained that they often have informal meetings between the four executive directors without inviting the non-executives. They make decisions at those meetings, which are then rubber-stamped at the monthly formal board meetings.

She is also not worried about not having an in-house internal audit function. She says the accountants are perfectly adequate and are brought in when needed to investigate any particular issues the board or her department require.

Discuss

- What is the UK Corporate Governance Code, where did it come from and why should companies comply with it?

- In what ways does Expansive not comply with it?

- Does it matter – is Georgia Tickett right about it improving decision-making?

- Internal audit – is the service provided by the accountants enough?

Bibliography

Cadbury, Sir A (1992) *Financial Aspects of Corporate Governance*, Gee & Co, London

Chartered Institute of Internal Auditors (nd) Corporate governance [Online] http://www.iia.org.uk/en/Knowledge_Centre/Resource_Library/corporate-governance.cfm#What_is_Internal_Audit_s_role_in_corporate_governance

Chartered Institute of Internal Auditors (2009) *Definition of Internal Auditing Code of Ethics International Standards for the Professional Practice of Internal Auditing*, IIA, London

FRC (2010) *Main Principles of the UK Corporate Governance Code* [Online] http://www.frc.org.uk/documents/pagemanager/Corporate_Governance/UK%20Corp%20Gov%20Code%20June%202010.pdf

Greenbury, R (1995) On Board Meetings, *Corporate Governance: An International Review* 3 (1), pp 7–8

Hampel, R (1998) *Committee on Corporate Governance: Final Report*, Gee & Co, London

Higgs, D (2003), *Review of the Role and Effectiveness of Non-Executive Directors*, The Department of Trade and Industry, London

Nolan, M (1995) *Summary of the Nolan Committee's First Report on Standards in Public Life*. Available at: www.archive.official-documents.co.uk/document/parlment/nolan/nolan.htm

Organisation for Economic Co-operation and Development (1999) *OECD Principles of Corporate Governance*, OECD, Paris

Sarbanes–Oxley Act (2002) H.R.Rep 107-610 25 July 2002. US Government Printing Office, Washington DC

Smith, Sir R (2003) *Audit Committee: Combined Code Guidance*, FRC, London

Turnbull, N (1999) *Internal Control: Guidance for Directors on the Combined Code*, FRC, London

Tyson, L D (2003) *The Tyson Report on the Recruitment and Development of Non-Executive Directors*, London Business School, London

UK Independent Commission for Good Governance in Public Services (2004) *The Good Governance Standard for Public Services*, OPA/CIPFA, London

The role of the senior executives/board

LEARNING OBJECTIVES

The material in this chapter covers:

- the responsibilities of directors/senior executives;
- the importance of ethical behaviour for senior management;
- the structures of controlling boards;
- alternative board structures;
- the role of the chair, CEO and non-executive directors;
- the need for and structure of sub-committees.

Introduction

The previous chapter provided the background to the principles of corporate governance and gave an understanding of the issues that have brought about its development over the last twenty years. This chapter goes into more detail about some of the specific areas affected by the corporate governance principles.

The responsibilities of directors/senior executives

The main principles of the Code highlight the importance and responsibility of the board in terms of running the company and being responsible for its long-term success. The Companies Act 2006 incorporates within it specific duties of directors. Section 172 of the Act lays down a specific duty on a company director to:

> Act in a way he considers, in good faith, would be most likely to promote the success of the company for the benefits of its members as a whole.

The Act goes on more specifically to specify that directors in their role must have regard to the interests of the company's employees, foster the company's relationship with suppliers, customers and others and ensure that the company maintains a reputation for high standards of business conduct. This implies that directors must act responsibly and use good ethical judgements in their behaviour and activities over and above the need for growth and long-term profitability.

The Combined Code also features key issues that affect the roles and responsibilities of the board, which therefore means that directors both as individuals and as part of the board have a duty of carrying out good corporate governance. Directors have to manage the conduct and behaviour of a company's activities and ensure that the business abides by procedures that adhere to good corporate governance. In order to carry out these responsibilities the Code provides detailed expectations of directors that will ensure that businesses generally focus their activities in the correct manner.

Acting as agents, they manage the business on behalf of the owners, the ordinary shareholders, so they need to ensure the growth of the business and its long-term survival. From the Companies Act and Combined Code they also have a duty of care to all stakeholders not just shareholders, so their activities are not just about profit and growth but must ensure that the businesses activities are undertaken with due care and consideration.

The following list summarizes the key expectations of directors and the board in order to meet the requirements of their role:

- They must lead the business and set out its strategic aims and plans.
- They must ensure that the management of the business is carrying out its role correctly.

- The board must consist of a chief executive, chairman and a suitable mix of executive and non-executive members who are appointed and selected appropriately following the company's procedure for appointment.

- They must make sure that the business has appropriate risk management techniques and necessary internal controls to reduce the risk of inappropriate activities taking place.

- Shareholders' and other stakeholders' needs must be met by the company.

- They must meet regularly and keep minutes of all decisions.

- Directors must have a clear list of their responsibilities.

- Their pay should be decided by the remuneration committee with their pay linked in to their abilities and performance.

- The role of the chairman and chief executive should be separated.

- There should be a strong presence of non-executive directors on the board.

- The chairman and non-executive directors need to meet regularly to review board performance and the non-executive directors need to review the performance of the chairman.

- All board members have a duty to update their skills on a regular basis.

- They should receive information in a timely and efficient manner.

- The board should review the effectiveness of their performance on a regular basis.

- New directors should be brought in regularly and re-elected every three years, with long service contracts discouraged (12 months being optimal).

So directors have a long list of responsibilities to adhere to if they are to undertake their role in line with the expectations and requirements set out for them.

The importance of ethical behaviour for senior management

Due to the number of worldwide scandals and the review of corporate governance in the UK through the reports listed in the previous chapter, the roles and responsibilities of the board have been developed to meet the requirements of the findings of these reports, as listed above. It follows that part of being a director is to have good ethics and that the underlying reasons behind major corporate collapses have been due to a lack of controls and specific requirements of the structure and operation of a business as it should be managed by the board.

Despite all of the guidelines and recommendations, a general requirement of good ethics and good principles can come a long way in addressing the risk of bad corporate behaviour and fraud and if followed by every board member, manager and employee of the business can help to ensure businesses operate as good citizens in all activities. However long the list of requirements and responsibilities, it can never cover all eventualities. A general requirement of good ethics can be a safety net for senior management to follow when all else fails.

The structures of controlling boards

Controlling boards can largely follow two basic structures, namely a unitary basis or a two-tier one. Countries like the UK and US follow the unitary board basis whilst the two-tier approach is used in countries such as France and Germany. As the term 'unitary' suggests, this is a structure whereby a company consists of one board made up of executive and non-executive directors. A two-tier board is a structure whereby a company has a board for management and a board for supervision.

Other multi-tier structures can exist, such as in Japan where a multi-tiered structure is used comprising a policy board that considers strategic issues, a functional board that considers different business functions and executive director roles and responsibilities, and monocratic boards with few responsibilities and a largely symbolic role.

Alternative board structures

The unitary board

This is where one board of directors exists that is responsible to the company's shareholders. The board both manages and controls the business. The one board is made up of both executive and non-executive directors. In the US over half must be non-executive directors and in the UK at least half, to meet the requirements of Sarbanes–Oxley (US) and the Combined Code (UK).

Within this board structure the role of chairman and chief executive is separated. Therefore, although there is one board carrying out management and control effectively, management is the role of the executive directors and chief executive, and supervision and control are the roles of the non-executive directors and chairman. Although this appears to all rest as the responsibility of the one main board, in essence in larger companies some of these duties would be devolved down to sub-committees and managers further down the chain of command in the business.

In law all directors on the board have responsibilities, be they executive or non-executive, and so can be seen as being accountable for their actions and decisions, and they all have a duty of care in the decisions and activities they undertake. Putting all directors into one board gives a greater sense of collective responsibility and means that the skills non-executive directors have gathered from their experience and expertise can be better utilized in the functions and decisions made by the board.

The board will be larger than the two-tier approach so may be more difficult to manage and organize but at the same time means that decisions are viewed and discussed by more members, so hopefully giving rise to the greater chance that fraud opportunities are minimized and abuse of power by board members is less likely.

The two-tier board

This structure comprises a board to carry out the management of the company and a board to supervise the business.

The supervisory board is led by the chairman of the company and is responsible for a general oversight of the company in terms of its compliance with regulatory law and guidelines plus the articles of association of the business. It also reviews the activities of the management board and ensures that it is operating in line with necessary procedures and generally reviews the company's activities and business strategies. It is also responsible for ensuring that management board members are appointed, supervised and removed in an appropriate way.

The management board is led by the chairman and is there to check that the business is generally run and managed effectively.

As the company is effectively in the hands of two boards there must be a link between the activities of the two tiers – this link is in the hands of the chairman of the supervisory board who has a key role in ensuring overall good, ethical and effective governance, good administration and collective operations of the two boards in acting in the best interests of the shareholders and other key stakeholders.

The two-tier approach splits the interests of the company in two and enables a cross-checking of board activities between one board and the other. However, questions as to how efficient this structure is, and how much conflict exists due to the monitoring of each other's activities, may be an issue in reality. The separation of supervisory activities from management also brings into question how accurate and clear the picture of the company's management is when it is effectively gained second hand.

The role of the chair

As part of the requirements of corporate governance a company must have a separate person carrying out the role of chairman to that of chief executive. The chairman runs the board of the company and the chief executive runs the company to ensure that no one person has too much power and control over the business.

Exactly what is required in the role of each person should be clearly established in writing for the two individuals concerned. As chairman of the board the position comes under the heading of non-executive director, ie they are not actively involved in the day-to-day running of the company and as such this role can be full-time or part-time, depending on what suits the company concerned. As chairman and a non-executive director this leads to the chairman having a greater say in the appointment of other non-executive directors whereas the chief executive has a greater influence in the appointment of executive directors. The chairman is appointed by other board members.

In summary, the chairman has an overall responsibility for the board carrying out the company's strategy in an appropriate way and ensuring that it is implemented appropriately. The chairman is also the key voice of the company to the outside world, explaining what the business's policies and objectives are to any interested outside parties.

As part of the chairman's duties they should:

- chair all board meetings;
- produce agendas for board meetings;

- meet with non-executive directors regularly to review board performance;
- chair annual general meetings and shareholder meetings;
- work closely with the chief executive;
- be responsible for the composition of the board reviewing its size, split of non-executive and executive members and overall effectiveness;
- ensure appropriate information is received by board members on a timely basis;
- ensure a contribution is being made by non-executive directors;
- ensure shareholders' views are communicated to the board and any major decisions in terms of strategy and governance are discussed with them.

The role of the CEO

The chief executive officer effectively runs the company and is a full-time employee of the business. The chief executive comes under the heading of an executive director and has a great influence in the appointment of other executive directors.

In their role as chief executive they must report directly to the chairman and other members of the board and have overall responsibility for ensuring that the company is managed in such a way that its performance meets the objectives of the strategy developed by the board. As such the chief executive has a very important and key role within the business. The company strategy, as determined by the board, has to be reviewed by the chief executive and developed into policies that, when implemented, meet the criteria set out by the board.

The chief executive takes full responsibility for the company operating in a way to meet the requirements of the board in terms of performance and all necessary controls. To do this job effectively the chief executive will need to develop a strong team of appropriately skilled management to carry out business activities.

The role is all about providing the link between day-to-day business activities and the operation of the board. Therefore the role needs to ensure that systems have been put in place to plan, manage risk, monitor finances, control physical resources, develop suitable internal controls and review operations to check that goals and budgets are being met.

The chairman is the key representative to the outside world in terms of the 'general public'. The chief executive is the link to more specific stakeholder groups such as customers, suppliers etc. Alongside the chairman, the chief executive has to assist in the appointment and monitoring of board members with a stronger emphasis on executive directors.

The role of non-executive directors and the importance of their independence

Executive directors are usually full-time employees of a business involved in the day-to-day running of the company. They are board members but also senior managers within the business such as a finance director, sales director, etc.

Non-executive directors are board members but are not involved with the day-to-day running of the business. They are not full-time employees with specific senior manager roles like executive directors. So why are non-executive directors required as part of the board structure?

They are required according to provisions in the Combined Code, which states that in the UK at least 50 per cent of a board should be composed of non-executive directors. As executive directors manage day-to-day activities, non-executive directors are there to ensure corporate governance processes are followed and to monitor activities and strategy development.

They are engaged due to their experience and knowledge gained through other business activities and employment. As part of their duties they will contribute to the development of strategy, scrutinize performance to check that it is meeting agreed goals and targets, ensure that risk management procedures and controls are adequate such that financial information produced is accurate. They will also be called upon to review board performance generally, the performance of the chairman, to ensure appointments to the board are carried out correctly and that succession planning is monitored to ensure that no one member serves for too long a period as a suitable replacement is in hand. They are also involved in deciding the remuneration packages provided to executive directors.

To do this job effectively they need to be 'independent' so that they have a corporate conscience which means that they should not have been employed by the business within the last five years and they should not receive any other remuneration from the company apart from their non-executive director's fee. There should also not have been any material relationship with the business for at least three years and there should not be any close family ties or significant shareholdings as any of these factors could impinge on their independence and decision-making abilities.

By the board consisting of a mixture of executive and non-executive directors with a balance of day-to-day involvement and general oversight, no one group dominates and more objective decision-making should take place as a consequence.

In effect, they should be more independent in their views and lack bias as they are that step away from direct involvement in business activities. In reality, however, as they are not permanent full-time employees, will they have the time to devote to gaining enough understanding of the business to conduct their responsibilities effectively and will they have to rely on executive directors' knowledge and information a bit too much when making decisions?

Non-executive directors need to have high standards of integrity and good business ethics alongside a good level of business expertise to conduct themselves in accordance with the requirements of the Combined Code and to achieve respect from the other board members. As they are 'independent' they are asked to make up the membership of a number of sub-committees – namely the remuneration, nomination and audit committees, as discussed below.

The need for and structure of sub-committees

To meet all the requirements of the Code effectively, the board does not have enough time to meet all the provisions in as much detail as is necessary. Therefore to ensure that good corporate governance exists, a number of sub-committees from the main board need to exist. These committees include:

- the audit committee;
- the remuneration committee;
- the nominations committee;
- the risk committee.

The audit committee

The board has an overall responsibility to ensure that adequate risk management processes exist within the company. Key factors that determine the role of the committee are major corporate scandals such as Enron where the accounts produced were not accurate and hid vital information to protect shareholders' and other investors' investments. As a consequence the spotlight was placed on the need for monitoring the integrity of financial information to restore public confidence in published accounts. Key to good audit is independence; therefore the audit committee has to meet separately to the main board and consists entirely of non-executive directors (at least three for larger companies) of whom at least one must have appropriate and up-to-date financial experience.

Their role (as discussed in more detail in the previous chapter) is to monitor the integrity of the financial statements, review internal controls and audit effectiveness, monitor the appointment of and removal of external auditors, ensuring their independence, and provide a forum that facilitates confidential whistleblowing. The key to their role is 'oversight', 'review' and 'assessment' – so they are a safety net to try to minimize risks happening and errors taking place.

The role of the audit committee came about from the findings of the Smith Report in 2003, which gave rise to the Smith Guidance, which covers the points listed above.

The audit committee should reinforce the position of internal auditors by overviewing their work and providing them with a channel of communication to the main board. The audit committee also ensures that external auditors are properly appointed, engaged and remunerated, ensuring that they are not engaged for other non-audit work, are properly experienced and qualified, with no reasons to jeopardize their independence or quality of work.

The remunerations committee

Excessive pay is corporate abuse and has been the subject of many news headlines. To try to ensure fair remuneration packages for directors a separate remuneration committee needs to exist, consisting entirely of non-executive directors who set out the policy and specific packages for each director.

This committee reports to the main board and is there to ensure that executive directors are not responsible for setting their own pay. The committee reviews pay scales, the proportion of different types of pay, the period in which performance-related pay becomes payable, what proportion of a pay package consists of a performance-related component and ensures that the rewards are disclosed and transparent.

The aim is to try to tie in performance to overall company goals and objectives that have a long-term view by using rewards such as share options and other benefits in an appropriate manner.

The nominations committee

This committee is all about getting the structure of the board right and largely consists of non-executive directors. It exists to try to ensure that any appointments made are not biased and are in line with the specification of the roles concerned.

The activities of this board cover:

- ensuring that the board members cover the appropriate balance between executives and non-executives;
- ensuring the current board has the right mix of skills, knowledge and experience;
- ensuring continuity and succession planning take place as contracts come to an end and board members need replacing;
- ensuring diverse backgrounds and the right gender mix exists – the gender imbalance on boards was a specific provision of the 2010 Combined Code, which sought to ensure that at least two members of a board are female;
- reviewing leadership needs of the company;
- reviewing general board size and structure on an ongoing basis and when appointments are made;
- monitoring non-executive directors to ensure they are spending sufficient time on their duties.

The risk committee

This committee again should consist largely of non-executive directors and is all about assessing the company's risk exposure and risk management strategy.

To do this, internal controls need to be reviewed and risk assessments taken of key functions of the business. Risk strategy and procedures are recommended to the main board to introduce and then, once implemented, reviewed by this board to ensure that they are adequate and sufficient in terms of their effectiveness.

There may be some overlap with the work of this committee and the audit committee and where appropriate areas of internal control risks may need bringing to the audit committee's attention.

There are a number of mechanisms in place to enable companies to try to establish good corporate governance activities. By understanding the requirements of the board and committee structures of companies, and ensuring that the key roles of the members of these groups are carried out effectively, organizations should be managed in a way that is in line with good corporate governance practice.

CASE STUDY

Handbag *et al* produce handbags. They also supply them internationally and through a network of sales outlets throughout the UK. They traditionally only made handbags but have latterly moved into a broad range of accessories to take advantage of the latest trends in the market place. In particular, purses now make up 40 per cent of their sales. They have expanded rapidly over the last two years and are now a major UK producer.

You are the auditors of Handbag *et al* and have been approached by the directors for advice on corporate governance and internal controls. They are aware that with their rapid growth, their obligations as directors have increased and they should be taking much more interest in the level of controls within the company. They are also considering establishing an audit committee and would like your advice in this area.

You have recently completed the annual audit of Handbag *et al* and are aware that very little has been done to promote sound governance within the company.

Discuss

- the role of the directors in relation to corporate governance and controls;

- the potential role of the audit committee and the factors that Handbag *et al* should consider in making a decision on whether to go ahead with the formation of the committee.

Bibliography

FRC (2010) *Main Principles of the UK Corporate Governance Code* [Online]
   http://www.frc.org.uk/documents/pagemanager/Corporate_Governance/
   UK%20Corp%20Gov%20Code%20June%202010.pdf

HMSO (2006) *Companies Act 2006*, HMSO, London

Sarbanes–Oxley Act (2002) H.R.Rep 107-610 25 July 2002. US Government
   Printing Office, Washington DC

Smith, Sir R (2003) *Audit Committee: Combined Code Guidance*, FRC, London

Turnbull, N (1999) *Internal Control: Guidance for Directors on the Combined
   Code*, FRC, London

06 Assessing performance and remuneration of directors and senior executives

LEARNING OBJECTIVES

This chapter will enable you to:

- understand the approach to assessing individual and collective performance;

- discuss the advantages and disadvantages of performance-related remuneration;

- appreciate the role of the shareholders in approving directors' remuneration;

- understand the role of non-executives in performance review and evaluation – the remuneration committee.

Introduction

The UK Corporate Governance Code sets out the standards of good practice expected of boards of directors and the basis on which the remuneration of directors should be calculated.

Section D of the Code states unequivocally:

> Levels of remuneration should be sufficient to attract, retain and motivate directors of the quality required to run the company successfully, but a company

should avoid paying more than is necessary for this purpose. A significant proportion of executive directors' remuneration should be structured so as to link rewards to corporate and individual performance.

There should be a formal and transparent procedure for developing policy on executive remuneration and for fixing the remuneration packages of individual directors. No director should be involved in deciding his or her own remuneration.

It expands on this further, stressing the need for executive remuneration to be linked to the success of the company – in other words, reward systems should be geared to performance and should not simply be a fixed reward irrespective of the actual results of the entity they are managing.

The performance-related elements of executive directors' remuneration should be stretching and designed to promote the long-term success of the company.

As we will see, this element of performance-related pay comes in many forms and there are mechanisms designed, in theory at least, to ensure that pay is commensurate with success and that executives are not rewarded excessively for mediocrity.

As we have seen elsewhere, the directors are employees of the company, and it would be thought that, as agents, their remuneration should ultimately be approved by the shareholders. As we will see, this is not necessarily the case. Every now and then there is what the press likes to call a 'shareholder revolt' when, usually minority, shareholders attempt to vote down some monster bonus or compensation package awarded for what they see as failure rather than success.

In this chapter we will look at the factors influencing pay and reward structures and we will consider whether weighting executive reward to performance is necessarily a good idea, and whether or not a handsome reward package really does encourage loyalty to the business or whether it stimulates the mercenary instinct among top executives who will then sell their loyalty to the highest bidder and will change their allegiance as soon as a better offer looms over the horizon.

Assessing the effectiveness of directors

How then do we assess how effective directors are in carrying out their duties? The UK Corporate Governance Code says:

The board should undertake a formal and rigorous annual evaluation of its own performance and that of its committees and individual directors.

That is all good and fine but the Code does not set out any particular standards to be adopted or methodologies to be used.

It is necessary for the performance of each director to be formally evaluated annually. There is often a hierarchy for this, for example:

- Executive directors will be evaluated by the chief executive officer (CEO).
- The CEO will be evaluated by the chair of the board.
- The chair's performance will be evaluated by the non-executive directors.

The performance of non-executive directors (NEDs) is often not formally assessed. These people are usually appointed for a fixed term and have been chosen for their independence, objectivity and business skills. Clearly a NED who did not gel with their fellow directors or brought no benefit to the board would be unlikely to last long in the role.

The formal evaluation process should be agreed by the board in advance. It is necessary for the board to set down:

- the responsibility for carrying out appraisals;
- what form the evaluations should take;
- what expectations there are of those carrying out the appraisal and those being appraised;
- what performance criteria are to be applied – for example, criteria should be based on their performance as a director not as a technician or a generator of profit. There should be a common set of performance criteria for all executive directors;
- how information will be gathered and assessed – will it be in the form of a questionnaire? If so, has this been properly evaluated and discussed between senior members of the board?
- how the appraisee will be able to respond to any points raised in the appraisal;
- will the appraisal process be monitored to ensure there is no bias or favouritism shown? Non-executive directors should be involved at every stage in the process to ensure fair play;
- how the success or otherwise of the appraisal process will be evaluated.

Goals and objectives

As part of the induction process new directors should be given goals and expectations and part of the appraisal process should be in measuring achievement of those goals. There is much literature written about goal setting and performance appraisal and this is, generally, outside the scope of this book. However, a common mnemonic for goal setting that sums up the objectives of setting goals but does nothing about the methodology is that goals should be:

Specific
Measurable
Achievable
Realistic/Results oriented/Relevant
Time bound ie within a time frame

SMART

It is critical that these individual goals and objectives cohere with the strategic objectives for the organisation so that all parties are working towards the same target – something that organisational theorists call 'goal congruence'.

When setting goals research highlights two key issues:

- Goal setting improves performance – more difficult goals result in higher levels of effort and, providing individuals have the skills to meet the goals, in improved performance. Clearly the setting of goals has to be balanced with the ability to achieve them.

- Specific goals are better than 'just do your best' goals. Goals should be specific and measurable as far as possible, although it is recognized that, at director level, progress towards achievement of some goals may not be so easily measured. For example, improving morale amongst staff may be recognized as having been achieved but may not be capable of being measured except through monitoring of indicators such as reduction in absenteeism or resignations or lower levels of petty theft and vandalism etc.

The board should thus set goals for itself as a board linked to strategic corporate objectives and, within that context, individual directors should have individual, business-orientated goals. They should also have some personal goals and individual performance-related goals decided by mutual agreement between appraiser and appraisee.

Goal setting helps to motivate and energize individuals towards achievement providing they have faith in the process and are convinced they can achieve what has been asked of them. Unrealistic goals and impossible targets are simply demotivating, however aggressively they are presented. Goals, or objectives, are not the same as targets. A target is something to be aimed for but not necessarily achieved; for example, a sales team may be given a target of sales of £1m per month and it will be rewarded for hitting that target. The sales director may know that the target is an extremely challenging one, albeit achievable, so would plan and budget for a lower level of sales that is realistically achievable. This would be the actual goal or objective the director was trying to achieve.

Directors should not be set targets, they must be set objectives linked to corporate strategies – they are not rewarded for hitting a target but for contributing to the achievement of corporate objectives and performing well as directors. It is also important that the whole board is accountable, including the CEO and the chair of the board so that all the directors, except the non-executives, are part of the process.

Individuals are not being assessed on technical ability; for example, the financial director is not being assessed on their knowledge of financing techniques or their ability with numbers; they are being assessed as directors. Many of the goals will consist of managerial skills such as:

- their ability to build a strong organization in their area of influence with high staff morale and improved productivity;
- their contribution towards achieving corporate objectives;
- their contribution towards innovative thinking and initiative;
- economic capabilities such as cost reductions or making the most of available resources;
- reporting and communications skills.

The UK Corporate Governance Code requires that, every three years, an independent external facilitator be appointed to evaluate the board. Any connection with the company has to be disclosed so the intention is to make this appraisal as independent and transparent as possible.

Initial goals are set which relate to corporate objectives and company strategies. It may be that, at this stage, the process will also include indications as to how the goal is to be achieved. For example, a strategic goal might be to increase market share in a defined area. This could be achieved by organic growth, marketing campaigns, promotions etc or by acquiring a competitor firm with strong links to that area. The 'how' part might exclude

FIGURE 6.1 Directors' performance appraisal, goals and development

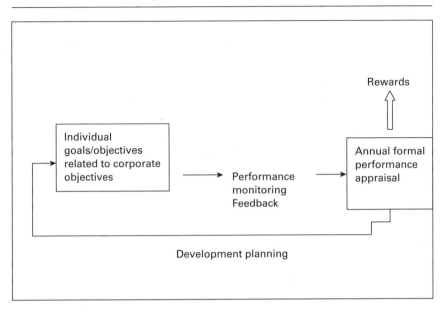

any element of acquisition and specify purely to organic growth – it is then up to the director as to what tactics they adopt to achieve the objective. The sales director's objective will be linked to production objectives, financial requirements and other aspects of the overall strategy of the business over the short term.

The director may also be set longer-term objectives to be achieved over, say, two to three years, which, again will relate to the longer-term strategy and growth of the organization.

Performance evaluation

From the day of appointment the new director is under scrutiny and their performance should be evaluated. These are often informal evaluations and they can come from a variety of sources including:

- evaluations of performance at formal meetings and sessions and at informal gatherings;
- views and comments from customers, clients or professional contacts;

- observations from stakeholders such as suppliers, customers, financiers etc;

- conversations or feedback from staff.

This feedback should be documented and included as part of the appraisal process (Figure 6.1).

Appraisal systems should evaluate the director's performance both in achieving goals and as a director with an appreciation of the wider corporate perspective. For example, a director who goes all out to achieve their objectives with little thought to cost or the implications of their actions on other parts of the organization is actually failing in their role – they have to think corporately and strategically and should not be incentivized in such a way that achievement of the goal becomes all-consuming because this is what brings in the biggest personal reward. Remember that in addition to business objectives directors should be set personal and management goals and these should be considered to be as important as the ones related to the business.

Sadly, as we will see, there is a view that reward systems have lost touch with these principles and that the links between performance and reward have broken.

Corporate governance and directors' pay

First of all let us look at the principles of good corporate governance as they affect the rewards of directors.

Clearly directors have always been rewarded for their efforts and, if we have regard to the principles of agency theory (Chapter 1) they are more likely to order the company's affairs in such a way as to maximize their own rewards often at the expense of their principals, the shareholders.

We can date modern principles of rewarding executives, as with so many other things, to the Cadbury Report in 1992. The enormous conflict of interest inherent in directors setting their own reward structures has been recognized for many years and the solution to the problem suggested by Cadbury was to adopt a system first used in the USA, namely that of setting up a remuneration committee, comprising solely non-executive directors, to decide on the pay and benefits of the executive directors.

Cadbury stressed the principles of openness and accountability. Shareholders are entitled to a full and clear statement of directors' present and future benefits, and of how they have been determined.

Cadbury recommended that:

- Separate disclosure should be made of salary and performance-related elements.
- The criteria on which performance-related pay is based should be fully explained.
- Information about stock options and pension rights should be given to the shareholders.
- Service contracts should be for no more than three years.
- A remuneration committee staffed and chaired by non-executive directors should be set up to determine suitable pay and benefits for each director. No directors should decide their own pay.

In the early part of the 1990s concerns were being raised about the remuneration levels of directors. Politicians and the press were eager to point out that directors were 'awarding themselves' big pay rises, that if they left office they were being compensated and that they were gaining handsomely from share options, particularly those who came from recently privatized utilities – water, gas and electricity. Socialist politicians threatened dire legislation when they returned to power, particularly where privatized public utilities were concerned. This became a serious political issue focusing on the pay rises executives in privatized utilities had received.

Gordon Brown, then Labour's treasury spokesman, highlighted the fact that utility privatization had created 50 millionaires among executives including all 14 of the chairmen of the regional electricity companies. A rallying point became the 75 per cent pay rise announced in 1994 for the chairman of British Gas, Cedric Brown, who then became the target of a 'Cedric the Pig' campaign at the May 1995 British Gas AGM. This campaign struck a nerve with the public at a time of relatively high unemployment, and independent evidence that revealed that there was no discernible link between pay increases and company performance (Cope, 1996). At the end of 1994 it was reckoned that £7bn of a total of £10.5bn of executive share options in listed UK companies did not relate to performance. As it happened Labour returned to power in 1997 under the leadership of Tony Blair so no legislation was forthcoming.

Greenbury and the remuneration committee

In 1995, the government approached Sir Richard Greenbury, then chairman of Marks & Spencer, to consider the whole thorny issue. The terms of reference were:

To identify good practice in determining Directors' remuneration and prepare a Code of such practice for use by UK PLCs.

Greenbury concentrated on the Cadbury principles of disclosure, transparency and performance rather than recommending any statutory controls. The Committee recommended:

- the setting up of a remuneration committee of non-executive directors to determine pay levels. The chairman of the committee should be accountable directly to the shareholders;

- enhanced disclosure of emoluments for all directors including bonus and incentive schemes based on performance and the criteria by which these are determined;

- directors' service contracts to be for one year;

- full disclosure of all aspects of share option schemes, including the number of shares, the price of all options, the market price of the share at the exercise date and a summary of the performance criteria on which the option is conditional.

The reaction to the report was less than enthusiastic. Companies complained about the increased regulatory burden of disclosure, the CBI worried that it had not gone far enough in regulating business behaviour and the Labour Party discussed banning share options altogether for privatized utilities. It has been argued that, if the intention of the Greenbury Committee was to regulate executive pay through enhanced disclosure, it has largely failed. Instead the enhanced disclosure in the financial statements has enabled directors to discover what their counterparts in similar organisations are earning and this has tended to raise the bar as successively lucrative pay deals are negotiated by directors.

However, the proposals were adopted and the UK Corporate Governance Code is quite unequivocal on the subject. Articles D2.1 and 2.2 state:

D2.1 The board should establish a remuneration committee of at least three, or in the case of smaller companies two, independent non-executive directors. In addition the company chairman may also be a member of, but not chair, the committee if he or she was considered independent on appointment as chairman. The remuneration committee should make available its terms of reference, explaining its role and the authority delegated to it by the board. Where remuneration consultants are appointed, a statement should be made available of whether they have any other connection with the company.

D2.2 The remuneration committee should have delegated responsibility for setting remuneration for all executive directors and the chairman, including pension rights and any compensation payments. The committee should also recommend and monitor the level and structure of remuneration for senior management. The definition of 'senior management' for this purpose should be determined by the board but should normally include the first layer of management below board level.

These requirements are mandatory for listed companies and are recommended good practice for other organizations. The remit of the remuneration committee extends as far as the first tier of senior managers below director level.

The process is intended to conform to the basic principles of corporate governance – it should be open and transparent and free from bias or influence. Whether this is so, however, may be open to question as there have been a number of disagreements between directors and shareholders, which has called into question, by implication, the judgement, and possibly even the independence of some NEDs where shareholders have objected to what they see as excessive rewards.

Accounting requirements

In 2002 the government passed legislation, the Directors' Remuneration Report Regulations 2002, which sets out the disclosure to be made in the annual financial statements. Listed companies must also follow the requirements of the UK Corporate Governance Code.

Disclosure now runs to several pages of the annual financial report and accounts and the amount of detail contained in these reports is extensive. Some of the information required to be disclosed has to be audited and some does not. Interestingly there is an emphasis, in the regulations, on disclosure of the links between performance and remuneration – even to the extent of requiring the directors to prepare a graphical representation of the performance of the company's share price against that of a notional bundle of shares similar to those on which an equity market index might be calculated.

Thus performance is linked not to the real performance of the business but to its share price. As this is a function of a market place it might be considered that the share price is a reflection of the value of the business, but stock markets are subject to outside influences such as political factors, economic performance and crises of confidence which can affect share prices. It does however go some way to explain why directors take such an inordinate interest in their company's share price.

Non-audited information

The Regulations set out key disclosure requirements that are *not* required to be audited. These include:

- the names of the members of the remuneration committee;
- the names of any individuals who materially assisted the remuneration committee and, if any of those who assisted were not themselves directors of the company (ie were consultants), information on the nature of any other services they provided during the year;
- a statement of the company's policy on directors' remuneration for the forthcoming and subsequent financial years. The policy statement must include, for each director, a detailed explanation of the performance conditions applicable to his or her entitlements to share awards including whether an award was granted under a shareholder-approved option scheme or long-term incentive scheme or was granted under a deferred bonus scheme set up without shareholder approval.

The detailed explanation must show:

- why the performance conditions were chosen;
- a summary of the methods used to assess performance (and why such methods were chosen);
- details of any performance conditions involving comparison with external factors together with details of any comparator group;
- an explanation of any significant amendment proposed to be made to any entitlement of a director to a share award (actual amendments to share awards require disclosure as audited information);
- where an entitlement to a share award is not subject to performance conditions, an explanation as to why this is so.

In relation to each director's remuneration, the policy statement must explain 'the relative importance of those elements which are, and those which are not, related to performance'.

The policy statement must also include information on the company's policy on length of contracts with directors and notice periods and termination payments under those contracts. Listed companies must disclose their policy on the length of non-executive appointments and whether they can be terminated by giving notice of termination. Note that institutional investors have expressed concerns about companies being able to terminate by notice because they regard it as weakening the non-executive director's position.

A performance graph must be produced illustrating actual shareholder return on a holding of the company's listed shares over the last five years compared with the notional shareholder return over the same period on a basket of shares 'of the same kind and number as those by reference to which a broad equity market index is calculated'.

The report should include details of directors' service contracts and/or contracts for services, and, in the case of non-executive directors, letters of appointment. Any 'significant award' made to a former director must also be explained. This would include any compensation package for loss of office and details of whether (and why) any discretion was exercised in favour of a director to enable that director to exercise options or receive other share awards.

Audited information

The company must disclose very detailed information, which has to be audited, to be set out regarding:

- the actual amounts received in the financial year by way of salary and fees, bonuses, expenses and other non-cash benefits;
- any compensation for loss of office or other termination payment;
- information on each director's share options and interests under long-term incentive schemes;
- information on each director's entitlements under pension schemes;
- sums paid to third parties for directors' services.

The auditors are required to report to shareholders and to state whether, in their opinion, it has been properly prepared in accordance with the Companies Act 2005 ('the Act'). The auditors are also required to provide a statement giving details of any non-compliance with the Act.

However, all this disclosure does not appear to have limited the remuneration of directors at all since Greenbury. Successive headlines have highlighted the fact that, generally, increases in pay of executives in the UK's largest companies have outstripped those of their employees by a considerable margin. In 2011 the Hutton Report revealed that average pay for directors of FTSE 100 companies has risen from 47 times average earnings to 88 times over the past decade, and from 124 times the minimum wage to 202 times. The perception among the investing public that levels of directors' remuneration may be becoming unreasonable has resulted in some displays of shareholder power. These, generally, cause directors to lose little sleep as they are, more often than not, revolts by small investors who have no real level of power or influence; however, in recent times, some of the major institutional investors have been turning their attention to this issue, particularly in underperforming companies, and, as we saw in Chapter 1, these bodies do have the ability to influence boards.

Executive pay: revolt of the shareholders

There has been, not unnaturally, public outrage at the enormous bonuses paid to City bankers who have seemingly walked away from a potential financial collapse avoided only by an injection of eye-watering amounts of public money without any sanction against them. Bankers' bonuses dipped a little during the worst of the crisis but are rapidly being restored to pre-crisis levels.

Such bonuses reach astonishing levels. For example, in 2011 two Barclay's Bank managers, in the investment banking arm and not the high street branch network, received almost £40m each after the maturity of share options awarded some five years previously and they also share in a bonus pool pot of £10m that could be worth considerably more in a few years' time if performance targets are met. The chief executive received £27m, mostly made up of performance-related and loyalty-based bonuses.

At the same time it was pointed out that the shareholder who invested £100 in 2007 would be faced with a loss of £47 by 2011 as the share price collapsed. This huge disparity between what company managers reward themselves with and the results for the shareholder is an extreme case but it is not an isolated one.

However, there are signs that the shareholders, particularly the small investors, are fighting back. For example, the press reported a shareholder revolt at the AGM of Lloyds Banking Group, which had to be bailed out by the government in 2009. In that case the directors' remuneration was approved because a big institutional investor (UKFI) threw its voting power behind the directors – this time – although it did hint darkly at remuneration reforms. However, other institutional investors have not been so relaxed about what ordinary shareholders see as excessive remuneration in difficult times. The Association of British Insurers, representing about 20 per cent of institutional investors, has issued an alert over what it sees as excessive rewards for directors (Davey, 2010). They have expressed concerns over, for example, a bonus scheme at a company called Wolfson Microelectronics plc whose reward system is designed to pay out handsome bonuses for growth in only four consecutive quarters, pointing out that this is hardly long term. Shareholder revolts also happened at a range of commercial companies (Table 6.1). Newspaper articles indicate that smaller investors are not prepared to see directors receiving comfortable pay and large bonuses in times of hardship or crisis when workers are being laid off or company performance is, at best, mediocre.

TABLE 6.1 Shareholder revolts over pay in 2011

Company	Activity	Grounds for Revolt
Reckitt Benckiser	consumer cleaning and health products	incentive- and performance-based share scheme not challenging – no absolute upper limits apply to awards under the long-term incentive scheme
Xstrata	mining	chief executive's 41 per cent pay rise and retention bonuses to other directors
William Hill	betting	50 per cent pay rise for chief executive
easyJet	airline	payment to retain chief executive of £1m to stay for one more year and defer retirement for one year; opposed by major shareholder (Davey, 2010)
Thomas Cook	holiday company	bonus scheme to directors based on profits ignoring effect of losses that affected share price so profits artificially inflated
Standard Life	insurance	excessive pay including £1m bonus to CEO

Where small investors tread, larger institutional investors will follow. Shareholders who have seen the value of their investments hit by a downturn will be reluctant to invest and this, in the longer term, could affect larger investors. So warning notes are being sounded that the days of wine and roses for 'fat cat' directors may be coming to an end.

In May 2011 the High Pay Commission, a body set up in November 2010 to investigate the pay of top earners, published an interim report on executive pay. The report revealed that during the decade to 2011 executive pay rose on average by 64.2 per cent whilst average earnings rose 7.2 per cent.

In its report the Commission argues that attempts to introduce a greater performance-related element to pay have exacerbated the problem and that, far from rewarding success and punishing failure as the Greenbury Committee no doubt envisaged originally, the report claims that too much emphasis has been placed on a notional performance linkage, and not enough on scale or reward. The problem is, undoubtedly, that the individuals who determine the performance measures and the level of pay linked to these measures are the directors themselves – there is no independent arbitration and no mechanism for prior shareholder approval.

The Commission also argues that the existing governance arrangements for pay, including the creation of remuneration committees and shareholder oversight, have failed to exert proper control; indeed the report suggests that, again, they may have even helped push pay up further. The Commission's interim report also sets out that its proposed reforms will focus on the themes of transparency, accountability and fairness, which could include 'reforms of the remuneration committees and the inclusion of other stakeholders'. The introduction of dissident elements into remuneration committees may restrict excessive pay awards.

Excessive rewards and shareholder rights

The failure of effective oversight by shareholders of executive pay raises deeper questions about company ownership and the rights of shareholders.

We stated, in Chapter 1, where we looked at agency theory, that managers, as agents, tend to make decisions that benefit them at the expense of their principals, the shareholders, and this awarding to themselves of what is considered to be excessive remuneration is a case in point. What remedies do shareholders, as owners, have to stop directors voting themselves huge bonuses based on what might be spurious performance criteria?

What does the law say, first of all?

Shareholders have surprisingly little power over the directors when it comes to their personal terms and conditions. Originally directors' pay awards had to be approved by the shareholders at the annual general meeting but gradually this right was eroded such that the Companies Act 2006 only requires the directors to have the directors' remuneration report approved by an ordinary resolution at the AGM (s 439). Accordingly most of the revolts shown in Table 6.1 are against these so-called 'advisory' resolutions. If the revolt succeeds and the report isn't passed by the shareholders it matters not, as s 439 states:

> No entitlement of a person to remuneration is made conditional on the resolution being passed by reason only of the provision made by this section.
>
> (s 439 (5) CA 2006)

This means that the director gets paid anyway, despite shareholder objections. Clearly failure to obtain shareholder approval in such circumstances would be a vote of no confidence in the remuneration committee and would send a clear signal to the directors. Companies facing such a shareholder revolt usually have ample warning through the press or shareholder comment and this may well result in some action by the directors to forestall a negative vote.

Spurious categories of compensation are limited under s 215, by prohibiting payments for loss of office, except, under s 220, in respect of damages for existing obligations and pensions and these have to be approved by the shareholders (s 217) – so no US-style golden parachutes except those contractually committed! Long-term incentive schemes involving directors must be approved by ordinary resolution under the London Stock Exchange Listing Rule 9.4.1. Under the UK Corporate Governance Code, with which all listed companies must comply or explain why they do not, a binding vote on approval of a long-term investment plans is recommended.

Other than this the shareholders have no power to prevent directors awarding themselves excessive remuneration. The principles of corporate governance are that the remuneration committee composed of non-executive directors, appointed by the executive directors, decides the remuneration of the executive directors. In large companies only the individual determination of non-executive directors to try and stop unreasonable payments stands between the company executive and a lot of money, and any non-executive who displayed signs of being likely to do this would have been weeded out prior to pay day.

The point is an obvious one. If the directors are agents for the shareholders why can't the shareholders decide how much their agents get paid? It seems contrary to natural justice that someone who is acting as an agent can decide their own rewards.

The debate now is as to whether the resolution under s 439 should become binding on the directors such that if the remuneration report is not approved then the remuneration does not get paid.

The problem is that this rapidly becomes impractical. Directors deserve to be paid something and different people have different ideas of how much that something should be:

- If a bonus scheme is excessive, by how much is it excessive?
- If a CEO is to be voted a £1m bonus and some shareholders don't like it, is that CEO to get nothing, apart from a basic salary, or half the bonus, or three-quarters of the bonus?
- Who decides if not the non-executive directors? Do the shareholders debate amongst themselves and come to a consensus? If so – when? At the AGM – hardly practical – or at some date when thousands of shareholders can all assemble?
- If directors' pay is limited in this way will it be difficult to recruit competent or able managers or will they, as some claim, flee abroad or refuse to take the top jobs?

The problem is far from simple to resolve. Lurid newspaper headlines castigating 'fat cats' and 'exploiters' are all very well but the practicalities are somewhat less easy to resolve.

At the time of writing the government is proposing legislation to tackle the issue of excessive directors' pay. Speaking publicly in January 2012 Prime Minister David Cameron stated:

> The absolute key, and the thing I can confirm today, that does need to happen and will happen is clear transparency in terms of the publication in terms of proper pay numbers so you can really see what people are being paid, and then binding shareholder votes so the owners of the company are asked to vote on the pay levels and – absolutely key – votes on parts about dismissal packages and payments for failure.
>
> (Walker, 2012)

What form this legislation will take remains to be seen.

International pay and reward systems

How is the issue of the rewarding of executive directors handled in the rest of the world? The most significant influence on executive pay is undoubtedly the US model and researchers have been looking at the influence of this on executive remuneration in other areas of the world.

Suffice to say that levels of compensation in the USA, for executives of larger corporations, far outstrip those in the rest of the world. Commonly it is CEOs who benefit from the enormous salary packages that are on offer – one study found that the rewards given to the CEO were typically 4.7 times greater than those given to the human resources director. CEOs argue that the responsibility for company performance falls on them and if things go badly it will be they who are fired, not the human resources director. US compensations are generally very much performance-related and the basic salary forms quite a small proportion of total earnings, which are boosted by variable pay such as bonuses, stock options and long-term incentive pay.

Outside the United States there is a much lower emphasis on performance-related pay and the question has been mooted as to whether the rest of the world will move towards the US model. There are some influences on this which bear consideration:

- Increasing globalization is likely to spread the influence of US reward patterns particularly into countries with a degree of US inward investment.

- Countries with strong corporate governance structures (eg the United Kingdom) tend to favour performance-related pay structures, although perhaps not to the same extent as the United States.

- Patterns of share ownership differ. In countries like the US and the UK share ownership is widespread and institutional investors have considerable influence. The agency cost issues (the cost of employing agents to manage the business on behalf of owners) can be partially defrayed by linking the cost of managers to corporate performance.

- However, other countries (eg Germany, Japan) have much more controlled structures so shareholders may have the means and the motivation to control the directors much more and to limit their rewards.

- In many countries companies do not have equity traded to any meaningful extent on a stock market and valuation of equity interests is difficult and time-consuming, so reward systems based on share price performance will not be fully accepted as there is no independent arbitrator of price. Where only a small proportion of shares are traded and the balance is controlled by a small group of shareholders, the price of the freely available shares may not be totally influenced by company performance but by political and other issues.

- Marginal tax rates may have some influence on levels and types of pay; where these are high there is often a trend to reward executives with incentives that bear lower rates of tax such as perks or through the use of complex tax-avoidance structures, which adds to agency costs.

- There may be increased cross-border hirings. Those companies wishing to hire an American as CEO, for example, will be likely to have to pay them on US lines rather than on local pay levels, which will influence the pay of others by raising the norm for CEO pay to some extent. Similarly those companies wishing to avoid losing their top talent to US companies may incline towards US-style remuneration packages.

- The level of disclosure has an effect as research indicates that increased disclosure of remuneration levels tends to raise average rewards rather than reduce them. Countries with high levels of corporate governance and disclosure tend to correlate with high levels of executive pay, as far as can be ascertained. Clearly where there is no disclosure of executive pay rewards may be even higher but we would not know – all we can say is that the growth of disclosure tended to show increases in pay and rewards.

Clearly levels of pay and reward are sensitive issues as some of the vitriolic press coverage of executive pay demonstrates. Undoubtedly there will be a trend, in those jurisdictions where share ownership is diverse and shares are easily valued, to reward executives on the basis of share price performance as this is seen as a reflection of corporate worth. It is unlikely that the rest of the world, apart perhaps from some aspects of the Russian executive reward structures, will begin to approach US levels of reward but the trend towards remunerating executives largely on the basis of performance is unlikely to decline in the immediate future and may well spread into the developing world as their corporate structures grow and develop.

CASE STUDY

The directors of Megatron have decided to revise the executive pay structure to make it more performance-related. They have formed a new remuneration committee, which is to be chaired by Lord Footler, who is also chairman of Boxers Bank plc. Three other non-executive directors would be appointed, chosen by Lord Footler and Megatron CEO Sir 'Billy' Bustler. The performance measure used was to be based on the share price and the financial director was instructed to ensure that performance targets and profit forecasts were met and that there was no financial 'bad news' that might shake the confidence of investors. Sir Billy told him privately to transfer funds from the subsidiary companies based in low-disclosure tax havens to prop up profits if necessary.

The share price was to be measured against a moving average share price of a 'bundle' of shares in companies which comprised a 'typical portfolio'. These shares were carefully selected by Lord Footler and Billy Bustler. Most of the companies included in this share bundle were safe but unspectacular companies in declining industries or markets which were mature and in which no real growth was expected. Megatron's share price was confidently expected to outperform these by some distance.

In addition, all the executive directors were appointed through nominees as directors of two companies based in the Cayman Islands. They were to be paid fees and commissions by these companies but the Cayman Islands disclosure rules meant that the payments would go unrecorded in any financial statements as they were ostensibly paid to other parties.

Discuss

- How would the principle that directors' pay should be linked to performance actually affect the performance of the company in the short term and over the longer term?

- Explain the principles of agency theory and discuss the ethics of directors being able to decide their own remuneration, albeit through a remuneration committee.

- What mechanisms exist for dissatisfied shareholders to prevent what they see as excessive rewards to directors?

Bibliography

Bawden, T (2011) Thomas Cook shareholders stage pay revolt: Investors oppose remuneration policy in protest at bonus awards to top 100 executives, *Guardian* Online, 11 February

Cadbury, Sir A (1992) *Financial Aspects of Corporate Governance*, Gee & Co, London

Cheffins, BR (2003) Will executive pay globalise along American lines? *Corporate Governance: An International Review*, **11** (1), pp 8–24

Clark, N (2011) Executive pay triggers revolt at William Hill, *Independent*, 13 May

Cope, N (1996) Controversy over fat cats dogs Brown to the end, *Independent*, 1 May

Davey, J (2010) More blue chip shareholders revolt over pay, *Sunday Times*, May 16

Financial Reporting Council (2010) *UK Corporate Governance Code*, FRC, London

Greenbury Report (1995) Financial Reporting Council, London

High Pay Commission (2011) More for less: what has happened to pay at the top and does it matter? *Interim Report, 24 May*, High Commission, London

Hughes, JJ (1996) The Greenbury Report on directors' remuneration, *International Journal of Manpower*, **17** (1) pp 4–9

Hutton, W (2011) *Hutton Review of Fair Pay in the Public Sector*, HM Treasury, London

Locke, EA and Latham, GP (2002) *A Theory of Goal Setting and Task Performance*, Prentice Hall, Englewood Cliffs, NJ

Hurley, J (2011) Reckitt Benckiser's pay plans opposed by investor group PIRC, *Telegraph*, 2 May

Jones, IW and Pollitt, M (2001) *Who Influences Debates in Business Ethics? An Investigation into the Development of Corporate Governance in the UK since 1990*, ESRC Centre for Business Research, University of Cambridge Working Paper no. 221

Pensions Investment Research Consultants (2011) *A Challenge to High Pay*, PIRC, London

Press Association (2011) Standard Life shareholders rebel, 18 May

Robertson, D (2010) Revolt at Xstrata as barely half its shareholding backs bosses' pay, *The Times*, 5 May

Treanor, J (2011) Barclays hands five bankers £110m, *Guardian* Online, 7 March

Treanor, J (2011) Lloyds blasted by investors over pay, *Guardian* Online, 18 May

UK Listing Authority (2004) *Listing Rules*, Financial Services Authority, London

Walker, P (2012) Executive pay legislation likely in Queen's speech, David Cameron says, *Guardian* Online

Websites

www.frc.org.uk
www.hmtreasury.gov.uk
www.guardianonline.co.uk
www.pirc.co.uk
www.thetimes.co.uk

The audit function
Public and private sectors

LEARNING OBJECTIVES

This chapter will enable you to:

- understand the basic principles of auditing theory and understand how the auditing profession developed;

- understand the role of the external auditor and how the audit profession is regulated – principle vs statute;

- consider whether a self-regulatory approach is good enough;

- compare and contrast the role of internal audit.

Introduction

In August 2010 the Auditing Practices Board issued a discussion paper, 'Auditor scepticism: Raising the bar'. Their opening paragraph summed up the nature of the auditing profession quite well:

> Audit is essential to public and investor confidence in companies. It is far from easy to do it well, requiring judgment and technical competence, often in complex circumstances.

The role of the auditor is, primarily, one that serves to reassure the shareholders, to whom they report, that the financial statements which the directors of the company have prepared present a 'true and fair' view of the results of their company for the accounting period. Indirectly the report of the audit may also serve to confirm the financial numbers to banks, employees, suppliers and customers, all of whom have a stake in the company.

It is important to understand one fundamental point, which we will come back to later in this chapter, and that is that responsibility for the *preparation* of the financial statements and the presentation of the information included therein rests with the management of the organization (in the case of a company, the directors). The auditor's primary responsibility is only to *report* on the financial statements as presented by management – their role is only to express an opinion.

This is spelled out by the Auditing Practices Board (APB) in its International Standard on Auditing (ISA) *ISA 200: Objective and General Principles Governing an Audit of Financial Statements*, which states:

> The objective of an audit of financial statements is to enable the auditor to express an opinion whether the financial statements are prepared, in all material respects, in accordance with an applicable financial reporting framework.
> The phrases used to express an auditor's opinion are 'give a true and fair view' or 'present fairly in all material respects' which are equivalent terms.

The auditor is, broadly, accountable only to the shareholders (most of the time) and thus the role of the auditor is inextricably linked with the principles of agency theory (Chapter 1), of which more later.

Many see the role of the auditor as being that of the independent expert who helps safeguard the investment in the company made by the shareholders from the depredations of the directors and who checks, in detail, the directors' account of their financial trusteeship for the year of the company's assets, leaving no stone unturned in their quest for truth. But, of course, it isn't as simple as that.

Auditing theory

As with most topics in business, auditing has been the subject of a good deal of academic discussion in an attempt to divine a 'theory of auditing' and to fit auditing into the context of the business world. These theories consider the social purpose of auditing and attempt to establish some fundamental theories or truths.

There are three basic academic writings that are considered fundamental to this area. These are:

1 The Theory of Rational Expectations, developed by Professor Limperg.

2 Mautz and Sharaf's *Philosophy of Auditing*.

3 Professor David Flint's *Philosophy and Principles of Auditing*.

We will look at each of these in turn as they do set out a useful guide to the development of an academic underpinning to an area of business activity that has been seriously neglected by academics.

The Theory of Rational Expectations

What is now commonly known as the Theory of Rational Expectations was developed in 1926 by Professor Theodore Limperg of the University of Amsterdam, who called it the Theory of Inspired Confidence.

Limperg's theory states that the usefulness of the auditor's opinion is based on the general understanding society has about the usefulness of audit. Legal considerations aside, the necessity for and cost of an audit are borne by companies because of the need of investors and lenders for reliable information to aid their decision-making. If the audit process changed so that it ceased to inspire a uniform level of confidence in society, but instead inspired different levels of confidence in different users, society's confidence in the audit process would decline as the social usefulness of the audit was reduced.

So Limperg's theory is a dynamic one which holds that, as the business community changes, so the expectations it has of the auditor's function also changes; the value of the auditor's report derives from the expert nature of the auditor as an independent, competent professional. The theory postulates that the work carried out by the auditor should be governed by the rational expectations of those who use their reports so auditors should not disappoint those expectations; further, auditors should not seek to raise those expectations by any more than the work they do justifies.

The auditor, Limperg theorizes, must meet the expectations of the reasonably well-informed layman but should not create any greater expectations than can be justified by the work carried out. The auditor thus has a wider responsibility to society and is not simply a watchdog for the shareholders so, surprisingly perhaps, Limperg found a social usefulness for auditors in meeting society's expectations for reliable financial information. This has echoes of the contemporary trend towards enhanced Corporate Social

Responsibility reporting for the benefit of a wider range of stakeholders than simply the shareholders.

Mautz and Sharaf's Philosophy of Auditing

Over the years Limperg's theory has been somewhat neglected and the predominant text in this particular field is probably considered to be that of R.K. Mautz and H.A. Sharaf, who in 1961 published a monograph called *The Philosophy of Auditing* in the USA. This was the beginning of attempts to codify a coherent theory of auditing and included discussion on the philosophy of auditing, methodology and auditing 'postulates' or assumptions. Mautz and Sharaf attempted to create order out of a somewhat chaotic mix of practices and ideas and held that auditing is based on scientific logic because the auditing process is a rational process of examination, observation and evaluation of evidence. A full discussion of these ideas is not appropriate for this book but the essence of Mautz and Sharaf's approach is that auditing practice should be built on a sound philosophy of auditing because basing actions on an underpinning philosophy means:

- going back to first principles of what an audit is, what purpose it serves and what usefulness it has for society;
- that knowledge has to be ordered in a systematic way; and it
- defines auditing's place in and usefulness to society.

Broadly, Mautz and Sharaf adopted a scientific approach to auditing, claiming that auditing practice, with its heavy emphasis on probability and a scientific approach to evidence, has much in common with scientific method. They developed eight tentative 'postulates' or factors necessary for audits to achieve the desired result. These postulates or assumptions are:

1 Financial statements and financial data are verifiable.

2 There is no necessary conflict of interest between the auditor and the management of the enterprise under audit, ie both are working to the same end of producing reliable financial information.

3 The financial statements and other information submitted for verification are free from collusive and other unusual irregularities.

4 The existence of a satisfactory system of internal control eliminates the probability of irregularities.

5 Consistent application of generally accepted principles of accounting result in fair presentation of the financial position and the results of operations.

6 In the absence of clear evidence to the contrary, what has held true in the past for the enterprise under examination will hold true in the future.

7 When examining financial data for the purpose of expressing an opinion thereon, the auditor acts exclusively in the capacity of an auditor.

8 The professional status of the independent auditor imposes commensurate professional obligations.

Whilst these postulates are useful in many ways, there are some key factors that Mautz and Sharaf did not consider, which are of fundamental importance today. These are:

- The questions of risk and control, which were not considered to be as important in the 1960s as we consider them to be today.

- Mautz and Sharaf do not pay much attention to the concept of accountability between parties, eg the accountability of the entity to the public or to investors. This was considered more by Flint (see page 158).

- The basis of Mautz and Sharaf's approach is founded in scientific method, which refers to evidence-gathering processes, the testing of hypotheses and probability theory. There are problems with this, particularly in the exercise of an auditor's judgement in the absence of conclusive evidence and the fact that scientists are often able to repeat experiments when trying to validate a hypothesis, whereas auditors only get one opportunity to gather the evidence they need.

- Whilst auditing shares many common practices with scientific method, in particular the gathering of evidence to substantiate their opinion, in practice auditing calls for a substantial exercise of judgement and experience that the scientific method does not allow. Auditing, in many ways, is more of an art than a science.

- The approach didn't attempt to rationalize the relationships between auditing concepts in order to develop a general framework of auditing.

Whilst Mautz and Sharaf undoubtedly contributed greatly to the philosophy of auditing they were very much grounded in the idea of scientific method and paid less attention to the idea of auditing as a social phenomenon as Professor Limperg had done, ie that it had a value to society generally and not just to those involved in the commercial entity. It was Professor Flint who added this dimension.

Professor David Flint's Philosophy and Principles of Auditing

In 1988 Professor David Flint of the University of California published *Philosophy and Principles of Auditing: An Introduction*, which built on and updated the work of Mautz and Sharaf. He also developed a series of postulates as a basis for the development of a theory of auditing. Flint's postulates or assumptions are:

1 The fundamental condition for the existence of an audit is accountability, either private (eg between management and shareholders), or public accountability.

2 The subject matter of accountability is too remote, too complex and/or of too great a significance for the discharge of the duty (to be accountable) to be demonstrated without the process of audit.

3 Essential distinguishing characteristics of audit are the independence of its status and its freedom from investigatory and reporting constraints.

4 All aspects of an audit, its conduct, the work carried out and its conclusions must be capable of being evidenced.

5 There have to be standards of accountability for those who carry out audits, which form the standard by which actual performance can be measured. This means:

   – that there are standards of accountability for conduct, performance, achievement and quality of information;

   – actual conduct, performance, achievement, quality and so on can be measured and compared with these standards by reference to known criteria; and

   – that the process of measurement and comparison requires skill and the exercise of judgement.

6 The meaning, significance and intention of financial and other statements and data which are audited are sufficiently clear that the credibility which is given to it as a result of audit can be clearly expressed and communicated.

7 An audit produces an economic or social benefit.

Flint's postulates are based on the fundamental idea that auditing has a social benefit and is not simply a technical exercise for the purposes of regulation. It is not the place of this book to expand on these ideas but perhaps students could consider the value of reliable financial information to stakeholders in companies, for example:

- to potential investors;
- to regulators of companies;
- to employees;
- to suppliers and customers;
- to the taxation authorities.

In addition to the work of Limperg, Mautz and Sharaf, and Flint outlined above, there have been other academic writings on this topic. Interested students could consult the work of Professor Tom Lee in his book *Corporate Audit Theory* (1993) but this appears to be aimed largely at the US market and, whilst of interest, is too complex and academic for this work. He has expanded the number of postulates to fourteen quite wordy ones that occupy too much space to detail here.

It has to be said that, in practice, the major auditing bodies, which are the three Institutes of Chartered Accountants and the ACCA, have not really shown a great deal of interest in academic auditing theories and there is still no real universally agreed conceptual framework for auditing beyond some rather vague statements broadly drawn from the postulates and theories outlined above. What framework there is has been set down in the International Standards on Auditing (ISAs), originally drafted by the International Auditing and Assurance Standards Board (IAASB) and adopted in the UK by the Auditing Practices Board (APB). These broadly define what an audit is, what responsibilities auditors have and how they must set about gathering the evidence they need to satisfy their objective of being able to give an opinion on a set of financial statements (see page 154).

These are coldly practical documents and, whilst they give the audit profession guidance and objectives, they make no comment on any philosophy of auditing or statement of universal principles, or even where audit's value lies in the wider scheme of things. They are simply a set of rules and an instruction manual.

The development of the auditing profession

What most people don't realize is that auditing as a regulated professional activity in the form we know it today is a relatively new phenomenon.

Naturally where one individual had to account to another for their financial stewardship there has always been some form of review or check that we could loosely describe as an audit – indeed the very word goes back to a time when a medieval steward would read out the accounts of his stewardship to an auditor who would check that he had not been careless or committed a fraud on his lordship. There is an audit report, which would terrify a modern auditor if they had to sign it, which simply says:

Examined and found right. Bristol, December 20 1797

from the records of the earliest known professional accountancy practice formed in 1780 when one Josiah Wade founded Tribe Clarke and Company in Bristol, whose main source of income appeared to be auditing merchants' accounts. The position was neatly summed up in 1905 by accounting historian Richard Brown:

The origin of auditing goes back to times scarcely less remote than that of accounting ... Whenever the advance of civilization brought about the necessity of one man being entrusted to some extent with the property of another the advisability of some kind of check upon the fidelity of the former would become apparent.

It was the passing of the Companies Act 1948 that, for the first time, required auditors to have a professional qualification and it was that Act which laid the foundations of the modern auditing profession.

Various Companies Acts have followed since then. In turn each one made its mark by tightening the legal restrictions on directors and on the company itself and regulating the content of accounts, increasing accounting disclosure, the requirements for accounts preparation and the records to be kept, culminating in the mammoth Companies Act 2006, the largest piece of legislation ever passed in the UK. This expansion of legislation increased the level of compliance required of organizations and consequently companies needed to create financial systems to both gather and present the information legally required in addition to controlling their internal financial procedures and producing management information.

The whole basis of auditing is that it is a process of checking the work of other people, but historian of the auditing profession Derek Matthews argues that the practice of auditors completing the accounts and then auditing them was common well into the 1960s. In theory, textbooks advised professionals and students to separate audit from accounting but Matthews argues that there was, de facto, a conspiracy of silence that allowed the practice to be widespread. The conflict of interest, what is today known as the 'self-review' threat, is obvious – the auditors cannot independently check their own work.

What is even less appreciated is that the standards by which the audit profession derives the authority for its audit approaches and techniques are also comparatively recent. The Auditing Practices Board (APB) was only formed in 1976, as the Auditing Practices Committee (APC), and it was not until 1978 that it issued its first booklet of draft auditing standards, for comment, comprising three auditing standards and seven auditing guidelines, which it claimed at the time to be codifying best practice.

It was in 1980 that the first auditing standards and guidelines were released, followed in 1989 by practice notes designed to deal with particular audit issues. Standards and practice notes trickled out until 2004 when the first international standards were issued, replacing most of the home-grown variety.

Internationally the process of standard setting began in 1978 with the establishment of the International Auditing Practices Committee, which began issuing internationally acceptable standards in an attempt to standardize audit practice and ensure consistency of approach and technical competence among auditors, something it is carrying on to this day as the International Auditing and Assurance Standards Board (IAASB).

The latest set of auditing standards was issued in 2009 following the completion of what the APB called its Clarity Project. These new standards, known as International Standards on Auditing, or ISAs, replaced the standards issued in 2004 with a revised set of international standards developed by the IAASB and adopted in the UK. Auditors now have to comply with these in their auditing practice.

The standards use the term 'entity' as a general term embracing all types of business, enterprise or undertaking including companies, charities, local authorities, government agencies etc. Some are profit-oriented and some are not but the same standard of audit practice applies to all.

The role of the external auditor

As soon as the directors were required by law to prepare annual financial statements shareholders were able to access some financial information about the company they owned. The question was, and to some extent still is, is the information the directors supply reliable given the basic tenets of agency theory outlined in Chapter 1, which highlights the conflict between the objectives of the directors (agents) and the objectives of the shareholders (principals)? In other words, can the directors be trusted to tell the shareholders the truth, and the whole truth, about what they have done with the money the shareholders entrusted to them?

In theory the directors act in a fiduciary capacity towards the shareholders. What that means is that they are in a special position of trust charged with preserving the assets of the business and, hopefully, running it for the benefit of the shareholders so that it increases shareholder value and pays them some dividend. The fiduciary relationship between the parties places the onus firmly on the directors to be accountable for their actions and to be transparent in their reporting.

The practical problem that emerged when owners began delegating the running of an entity in which they had invested to managers and thus sacrificed any involvement in the day-to-day control of the organization, is – can the owners believe the financial report prepared by their managers? The report may:

- contain errors;
- not disclose fraud;
- be inadvertently misleading;
- be deliberately misleading;
- fail to disclose relevant information;
- fail to conform to regulations.

Financial statements in the UK, prepared by the directors, must now comply with the relevant financial reporting framework, which is based on the Companies Act 2006 together with all the associated accounting standards etc which comprise UK Generally Accepted Accounting Practice (UK GAAP). Even in the modern era, despite the developments and expansion of disclosure in the financial statements and the growth of accounting standards, practical access to detailed financial information by shareholders remains limited.

As we saw in Chapter 1 owners of companies must be protected from:

- unscrupulous management who would use the owner's investment for their own benefit and not that of the owner; and
- abuses of limited liability where companies are deliberately set up for speculative or high-risk ventures because the initial investors have very little to lose and the managers perhaps nothing at all apart from their employment.

If later investors are not aware of company activity they could be induced to invest in a project that carries a much greater level of risk than the rewards they might achieve would warrant. The audit helps to reduce these so-called agency costs as it helps to protect investors from the actions of predatory managers.

Shareholders, or potential shareholders, may come to believe that they are not getting all the information, or the right information to enable them to make investment decisions. Financial analysts working for major institutional investors may have rather more access to the directors of major corporations than the small investor but even they have made mistakes and many of them have still lost their employer's money despite their abilities and the access to information granted to them. Consequently the role of the auditor, as agent for the shareholder, becomes crucial and the costs of the audit are as nothing compared with the comfort and reassurance the audit affords the shareholders. The auditor's report on the financial statements also becomes crucial to the managers of the business as a favourable opinion from the independent auditor confirms their actions and reinforces their credibility and reputation as agents for the shareholders.

So the primary aim of an audit is to enable the auditors to say 'these accounts show a true and fair view' or, of course, to say that they do not. Note they are not certified as being 'accurate', because they include assumptions and estimates, nor are they certified as being 'correct' for the same reason.

They also must report on:

- whether or not the financial statements are supported by the underlying records;
- whether they have received all the explanations and information they deem necessary for the audit;
- whether or not the information required to be disclosed in respect of directors has been properly disclosed;
- in the case of companies listed on the London Stock Exchange, whether the provisions of the Stock Exchange Listing Agreement have been complied with.

This latter point brings the auditors directly into corporate governance as the Listing Agreement includes the UK Corporate Governance Code (Chapter 4).

Conflicts of interest

There is another, larger, problem – one with which the audit profession has wrestled from time to time and one which it has come to the conclusion is best left alone. That problem is the inherent conflict of interest between:

- the auditor who acts for the shareholders as the guardian of its investment and the wielder of the stamp of approval of their agent's reports; and

- that very same auditor whose fees are paid by the directors and who is able to solicit non-audit work from those very same individuals.

The problem is this. Audit firms are able to garner considerable sums in fees from carrying out a whole range of non-audit consultancy-type work from their clients. Of course there are safeguards to ensure ethical behaviour that firms should scrupulously observe – Chinese Walls, use of different teams etc – but the fact remains that, at the accounting firm level, these audit clients are valuable generators of large amounts of income (Figure 7.1).

This is the 'elephant in the room' that audit regulators hate to acknowledge – this conflict of interest that can ultimately place seen or unseen pressure

FIGURE 7.1 The auditor's conflict

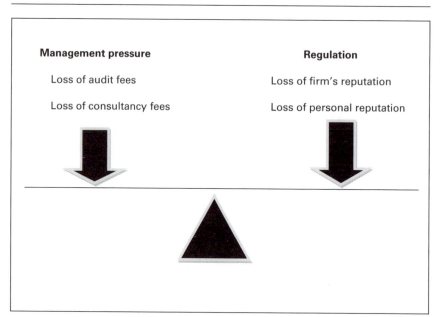

on an audit partner to maybe accept an accounting treatment which perhaps bends the rules rather further than good practice would indicate, or to accept directors' explanations a little more readily and with a little less corroboration than a more prudent auditor might.

This duality of auditor/advisor is what destroyed Arthur Andersen in the Enron case and is what has tainted the profession's purity throughout its existence. In the USA audit firms are now banned under the Sarbanes–Oxley Act 2002 (known colloquially as 'Sarbox') from carrying out non-audit services for precisely this reason; in the UK the framework still holds and, as far as we know, has not been broken by an Enron-sized scandal – yet.

Audit firms, and individual partners, must strike a balance between the lure of large fees and the consequences of any revelation of what might amount, at best, to sharp practice and at worst to a criminal activity.

Auditors come back to their clients every year; they have an ongoing relationship with them so these kinds of decisions may have to be faced more than once. However, there is time, the auditor does not have to make a snap decision. The cost/benefit analysis, the risk/reward equation is a carefully considered rational choice.

Globalization

The developments in technology that have made possible increasing global trading and the expansion of capital markets have resulted in:

- Regulators requiring an improved standard of information, in terms of accuracy and timeliness, in order to protect investors. This applies particularly to banks.

- Greater accountability and control over corporate executives running companies that may have revenues considerably greater than some countries, resulting in increased corporate governance requirements designed to enhance accountability and disclosure.

- Conflicts between the US rules-based approach to control audit firms, based on the Sarbox legislation (see page 172), and the UK and other countries that have adopted a non-legislative audit framework based on self-regulation.

- The need for auditors to use technology and to develop new approaches to the audit of large, multinational businesses.

- The problems faced by auditors and accountants in producing consolidated financial information in compliance with an appropriate accounting framework where the component information is prepared under a range of differing standards of quality and disclosure. Increased global trading means that audit firms have experienced an increase in the range and significance of group component companies trading in low-cost economies where standards of corporate governance are low and which produce information that has not been prepared under recognized accounting or auditing standards.

- The growth of internet-based online trading, which has challenged conventional audit approaches. Companies may trade globally and, apart from huge technical problems in auditing computer-based entities it may be difficult to establish which legal jurisdiction applies to such businesses and which set of standards and rules applies to them.

- Audit firms are being increasingly required to carry out assurance-type assignments. These require a lower standard of evidence than does an audit. There are moves among international regulators to separate the audit function from other types of audit work in order to reduce the inherent conflict of interest this creates in audit firms – ie that of acting both as auditor and advisor.

- The development of auditing mega-firms who, they claim, are the only firms with the resources to audit modern corporate behemoths. The audit profession is thus dominated by the 'Big Four' (PricewaterhouseCoopers, KPMG, Ernst & Young and Deloitte). Smaller firms with a lower level of global reach and those that have developed international networks claim that this reduces competition in the audit market for the biggest clients. The Big Four claim that they compete ferociously between themselves.

Companies or groups can be very large with multinational activities and comprising many subsidiaries and related activities. The preparation of the accounts of such entities is a very complex operation, perhaps involving the bringing together and summarizing of accounts of subsidiaries with differing conventions, legal systems and accounting and control systems. The examination of such accounts by independent experts trained in the assessment of financial information is of benefit to those who control and operate such organizations, as well as to owners and outsiders. Consequently the existence of a strong auditing profession is important to global markets because:

- Reliable financial reporting promotes confidence and stability in the market.

- Markets need the confidence and the assurance a strong audit function can bring in order to enable participants in the market, including the entities themselves, investors and potential investors, to make informed decisions.

- This involves reducing risk to potential investors by providing them with 'sound' information.

- Corporate failures, particularly those involving fraud by senior management, reduce confidence and create instability. They also tend to encourage increased regulation, which may restrict market operations or encourage further deception.

- The concepts of agency highlighted in Chapter 1 require an auditing profession that is able to enforce standards of accountability on company managers through the mechanism of the auditors' report.

Regulation of the audit profession

Clearly as the audit profession has such a crucial role to play in the validation of financial information it is vital that it is seen to possess the qualities of integrity and independence that enable the investing public to trust the certificates they sign. The whole *raison d'être* of the auditor fails if the audit profession is seen to be in the pockets of their clients, and is merely there to rubber-stamp the numbers and add a veneer of respectability to them. The profession must be, and must be seen to be, above suspicion and truly independent and objective, otherwise it has no validity.

Thus any scandal that casts doubt upon the integrity of the auditors fills the profession with horror as regulators may feel that the present system has failed and replace it. The collapse of audit mega-firm Arthur Andersen after the Enron and WorldCom scandals was the most recent example of a loss of trust in audit firms and, as we shall see, resulted in the US government passing legislation that severely restricted the activities of auditors in the services they can offer to audit clients.

There are two general approaches to regulation of the audit profession: one is primarily rules-based and the other is based on concepts and principles and is known as the 'framework approach'.

Contrast rules-based and framework approaches to regulation

The legalistic rules-based approach clearly requires laws and rules that delineate precisely, or as precisely as legal interpretation allows, what members of regulated bodies can and cannot do. The UK has adopted this approach with members of the financial services profession, regulated by the Financial Services and Markets Act 2000, but it has not done so for the auditing profession, unlike their colleagues in the USA.

The second approach to regulation is what is known as the 'framework' approach. A series of guidelines, recommendations for best practice or professional standards are produced, backed by some fairly broad-brush legislation and a duty to comply with the recommendations or explain why you haven't done so. This is the basis of regulation in the UK.

The broad-brush legislation is the Companies Act 2006, which:

- states that companies over a certain size have to be audited; and
- sets out the rules for who can or cannot be accredited as an auditor.

The standards and rules are set out by the Financial Reporting Council and its satellite body the Auditing Practices Board.

Whilst these are rules in the sense that they set out a series of 'dos and don'ts' for practising auditors, they are not a prescriptive set of requirements that attempt to cover every situation. Rather they form a conceptual framework based on fundamental principles. What this means in practice is that there are fundamental ethical principles that, taken together as a code of conduct, will enable the auditor to retain the required level of independence from their client and observe appropriate standards of competence and behaviour. We look at these in more detail below.

For example, one of the fundamental principles is integrity. In the UK the framework-based ethical code defines it and says auditors must have it and so behave in an appropriate way. For example, the ethical standards point out one obvious problem, that of conflicts of interest. It deals with this problem by:

- defining what they are; and
- requiring auditors to avoid them wherever possible,

and that is about it.

In contrast, a legislative, rules-based approach involves a lot of convoluted definitions and attempts to set out for the auditor how to behave in

TABLE 7.1 Approaches to ethical codes – principles- or rules-based?

Principles-based Conceptual Framework	Rules-based Conceptual Framework
Advantages <ul><li>flexible – capable of fitting changing situations and circumstances</li><li>can be applied across boundaries</li><li>onus is on the auditor to prove they have considered everything and comply</li><li>can include specific prohibitions</li></ul>	**Advantages** <ul><li>provides certainty – auditors are told what to do</li><li>contains definite prohibitions, which reduces ambiguity and the scope for personal 'interpretations' of the requirements</li></ul>
Disadvantages <ul><li>lack of precision may lead to 'interpretations' of rules</li><li>requires judgement on the part of the auditor, which can lead to differing interpretations</li></ul>	**Disadvantages** <ul><li>encourages a legalistic approach to redefining or reinterpreting the rules to fit a situation where there are no rules</li><li>can't deal with every situation</li><li>inflexible</li></ul>

specific situations or when dealing with specific types of client. The accountancy bodies in the USA have adopted this approach, particularly in the light of the Sarbox legislation (see page 172). Such rules-based codes tend to be much bigger and contain pages and pages of prescriptive requirements. There are advantages and disadvantages on both sides of course, which can be summed up in Table 7.1.

As can be seen from Table 7.1, rules-based codes are generally seen as inflexible and encouraging of legalistic-style quibbling and 'bending' of the rules. Principles-based approaches are seen as flexible and place the onus on the auditor to demonstrate compliance, rather than simply ticking a legal box, but their very imprecision may lead to misinterpretation or rule-bending without there being much in the way of possible sanctions. It is difficult to discipline an auditor when the rules they are supposed to observe are ambiguous or imprecise and use words such as 'appropriate'.

For example, what might be considered to be an 'appropriate' level of corporate hospitality from a client? Is it none at all, which is the rule in the public sector, lunch in the pub, a box at the opera, tickets to the cup final, a holiday in the Maldives? Clearly that last one would be inappropriate but what about the others? If you are the senior partner of a multinational accountancy firm dealing with a huge client, cup final tickets may not be classed as inappropriate, but if you are a partner in a small auditing firm dealing with a small client with financing issues it might well be totally inappropriate to accept an expensive gift from them.

The auditor is always required to exercise judgement and discretion in such matters. Whether a code is a principles-based conceptual framework or contains a prescriptive set of rules they both require the auditor to maintain their independence from their client and any action that might possibly compromise that must be resisted whether it is technically permitted by the rules or not.

Professional regulation and ethical codes

In the UK there is no body analogous to the US Securities and Exchange Commission (SEC), which regulates the profession in the USA. The government has no hand in regulating the audit profession nor do any of its satellites such as the Financial Services Authority. Instead auditors are regulated by their own trade bodies. Individual auditors have to be accredited by what are known as Recognized Supervisory Bodies (RSBs), which:

- establish the ethical standards expected of members;
- control admission and the standards of technical ability expected of members;
- reinforce behaviour through a disciplinary code;
- provide advice and support for members.

In the UK there are, basically, four such bodies:

- the Institute of Chartered Accountants in England and Wales (ICAEW);
- the Institute of Chartered Accountants in Scotland (ICAS);
- the Institute of Chartered Accountants in Ireland (ICAI);
- the Association of Chartered Certified Accountants (ACCA).

Their members, suitably accredited by their RSB, are empowered by the Companies Act 2006 to carry out statutory audits. These individuals are known as Registered Auditors.

These regulatory bodies each have a code of ethics and the Auditing Practices Board issues one as well. In brief, all of these ethical codes emphasise five things:

- integrity – which comprises honesty and fair dealing;
- objectivity – the auditor must not become too embroiled in client affairs;
- confidentiality – client's affairs may not be divulged except in specific circumstances;
- professional competence – the auditor must be technically able and up to date;
- professional behaviour – the auditor must do nothing to bring the profession into disrepute.

As we saw above, the approach in the UK is that of a non-regulatory framework, a code of practice that the profession feels is best policed by itself, a gentlemanly way of conducting affairs, moderated at the bar of professional and personal reputation rather than in the courtroom. The alternative to this honourable approach, which has after all served us well for many years, is to have, the profession points out wincing painfully, a situation where some jackbooted regulator crashes in stamping all over the delicate porcelain of the relationship between an audit firm and its client.

The argument the profession uses for maintaining self-regulation is this – the consequences of being thought of as being so venal that the standards of the profession are compromised or betrayed are likely, in practice, to amount to financial penalties from a regulator, which often the large firms may be well able to afford, but the greater loss is that of reputation. Ultimately the transgressing individual may have sanctions against them, have their audit licence taken away, maybe even their professional qualification if their crimes are egregious enough, but the cost of the loss of reputation to the firm as a whole can be immense – as the fate of mega-firm Arthur Andersen, destroyed by the Enron and WorldCom accounting scandals, among others, now bears mute witness.

The loss of clients, the scorn of the financial press, even the opprobrium of the public can be far more damaging than mere loss of money. The whole firm can be damaged by the actions of a few so, generally, it pays off for firms to maintain the standards of the profession and maintain a clear, objective, independent line with their client no matter what the temptation.

Sarbox: the American way

In contrast to the form of regulation in the UK, the 'comply or explain' framework approach, the USA decided that legislation was the only way to prevent the shocking corporate scandals that had plagued US business in the early part of this century.

The whole question of corporate governance in the USA was dominated by the financial scandals, Enron being perhaps the most well known, and other egregious frauds and failures by company directors at WorldCom, Tyco International, Global Crossing and many others. All of the major accounting firms had clients who were caught up in these scandals, the apotheosis being the destruction of the worldwide accounting firm of Arthur Andersen.

In 2002 this resulted in the USA publishing the Sarbanes–Oxley (Sarbox) legislation, which does not affect UK companies unless they are subsidiaries of US firms or are listed on US stock exchanges, but is a paradigm for the legal approach for restricting auditor activity.

The Act is designed to enforce corporate accountability through new requirements, backed by stiff penalties. Under the Act, chief executives and chief financial officers must personally certify the accuracy of financial statements, with a maximum penalty of 20 years in jail and a $5m fine for false statements. In addition, and of great significance to auditors, under s 404 of the Act, executives have to certify and demonstrate that they have established and are maintaining an adequate internal control structure and procedures for financial reporting. This requires them to ensure that all the financial reporting systems, including the ancillary systems such as procurement and HR, are functioning in such a way as to prevent material misstatements appearing in the financial accounts – and it is a personal liability.

It should be pointed out that this legislation, passed in haste, is seen as being too prescriptive and too inhibiting of US business freedoms; however, so far the US government shows no real signs of weakening any of its provisions and the recent scandals involving US banks, which were caused by greed and incompetence rather than deliberate fraud, are unlikely to prompt a change of mind any time soon.

Is self-regulation good enough?

There is no movement in the UK for the adoption of a similar piece of legislation to Sarbanes–Oxley, yet there is disquiet that the system of self-regulation and the rather hands-off approach of regulators has promoted a rather cosy feeling of invulnerability among the bigger audit firms. Their view tends to be, judging by their public pronouncements, that providing they can substantiate that they carry out their audits in accordance with the auditing standards, they can feel that their remit has been fulfilled. Any wider consideration of what audit is actually for, inspired perhaps by an academic theory of auditing, isn't relevant because what it is for is set out in the Companies Act so there is no need for any intellectual debate on abstract issues. Audit firms have simply to demonstrate compliance and nothing more.

Since the early 1990s the UK has, generally, not been troubled by audit failure on a scale large enough that the non-investing public became concerned about it and it moved out of the pages of the financial press and into tabloid headlines. It was the collapse of a company called Polly Peck in 1990 and the accounting manipulations revealed subsequently which prompted the setting up of Sir Adrian Cadbury's committee, which, as we have seen, resulted in the Cadbury Report and all that followed. The subsequent collapses of the Bank of Credit and Commerce International and the Maxwell fraud outlined below strengthened the calls for increased regulation of the audit profession.

As there has been no recent major auditing scandal in the UK to compare with the likes of Enron and WorldCom in the USA we have to look at the response of the profession's regulators to the last scandals that came to the attention of the investing public in the early 1990s. We will look at three cases as it is illustrative to review the response of the regulators to these major scandals.

Maxwell Communications Corporation

In 1991 Robert Maxwell was revealed to have stolen £400m from the Mirror Group pension scheme. An investigation carried out by what was then known as the Department for Trade and Industry (DTI) revealed that from 1985 until 1991 Maxwell was:

- plundering the Mirror Group (part of Maxwell Communications Corporation (MCC)) pension fund;
- selling assets pledged as collateral for loans; and
- transferring cash and assets from within Mirror Group to companies controlled by Maxwell personally.

Throughout this period MCC had received unblemished auditors' reports and the failure of auditors Coopers & Lybrand, now part of audit behemoth PricewaterhouseCoopers, to identify or in any way detect or prevent these abuses caused no little criticism and comment. The response of the profession's regulators was rather muted. The Joint Disciplinary Scheme (JDS), as it then was, investigated the actions of the auditors. A paper by Prem Sikka of Essex University summarized what happened (Sikka, 2001). According to the JDS report, which was not published until 1999, four partners of former Maxwell Communications Corporation auditors Coopers & Lybrand failed to meet the required professional standards in auditing various parts of the Maxwell empire. As the senior audit partner who led the audit had died in the interim the next senior partner, against whom twenty complaints were listed, was censured and ordered to pay costs of £75,000 and fined a total of £35,000. The report stated that he had never encountered fraud before and criticized him for too easily accepting management explanations. Of the other three partners involved, two paid costs of £10,000 each and were admonished.

Another partner paid costs of £5,000. In what is considered to be 'the loudest tut-tut [the JDS] has ever emitted' (*The Times*, 3 February 1999, p 16), Coopers & Lybrand were fined £1.2m (at around £2,000 per partner for its 600 UK partners) and also ordered it to pay costs of £2.1m. The financial penalties were described as 'extraordinary in their triviality' (*Daily Mail*, 3 February 1999, p 67), 'not ... much of a burden' (*Financial Times*, 3 February 1999, p 23) and 'a derisory flea bite upon a partnership whose greed and reckless judgements had, over twenty years, allowed Maxwell to build – for the third time – an empire based upon fraud' (Bower, 1999).

What Sikka, in his paper, was at pains to point out was that he felt that there was a systemic reluctance on the part of the accountancy profession to punish failings where these were committed by the largest firms because they dominated the profession and its regulation. At that time Coopers & Lybrand was one of the big wheels in the accountancy profession in the UK.

Polly Peck

Polly Peck was a small company with interests in the clothing industry when a majority stake in it was acquired by a private company controlled by Cypriot businessman Asil Nadir. Polly Peck grew rapidly, acquiring businesses in Turkey and Northern Cyprus, an area of Cyprus controlled by Turkey. In 1989 it acquired the Del Monte fresh food business. Reported figures showed spectacular growth between 1982 and 1989; for example, turnover increased from £21m to £1.2bn and profits increased from £9m to £161m in that time. Reportedly holding cash and bank balances of £405m Polly Peck suddenly became unable to pay its creditors and collapsed in 1990 owing £551m – clearly the financial statements were extensively misstated (Jones, 2011).

Most of the blame for the audit failures was placed on the heads of the auditors of Polly Peck group companies based in Northern Cyprus who were struck off from the Institute of Chartered Accountants in England and Wales and fined £1,000 each. Having stuck it to 'Johnny Foreigner' the regulators fined UK firm Stoy Hayward, the group auditors, who were, after all, ultimately responsible for the group financial statements, a total of £75,000 with £250,000 costs. None of their partners were found to be negligent or fined individually.

It was pointed out that they had never fully checked out the suitability of the Cypriot auditors, they had accepted unsubstantiated assurances from CEO Asil Nadir, they had not properly queried the figures supplied to them by the Cypriot companies, most of which subsequently transpired to be fantasy and they had not carried out any form of rigorous review to account for the spectacular growth in these Cypriot subsidiaries. Stoy Hayward offered to hold training courses for partners and managers on how to carry out group audits, which was a novel form of atonement for a massive failure of the audit function.

Clearly these cases are exceptional and both were some years ago so it is tempting to say that, in the new corporate governance climate, things would be different and audit failures on such a scale would be severely punished.

TransTec

Any indication that this might, in fact, be so is indicated by the profession's response to a significant audit failure at a company called TransTec.

TransTec collapsed in December 1999 leaving hundreds out of work and debts of more than £100m. The company was a supplier to the Ford Motor Company and agreed compensation to Ford amounting to $18m following a claim by Ford for compensation from TransTec for the supply of defective cylinder heads for their Ford Explorer vehicle.

A payment schedule was agreed and some payments made but instead of these being expensed they were capitalized as 'tooling' and then written off as obsolete. The outstanding amounts of the claims unpaid were not included as liabilities, whether contingent (at the time compensation was being negotiated) or actual (once the schedule of compensation was agreed). The compensation payable to Ford was not disclosed in the accounts nor was it included in a letter of representation signed by the directors. The audit team from PricewaterhouseCoopers (PwC) had come across a series of debit notes issued by Ford relating to compensation payable to Ford Motor Company in restitution for the supply of defective cylinder heads but failed to act on this information and on conflicting explanations for these notes. Instead, audit partner Jonathan Lander relied on what the senior management told him and did not challenge that evidence fully.

In 2006 the Joint Disciplinary Tribunal, the profession's watchdog, ordered PwC and Jonathan Lander to pay fines and costs totalling £1.5m. Mr Lander was reprimanded by the chartered accountants' Joint Disciplinary Tribunal and fined £5,000. As PwC has some 800 profit-sharing members in the UK this equates to something around £2,000 per member or broadly the same as that imposed on Coopers & Lybrand in the wake of the Maxwell case.

The future of self-regulation

It remains to be seen whether or not the profession's self-regulatory function will continue into the future. As we will see there is an increasingly strident level of calls for some form of external regulator, perhaps on the lines of the SEC in the USA, to monitor the watchdogs of the financial world.

In June 2010 the Financial Reporting Council (FRC) and the Financial Services Authority (FSA) issued a joint discussion paper called 'Enhancing the auditor's contribution to prudential regulation'. In that paper they say:

> In some cases that the FSA has seen, the auditor's approach seems to focus too much on gathering and accepting evidence to support management's assertions and whether management's valuations meet the specific requirements of accounting standards. It is important for auditors to also consider if the standards' requirements have been applied thoughtfully so as to ensure that the objectives behind the requirements have been met.

The concern has been prompted by what these bodies perceived to be a too ready acceptance by the auditors of representations made to them by management and a lack of what ISA 200 calls an attitude of 'professional scepticism'. This is defined in ISA 200 as:

An attitude that includes a questioning mind, being alert to conditions which may indicate possible misstatement due to error or fraud, and a critical assessment of audit evidence.

The key words in that definition are 'a critical assessment of audit evidence'. Trainee auditors are taught that auditors need sufficient, reliable evidence to support their audit opinion and that good evidence consists of their own work and evidence supplied by third parties, not the representations made to them by directors who may have a vested interest in not seeing the figures challenged.

Another aspect of the auditors' role is a consideration of what is known as 'substance over form'. This means that auditors are supposed to look behind the appearance of a transaction, ie what it is being presented as, to decide what it really is. This brings us back to the opening paragraph of this chapter and the 'Auditor scepticism: Raising the bar' discussion paper mentioned there.

In it the Auditing Practices Board point out the criticisms of audit firms made following various investigations including those into Equitable Life Assurance Society, London International Group, Independent Insurance, TransTec, Wickes and ERF Holdings which identified audit failings. These include instances of:

- over-reliance on management representations;
- failure to investigate conflicting explanations; and
- failure to obtain appropriate third-party confirmations.

This may suggest that the auditors in these cases were not sufficiently sceptical and were too ready to accept superficial explanations.

The Audit Inspection Unit (AIU), which is part of the Professional Oversight Board, a satellite of the Financial Reporting Council, and which is responsible for monitoring the audits of all listed and other major public interest entities, has also reported on this lack of scepticism. One of the findings described in their 2009/10 annual report was that audit firms are not always applying sufficient professional scepticism in relation to key audit judgements. In particular, audit firms sometimes approach the audit of highly judgemental balances by seeking to obtain evidence that corroborates, rather than challenges, the judgements made by their clients.

The AIU also reported that auditors should exercise greater professional scepticism when reviewing management's judgements relating to fair values of assets, the impairment in the values of goodwill and other intangible assets and future cash flows relevant to the consideration of going concern, ie whether or not the company will be able to stay in business for the foreseeable future – broadly the next twelve months.

In the case of the collapses of various British banks in 2007–08, the criticism, refuted by firms that audited the major banks, was that they, as auditors, were too ready to accept weak evidence of the value of bank assets and that they didn't look beneath the appearance of some of these complex derivative instruments to see what they really were. The APB did not pull any punches in its discussion paper and recognized the reality of the situation. It accepted that whilst firms have policies and procedures in place to promote audit scepticism and that firms are well aware of the consequences to their reputation and the possibility of litigation arising from audit failure, the reality is that:

> audit firms place considerable importance on retaining their client base. Emphasis on client service planning and relationship management within the firms may act as a disincentive for auditor scepticism if audit teams believe that by demonstrating scepticism they risk having an 'unhappy client'.

They point to the disincentives to an overly sceptical approach such as:

- increased audit time; and therefore
- increased audit cost particularly where fee estimates are agreed in advance based on the assumption that all will be well; and
- delays in completion of the audit whilst questions are answered.

Audit firms, it must not be forgotten, are commercial firms and have bills to pay, staff to reward and partners or members to share in the profits. Thus the commercial imperatives of cutting down on audit time, and thus cost to the client, and not offending client sensibilities by asking too many awkward questions, may well play a part in the failure of external audit to be as rigorous as it might be.

This is not to say that any audit firm in the UK would tolerate or forgive deliberate misrepresentation of financial information or collude with directors in disguising malpractice or fraud. Rather it may be part of the culture of the firm that works subconsciously on audit partners and staff, particularly at audit manager level, as they await that all-important call to become a partner. As we saw in Chapter 2, socialization can play a big part in behaviour and employees can lose sight of the true purpose of what they are doing in an attempt to impress their employers. At Arthur Andersen, partners and employees lost sight of their true role and focused on commercialism, making as much profit for Andersen as possible. Barbara Lay Toffler, author of a book on the fall of Andersen, told a story of one partner at

Andersen who inflated fees to clients enormously, saying 'Relax. We're Arthur Andersen. They need us. They'll pay' – and they did.

The problems of the audit profession were brought to the fore when public concern was prompted by the catastrophic collapse of several UK banks, starting with Northern Rock in 2007, which required a huge injection of government money and the effective nationalization of several banks in order to avoid an even bigger financial disaster that would have had enormous implications for the UK economy. The finger was pointed quite firmly at the auditing profession and in particular what appeared to be their less than rigorous assessment of risk and their apparent willingness to accept the market bubbles which had resulted in high values for complex derivative financial instruments. As we now know these were founded on nothing more than bundles of very bad loans – the audit firms may not have questioned, when looking at these derivative instruments, what they were derived from.

Questions were posed as to whether:

- the auditors actually understood what they were auditing; and
- why, if they would have refused to allocate any value to a loan that wasn't going to be repaid, did they allocate value to some financial instrument that was nothing more than that loan dressed up as something else?

Financial journalists and others were quick to point out that the auditors of these banks, which had failed so spectacularly, were confined to three of the so-called Big 4 firms:

- PricewaterhouseCoopers (Northern Rock, Landsbanki, Glitnir, Lloyds);
- KPMG (HBOS);
- Deloitte Touche Tomatsu (Royal Bank of Scotland).

Ernst & Young, whilst not being involved in any UK bank audits, were hardly off the hook as they were being investigated in Ireland over the collapse of Anglo Irish Bank and are facing a lawsuit in the USA over the spectacular collapse of Lehman Brothers, which in no small way precipitated the financial crises of 2007/2008. In particular they were being questioned over the use of an accounting scheme, colloquially known as Repo 105, which enabled the bank to move huge amounts of borrowing off its balance sheet for a short time, which included its financial year end, thus, it is alleged, distorting its true position. No regulatory action was taken against them.

The European Union and regulation

The Big Four firms have a stranglehold on all major audits in the UK, auditing 95 per cent of the FTSE top 350 companies. They also have a significant presence on the councils of the chartered accountancy bodies that regulate the auditing profession in their role as Recognized Supervisory Bodies.

This situation has been recognized both by the Office of Fair Trading and the European Union (EU). In October 2010 the EU published a Green Paper, 'Audit policy: Lessons from the crisis' (European Commission, 2010). This was meant to stimulate debate on matters affecting the auditing profession and one of those was the dominance of the Big Four audit firms. The EU has taken a fairly strong line on this and in its wide-ranging proposals has suggested reforms that may well have horrified the cosy world of UK audit regulation.

The EU paper proposes:

- a single pan-European-led regulator for the industry;
- a 'European passport' for auditors that would allow them to provide services on an EU-wide basis;
- to enhance the role of auditors at banks and major companies;
- auditor appointment, remuneration and duration of the engagement would be the responsibility of a third party, perhaps a regulator, rather than the company itself;
- mandatory rotation of the audit firm and compulsory re-tendering of audits;
- prohibition on the sale of non-audit services to audit clients; and
- a limit on the proportion of fees an audit firm can receive from a single audit client.

These are revolutionary ideas in the audit world and, like many another EU initiative, may never come to pass or not for many years, but the fact that this paper exists does reflect the concern of politicians, reflecting no doubt the concerns of their constituents, that regulation of the audit profession is seriously flawed. Critics point to the USA's robust response to the Enron scandal, which resulted immediately in legislation banning auditors from accepting consultancy work and forcing directors to authenticate their internal financial processes as being free from serious fraud or error.

In September 2011 the EU revealed that it intends to take a tough line with the audit profession when a draft of another Green Paper revealed that possible EU legislation might include:

- outlawing the provision of consultancy and non-audit services even to non-audit clients – effectively splitting firms into two, audit and consultancy, with no connections between them;
- clarification and specification of the scope of the audit to aid clarity of perception by stakeholders;
- improved and expanded audit reports and improved communication between auditor and audit committee;
- regular discussions between auditors and regulators;
- mandatory rotation of audit partners every nine years;
- joint audits between a larger and a smaller firm;
- strengthening of national audit supervisory authorities.

Clearly some of these proposals will ultimately be shelved but the intent is clear. The audit profession must be more proactive in its role as watchdog and must be more challenging and sceptical in its audit approach. The EU for one clearly intends to try to break the monopoly of the Big 4 and to try to disturb what they see as a rather cosy arrangement between them and their clients by stimulating competition, breaking up these enormous firms and eliminating possible conflicts once and for all.

The response in the UK to the fact that all the banks that needed to be rescued had received clean audit reports was to, basically, state that it was not the job of the auditors to tell management how to run their business and that was it. In October 2008 the then chief executive of the Financial Reporting Council Paul Boyle stated, 'auditing has had a good crisis'. Mr Boyle stood down in January 2009.

However insensitive Mr Boyle's comment was, the truth remains that auditors were able to defend their actions by stating that their audits all complied with UK auditing standards and no blame could be attached to them for what occurred. In fact the blame became attached to greedy bankers, inept regulators and unscrupulous traders, but unsettling thoughts remained – if good audit practice could not flag up or assist management in preventing a crisis of such magnitude, what use is it?

The role of internal audit

The role and function of the internal auditor is defined by the Institute of Internal Auditing (IIA) as follows:

> Internal auditing is an independent, objective assurance and consulting activity designed to add value and improve an organization's operations. It helps an organization accomplish its objectives by bringing a systematic, disciplined approach to evaluate and improve the effectiveness of risk management, control and governance processes.

Establishment of an internal audit function is not a legal requirement for companies in the same way that they are required to be audited by external auditors. However, the principles of good corporate governance require that an independent, objective and capable internal audit function is established with a clear mandate to review not only the accounting function but also all aspects of the organization including corporate governance itself. For listed companies internal audit is mandatory under the UK Corporate Governance Code.

Internal audit is, however, a legal requirement in the public sector, including local authorities and the NHS, as well as for government departments. The overriding reason for this is that government and public sector bodies are funded by public money and must therefore be accountable for its use. Accordingly the public sector auditing process perhaps places a greater reliance on the effectiveness of internal audit than does the audit process in the private sector.

Internal audit differs from external audit in scope; it does not focus solely on financial statements or financial risks. Much of the work of internal audit considers operational or strategic risks and the management processes set up to address them. As can be seen from the IIA's definition, internal audit sees itself very much as part of the management function, particularly as part of the quality system. The best way to highlight this is by means of a table that will contrast the respective roles (Table 7.2).

Internal auditors look at how organizations are managing their risks. They provide the audit committee (if there is one – see page 187) and the board of directors with information about whether risks have been identified, and how well they are being managed.

The responsibility to manage risk always resides with management. Internal audit's role as part of that process of managing risk is:

- identifying potential problem areas, both financial and operational;
- recommending ways of improving risk management and internal control systems;
- monitoring corporate governance issues including ethics, performance management and accountability, communications

TABLE 7.2 Internal and external audit

	Internal Audit	External Audit
Objectives	• to evaluate the organization's risk management processes and systems of control and to make recommendations for the achievement of organizational objectives	• to provide an opinion on whether the financial statements show a true and fair view, and whether proper accounting records have been maintained
Responsibility	• to management • part of quality system and corporate procedures on an ongoing basis	• to shareholders • report on financial accounts on an annual basis
Carried out by	• frequently employees of organization • if outsourced, the provision is largely within management's control and direction	• external body independent of organization
Scope	• all aspects of the organization's activities, including operational considerations and compliance issues	• financial records and processes, risk management processes
Approach	• risk-based • evaluate internal control systems • test systems • evaluate operational efficiencies	• risk-based • test basis on which financial accounts produced and reliability of systems • verification of assets and liabilities
Legal Status	• report to management • no specific legal requirement but UK Corporate Governance Code for listed companies requires internal audit • mandatory in the public sector	• report to shareholders • Companies Act 2006

throughout the organization in connection with risk management and internal control and with firm-wide values and acceptable behaviours;

- reviewing operational procedures including, for example, value for money initiatives, procurement and supply-chain management or HR processes;
- reviewing compliance with laws and regulations.

Independence

The key to a successful internal audit function, which let us remember is seen as being of fundamental importance to good corporate governance, is the way the internal audit function is structured inside the organization. Internal auditors are bound by the same ethical rules as external auditors; the principle of independence of thought and function underpinned by the ethical values of integrity, objectivity and competence are as important to them if they are to carry out their role properly as they are to a firm of external auditors.

The problem is how to achieve this within the organization because, don't forget, internal auditors are employees and are therefore subject to the rules of the organization and the instruction of senior management.

To decide whether or not the internal audit function is likely to be effective, the observer should ask some key questions:

- What is the scope of the internal auditors' work – are they constrained by management in any way, or told to concentrate only on specific aspects of the organization's activities?
- How independent is the internal audit function:
  - Can it decide its own pattern of work?
  - Does it have unrestricted access to management at the highest level, ie the CEO or the audit committee?
  - Is it free of any operational responsibilities?
  - Can it communicate freely with the external auditors?
- Does the head of internal audit have a senior management or board-level position, independent of the financial director?
- How competent is the internal audit function? Does the department contain sufficient numbers of trained, competent professional

accountants to carry out the role effectively? Is it well enough resourced? Do they have professional qualifications and training programmes both for trainees and for continuing professional development?

These considerations apply whoever provides the internal audit role. Clearly matters of independence are more easily dealt with if the function is out-sourced to an external provider or, in the public sector, dealt with through some sort of consortium arrangement.

The public sector

Internal audit plays a much more significant role in local and national government, the National Health Service and bodies such as housing associations than it does in private sector organisations. Indeed internal audit is mandatory in local government and the NHS.

This is due to two factors:

- accountability – most public sector organizations are funded primarily through taxpayers' money – and so it has to be properly accounted for as they are accountable to the public for how the money has been spent.

- regularity – this is a term used in the public sector and it means use of funds for the purpose for which they were intended, ie capital funds cannot be used for revenue, grants for specific activities must be spent on those activities.

To a large extent these are not issues that affect private organizations who raise their income from selling goods and services in the marketplace and are accountable, primarily, only to their shareholders.

The strength of the audit function in the public sector does serve to act as a strong incentive to financial probity and promote performance savings. The problem in the public sector is that many of the services it delivers are difficult to measure in any meaningful way. For example, billions are spent on social services across the UK but measurement of outcomes in any meaningful way is virtually impossible as, by its nature, much of its work is preventative and the difficulty of proving a negative is well known. For example, a drug awareness and treatment programme may wean some addicts from heroin, some permanently, but it could not be known how many individuals were dissuaded from starting to take it through the awareness programme.

Both the soon to be abolished Audit Commission and the accountancy body responsible for training accountants with a specific role in the public sector, the Chartered Institute of Public Finance and Accountancy (CIPFA), have issued several bulletins on the role of internal auditing in the public sector that students should be aware of.

The role of external audit in the UK public sector is somewhat wider than that of an external auditor reporting on the accounts of a private sector company. The principles of how auditors carry out their work and the ethical standards they must apply are, of course, the same but there are some significant differences:

1 Most public sector bodies are not at liberty to choose which firm of auditors are appointed to carry out their work. This is decided by the government agencies. What they call public audit, comprising both financial audit and performance audit, is carried out by the national audit agencies, such as the National Audit Office, and Audit Scotland who appoint private firms of auditors to carry out the work.

2 The scope of public audit is rather wider in the public sector than the remit for the audit of a limited company. The audit is considerably wider than simply giving assurance on the financial statements of the public body and includes:

   – examination of aspects of corporate governance within the public body;

   – the effective use of resources (commonly described as 'value for money' initiatives and how they are applied). This is known as 'performance audit'.

In practice auditors adopt an integrated approach to delivering the different elements of this audit, whereby work in relation to one element informs work in relation to the other and vice versa. Financial audit covers the audit of the accounts and the underlying financial systems and processes including, in specific parts of the public sector:

- whether public money was spent for the purposes for which it was intended (known as 'regularity');

- the financial aspects of corporate governance, such as internal control and risk management;

- the probity and propriety of officers and officials.

Essentially, it provides assurance that public money has been safeguarded and accounted for properly.

Performance audit is concerned with the value for money of services, functions, programmes or specific projects, and the systems and processes put in place by the body to manage its activity and use of resources and to prepare and publish performance information. In local government in England and Wales it also includes auditors' work in relation to 'best value' performance plans. These relate to a process of improvement of delivered services through questioning the mode of delivery and carrying out cost comparisons in order to improve efficiencies and promote savings.

Both the financial and performance aspects of audit involve reporting on the stewardship of resources. Thus, the national audit agencies usually require auditors, in planning and carrying out their work, to take into account both financial and performance considerations, with respect not only to the business risks relating to a particular service or function, but also to its relative importance to the public and its representatives.

The audit committee

The UK Corporate Governance Code requires that all listed companies set up an audit committee. Ideally it should comprise at least three non-executive directors (two in the case of smaller companies) who are independent of management. The chair of the board of directors could be a member of the audit committee but should not chair it. In addition to this:

- the members of the audit committee should have a wide range of business and professional skills;
- the members should have a good understanding of the business yet should have had no recent involvement with direct management of the business;
- the committee should have clear written terms of reference setting out its authority and its duties;
- the members should be prepared to devote significant time and effort to the work of the committee.

Clearly this can sometimes be difficult to achieve. However, the objective is to create a committee that is competent to carry out its role, is independent and is free from bias. The key objectives associated with the setting up of audit committees, from the point of view of corporate governance, generally, are:

- to increase public confidence in the credibility and objectivity of published financial information;
- to assist the directors in carrying out their responsibilities for financial reporting;
- to strengthen the position of the external auditors by providing a channel of communication at board level without the constraint of any executive bias.

There are advantages to having an audit committee. These are:

- It can improve the quality of management accounting, as they are able to criticize internal reporting, which is not necessarily the responsibility of the external auditors.
- It can facilitate communication between the directors, internal and external auditors and management.
- It can help minimize any conflicts between management and the auditors.
- It can facilitate the independence of the internal audit role if the internal auditors report to the audit committee directly.

However, there are some disadvantages that the members of the audit committee have to avoid:

- It can be perceived that their purpose is to criticize or 'catch out' executive management.
- This can result in the perception, if not the reality, of a two-tier board.
- The non-executives can become too embroiled in detail and start to act like executive directors, thus losing their independence.

The role of the audit committee, specifically, is:

- to monitor the integrity of the financial statements of the company and any formal announcements relating to the company's financial performance, reviewing significant financial reporting judgements contained in them;
- to review the company's internal financial controls and, unless expressly addressed by a separate board risk committee composed of independent directors or by the board itself, the company's internal control and risk management systems;
- to monitor and review the effectiveness of the company's internal audit function;

- to make recommendations to the board, for it to put to the shareholders for their approval in general meeting, in relation to the appointment of the external auditor and to approve the remuneration and terms of engagement of the external auditors;

- to review and monitor the external auditor's independence and objectivity and the effectiveness of the audit process, taking into consideration relevant UK professional and regulatory requirements;

- to develop and implement policy on the engagement of the external auditor to supply non-audit services, taking into account relevant ethical guidance regarding the provision of non-audit services by the external audit firm; and

- to report to the board, identifying any matters in respect of which it considers that action or improvement is needed and making recommendations as to the steps to be taken.

In essence, the audit committee is designed to act as an independent voice on the board of directors with regard to audit and corporate governance issues and can be a valuable asset, particularly with respect to maintaining the independence and integrity of the internal audit function. They also act as a point of contact for external auditors and can be a powerful voice for the audit role in the organization.

CASE STUDY

The audit of Megatron plc is under consideration by the executive directors. The group has been audited by one of the international audit firms, Tickitt & Run, for the last fourteen years.

Tickitt & Run also carry out certain internal audit functions, have advised Megatron on several major acquisitions and also provide computer consultancy services and finance consultancy. The senior partner of Tickitt & Run is a regular guest at several Megatron corporate events and Tickitt & Run were joint sponsors with Megatron of a tennis tournament in Antigua where they entertained the board of Megatron at an end of tournament party, at which several major tennis stars were present.

After the corruption scandal that caused the downfall of previous CEO Sir 'Billy' Bustler and Chairman Lord Footler, the new CEO, a Scottish chartered accountant called McTavish, is reviewing all professional relationships with a view to enhancing the corporate governance in the group. He is concerned that the relationship with Tickitt & Run is too close and is of the view that a new firm should be appointed.

He is being opposed by his finance director who feels that Tickitt & Run are a trusted firm, that they are familiar with Megatron's complex group structure and that changing to a new firm would send a bad message to the City. He feels that a new audit partner and a reduction in the amount of consultancy work Tickitt & Run receive would be sufficient.

Discuss

● Would mandatory rotation of audit firms improve the quality of the audit or would it simply result in a costly game of musical chairs as audit firms simply swopped clients?

● Does a long-term relationship between an auditor and its client have the benefits claimed for it by the finance director or does it simply breed complacency?

● Would rotation of audit partner have the same result as rotation of the audit firm in terms of an improved audit function and benefit to the shareholders and potential investors?

● Does competition in the audit market for international clients improve the quality of audit or would it simply cause audit firms to cut costs and thereby reduce audit work in order to be competitive in bidding for work?

● How can regulators ensure auditors remain independent of their clients and approach their audits with a suitably sceptical attitude when the directors they may have to challenge approve payment of the audit fee?

Bibliography

Audit Commission (2002) *Code of Audit Practice*, Audit Commission, London

Audit Inspection Unit (2010) *Annual Report 2009/10*, Financial Reporting Council, London

Audit Quality Forum (2006) *Fundamentals: Audit Purpose*, ICAEW, London

Auditing Practices Board (2008) *International Standards on Auditing*, Financial Reporting Council, London

Auditing Practices Board (2009) *ISA 200: Objective and general principles governing an audit of financial statements*, FRC, London

Auditing Practices Board (2010) *Auditor Scepticism: Raising the bar*, Auditing Practices Board, London

Blackden, R (2010) Ernst and Young faces lawsuit over Lehman Brothers' accounts, *Telegraph*, 21 September

Bower, T (1999) Cover up, *Daily Mail*, 4 February 1999, pp 10–11

Brown, R (ed) (1905) *A History of Accounting and Accountants*, TT and EC Jack, p 75, reprinted 1968, Frank Cass, London

Cadbury, Sir A (1992) *Financial Aspects of Corporate Governance*, Gee & Co, London

Chartered Institute of Public Finance and Accounting (1992) *LAAP Bulletins*, CIPFA, London

Christodoulou, M (2010) Audit: Time for a change, *Accountancy Age*, 22 (7)

European Commission (2010) Audit policy: Lessons from the crisis, Green Paper, 13 October 2010, European Commission, Brussels

Financial Reporting Council (2010) *UK Corporate Governance Code*, FRC, London

Financial Reporting Council (FRC) and the Financial Services Authority (FSA) (2010) Enhancing the auditor's contribution to prudential regulation, Discussion paper, FRC and FSA, London

Flint, D (1988) *Philosophy and Principles of Auditing: An introduction*, Palgrave Macmillan, Basingstoke

HMSO (1948) *Companies Act 1948*, HMSO, London

HMSO (2000) *Financial Services and Markets Act 2000*, HMSO, London

HMSO (2006) *Companies Act 2006*, HMSO, London

Jones, A and Smith, J (2011) E&Y faces probe on Anglo Irish Bank audit, *Financial Times*, 14 September

Jones, M (ed) (2011) *Creative Accounting, Fraud and International Accounting Scandals*, John Wiley, Chichester

Lee, T (1993) *Corporate Audit Theory*, Chapman & Hall, London

Limperg, T (1932) *The Function of the Accountant and the Theory of Inspired Confidence*, Limperg Instituut, Amsterdam

Matthews, D (2006) *A History of Auditing: The changing audit process in Britain from the nineteenth century to the present day*, Routledge, Abingdon

Mautz, RK and Sharaf, HA (1961) *The Philosophy of Auditing*, New York, American Accounting Association

Millichamp, A and Taylor, J (2012) *Auditing*, Cengage, London

Prowle, M (2009) *Managing and Reforming Modern Public Services*, Prentice Hall, Harlow

Public Audit Forum (2002) *The Different Roles of External Audit, Inspection and Regulation: A guide for public service managers*, Public Audit Forum, London

Reed, K (2006) TransTec auditors pick up the second largest bill in JDS history, *Accountancy Age*, 13 December

Sarbanes–Oxley Act (2002) H.R.Rep 107-610 25 July 2002. US Government Printing Office, Washington DC

Serious Fraud Office (2006) *TransTec plc*, SFO, London

Sikka, P (2001) *Regulation of Accountancy and the Power of Capital: Some observations*, University of Essex, Essex

Spence, A (2010) 'Big four' maintain hold on UK audit market, *The Times*, 1 March

Staff [accessed 12 September 2012] Auditors are having a good crisis, *Accountancy Age* [Online] www.accountancyage.com

Taylor, J (2010) *Forensic Accounting*, Pearson, Harlow

Toffler, BL and Reingald, J (2003) *Final Accounting: Ambition, Greed and the Fall of Arthur Andersen*, Crown Publishing, New York

Websites

www.acca.org.uk
www.accountancyage.com
www.charteredaccountants.ie
www.cipfa.org
www.ec.europa.eu
www.ft.com

www.icaew.com
www.icas.org.uk
www.public-audit-forum.gov.uk
www.sfo.gov.uk
www.telegraph.co.uk
www.timesonline.co.uk

Corporate governance and other stakeholders

Introduction

The basic principles and implications of corporate governance have been addressed in previous chapters. Stakeholders such as the board and its directors and the impact that corporate governance guidelines have on their role were dealt with specifically in their own separate chapters. This chapter looks at other stakeholders that companies have to consider in their actions and the implications that corporate governance has on their rights.

Whether the main purpose of an organization is to look after their shareholders and achieve maximum shareholder wealth or to serve a wider range of stakeholders and their interests has been an issue of long debate. According to Milton Friedman in 1982, 'corporate executives are there to maximise the income and wealth of stockholders' (Friedman, 1982). However, he goes on to state that management is there 'to make as much money as possible while conforming to the basic rules of society, both those embodied in the law and those embodied in ethical custom'.

This implies that, although there is a debate between whether shareholders or other stakeholders should take priority, the two should run side by side and be considered alongside every decision made.

Definitions of stakeholders

There are numerous definitions and categories of stakeholders. Generally a company can consider a stakeholder as a person or group who has an interest in or can be affected by an organization's activities. As a consequence of this definition, a general list of stakeholders for a business to consider can be quite extensive, covering employees, shareholders, management, creditors, trade unions, customers, suppliers, investors, the government, the local community, future generations and so on. However, not all stakeholders have the same level of interest and impact on an organization or can be affected by the company's activities to the same extent and therefore it helps if a company can categorize and prioritize its stakeholders to ensure that it considers its impact on them in an appropriate way and carries out its activities in a way that keeps them happy.

One way of classifying stakeholders is to first split them into those who are inside the organization and those who are outside – namely internal and external stakeholders. Internal stakeholders would cover groups such as employees, management and trade unions.

External stakeholders would cover groups such as customers, competitors and suppliers.

Another way of classifying stakeholders would be to consider those who are most affected and/or dependent on the organization and those who are less affected/dependent on the organization. Those who are likely to be more affected by the organization are shareholders, employees, management, customers and suppliers. Those who are likely to be less affected are the government and the wider community.

Placing stakeholders under the heading of 'primary' and 'secondary' stakeholders can also help. Primary stakeholders are those who have a direct impact on the organization and without whom it would be difficult to operate. Stakeholders included in this category would be the government, shareholders and customers. Secondary stakeholders such as the community and management have a less direct impact on the organization and the company could survive without them to a certain extent.

Another useful way of categorizing stakeholders would be to consider those who are active, such as management, employees, regulators, suppliers and pressure groups, and those who are passive such as shareholders, local communities, the government and customers.

Whichever categorization of stakeholders is preferred by a business, they all help to prioritize the importance and impact of stakeholders and therefore will help a business direct its activities and decisions in a way that means their key stakeholders are considered. This can help when considering the implication of corporate governance for a business in terms of stakeholders and who to prioritize; however, there is also more formal guidance to help a business consider how corporate governance principles should be interpreted in light of stakeholder interests.

Guidance on stakeholder interests

The OECD 1999 principles and the UK Corporate Governance Code (June 2010) help to define and clarify the role of stakeholders in terms of corporate governance, which a business will need to consider.

According to the OECD 1999 principles, when a business is considering the impact of stakeholders on their corporate governance actions they first need to consider stakeholder rights established by law. The principles then go on to specify that under the corporate governance framework businesses need to co-operate with their stakeholders in a way that enables them to 'create jobs, wealth and sustain financially sound enterprises'.

The OECD principles help to clarify exactly what a business needs to consider with their corporate governance activities to look after their stakeholders and the concepts are summarized below:

- The rights of stakeholders protected by law need to be respected within the corporate governance framework.
- With any stakeholder interest protected by the law, stakeholders need to have the opportunity to obtain effective redress for violation of their rights.

- Performance-enhancing mechanisms for stakeholder participation need to be included in the corporate governance framework.
- Relevant information needs to be provided to stakeholders who participate in the corporate governance process.

Therefore, knowing who your stakeholders are and how the law protects them are key to ensuring that business activities comply with corporate governance guidelines. As a consequence the list of actions could be very wide-ranging to ensure shareholders, customers, investors, employees and so on are all looked after and have mechanisms to protect their rights and participate in corporate governance activities.

The UK Corporate Governance Code June 2010 emphasizes that corporate governance needs to be very well linked to investors. It covers the following summarized points:

- There needs to be sufficient engagement between investors and company boards.
- This engagement is vital to the health of the UK's corporate governance regime.
- It is the responsibility of both the company and shareholders to ensure that the 'comply or explain' principle remains an effective alternative to a rules-based system.
- Interaction between boards and shareholders has practical and administrative obstacles; however, increased trust between the parties could improve attitudes to the Code and its constructive use.

These points emphasise that shareholders have an important part to play in corporate governance decisions.

These guidelines form a starting point for considering the implications of stakeholders on corporate governance activities. The next section looks specifically at internal and external stakeholders and how they need to carry out their role in the best interests of corporate governance.

Internal corporate governance stakeholders

Within the section above defining stakeholders, one classification of stakeholders given was that of internal stakeholders. In helping to understand the implications of corporate governance and stakeholders this classification can specify key internal stakeholders and their involvement in corporate governance activities.

TABLE 8.1   Internal stakeholders' roles within the business and in respect of corporate governance guidelines

Internal Stakeholder	Defined Business Role	Corporate Governance Role
Executive and Non-executive Directors	responsible for the corporation's activities	ensure the company is controlled in the best interests of its stakeholders
Company Secretary	responsible for ensuring the business complies with company legislation and regulations update board members on their legal responsibilities	provide advice to the board on corporate governance matters
Management	manage business operations carry out policies determined by the board	highlight and evaluate risks faced by company ensure controls are developed and followed highlight concerns
Employees	follow job requirements and management orders	adhere to internal controls and report breaches
Trade Unions	look after employee interests	identify and take action against any breaches in corporate governance requirements such as the non-protection of whistle-blowers

Each internal stakeholder has a number of aspects to consider. First, they will have a defined role within the business and second, they will have a role in respect of corporate governance guidelines that they need to fulfil. Each internal stakeholder is reviewed in this way in Table 8.1.

External corporate governance stakeholders

Similarly, external stakeholders exist and have a role to play in ensuring that a company is complying with corporate governance guidelines. Each

TABLE 8.2 External stakeholders' role in respect of corporate governance guidelines

External Stakeholder	Corporate Governance Role
Auditors	independent review of company's reported financial performance and ensuring adherence to corporate governance guidelines
Regulators	compliance with regulations
Government	compliance with the law and guidelines
Stock Exchange	implementing and maintaining rules and regulations for companies listed on the stock exchange
Small Investors	limited power but can use voting rights
Institutional Investors	through considered use of their voting rights can influence corporate policy

external stakeholder can influence how a company operates in line with corporate governance, as is summarized in Table 8.2.

Institutional investors and corporate governance

Increased pressure is being brought on institutional investors to monitor corporate governance issues within the businesses they are investing in, as can be seen in the UK Corporate Governance Code detailed above. As a consequence companies need to consider institutional investors as key stakeholders and inform them of the corporate governance policies that they are following.

The reasons for this pressure are that institutional investors can have a large stake in a company due to the size of their shareholdings and consequently can exert significant influence on corporate policy and take an active role in bringing under-performing companies to task.

In 2002, the Institutional Shareholders Committee issued guidelines to encourage institutional investors to develop a policy on corporate governance and to apply this policy when voting in company meetings.

Just as directors have obligations to their shareholders, institutional investors have obligations to the many individuals such as pension scheme holders, unit trust investors and so on. They are investing money on these individuals' behalf and therefore need to ensure that the companies they are investing in are sound businesses that follow corporate governance guidelines, so as a consequence they have a need to monitor and ensure that guidelines are being followed correctly.

Therefore there are numerous and varied stakeholders that will influence and impact on corporate governance activities carried out by businesses. The list of stakeholders will vary from one organization to another, therefore organizations must list them, prioritize them, consider the law that protects them and how it impacts on their activities and take this on board and continually review it.

CASE STUDY

A company manufactures clothes in a number of towns and cities in the United Kingdom. These are then distributed to a network of retail outlets throughout the country.

The company is owned by two other companies that take an active interest in the profitability of the clothing manufacturing and retailing sides of the business. Other UK clothing businesses now source their products from overseas as manufacturing costs in the UK are extremely high and reduce margins on the sale of the final product.

The board of the business is currently considering closing the manufacturing side of the business and sourcing their garments from countries like China and India where manufacturing costs are half of those in the UK. However, there is some concern over the conditions for workers in these countries and the age of labour used.

Discuss

- Identify the stakeholder groups who will be affected and interested in the decision to relocate the manufacturing side of the business, and the impact of the decision on the group.

- Discuss the actions the board can take in respect of each stakeholder group.

Bibliography

FRC (2010) *Main Principles of the UK Corporate Governance Code* [Online] http://www.frc.org.uk/documents/pagemanager/Corporate_Governance/UK%20Corp%20Gov%20Code%20June%202010.pdf

Friedman, M (1982) *Capitalism and Freedom*, 2nd edition, University of Chicago Press, Chicago

Institutional Shareholders Committee (2005) *The Responsibilities of Institutional Shareholders and Agents – Statement of Principles*, IVIS, London

OECD (nd) OECD Principles of Corporate Governance [Online] www.oecd.org/document/49/0,3746,en_2649_34813_31530865_1_1_1_1,00.html

09 Corporate Social Responsibility and its reporting

LEARNING OBJECTIVES

The material in this chapter covers:

- the growth in importance of CSR reporting;

- definitions of CSR;

- corporate governance and its link to CSR;

- the history of CSR;

- the reality of CSR;

- auditors and CSR;

Introduction

The previous chapter covered corporate governance and its link to an organization's stakeholders. By having to consider a variety of stakeholders, this links into understanding the importance of why Corporate Social Responsibility activities and their reporting are becoming a growth area for businesses.

The growth in importance of CSR reporting

Corporate Social Responsibility (CSR) activities and reporting are important and carried out throughout the world, as can be seen by the number of companies producing Corporate Social Responsibility reports each year. For example, the KPMG International Survey on Corporate Social Responsibility showed that on:

> October 28, 2008 – Eighty per cent of the Global Fortune 250 now release corporate responsibility information in stand-alone reports or integrated with annual financial reports, up from 50 per cent in the three years since KPMG last conducted its survey in 2005 and from 35 per cent in 1999.
>
> (**www.kpmg.co.uk**)

In their 2011 survey, this figure had increased to 95 per cent of the 250 largest companies in the world reporting on their corporate responsibility activities (KPMG, 2011, p 6). Therefore there has been significant growth in CSR reporting from 1999 to 2011.

Corporate Social Responsibility guidelines and frameworks, such as the Global Reporting Initiative (GRI), are used to assist businesses in performing this reporting in a more standardized way. According to the KPMG 2011 survey, 80 per cent of G250 (the 250 largest companies in the world) and 69 per cent of N100 (the top 100 companies in the world listed by revenue) companies adhere to GRI Sustainability Reporting Guidelines (KPMG, 2011, p 20).

In 2010, the sports firm PUMA became the world's first major corporation to publish the cost of its activities in terms of their impact on the environment by producing an environmental profit and loss account that values the impact of its activities across its value chain (CIMA Financial Management, 2011, p 13).

The creation of the International Integrated Reporting Committee (IIRC) in 2010 catapulted the idea of integrated reporting onto the world stage and highlighted the fact that corporate responsibility should now be a board-level consideration for companies around the world. The IIRC was established to achieve a globally accepted integrated reporting framework. The committee consists of members from both the financial and the sustainability sectors who work together to develop a framework that brings together financial, environmental, social and governance information in a clear, concise, consistent and comparable format (KPMG, 2011, pp 23–4).

This evidence indicates a growing interest in reporting moving away from basic financial reporting and towards a more standardized approach to CSR-style reporting to assist firms in meeting their broader reporting requirements and including Corporate Social Responsibility in their main financial statements.

To understand the concept of Corporate Social Responsibility and its growing importance, it is useful to gain an insight into how the concept has developed and why. The following sections review definitions of Corporate Social Responsibility, which have evolved over time, the history of Corporate Social Responsibility and developments in the auditing of CSR-type activities.

Definitions of Corporate Social Responsibility

The term 'Corporate Social Responsibility' has been defined in many different ways by academics; however, there is still no common and absolute definition of this term, despite extensive research by academics. According to Rizk, Dixon and Woodhead the term 'Corporate Social Responsibility' 'is a brilliant one: it means something, but not always the same thing, to everybody' (2008, p 309). Definitions of Corporate Social Responsibility have also changed over a number of decades. These are summarized in Table 9.1.

According to these definitions, two different points of view about Corporate Social Responsibility have been highlighted by academics:

- The only responsibility of a business is towards its shareholders and to maximize profits (such as the definition of Friedman, 1982).

- Business has a responsibility towards society as a whole and not just to its shareholders who are interested in profit maximization (supported by most academics in the definitions in Table 9.1).

There are many more recent definitions of Corporate Social Responsibility but two commonly used sets of definitions are provided by the Business for Social Responsibility (BSR) and the World Business Council for Sustainable Development (WBCSD).

The Business for Social Responsibility defines Corporate Social Responsibility as:

> Achieving commercial success in ways that honor ethical values and respect people, communities, and the natural environment.
>
> (White, 2006, p 6)

The World Business Council for Sustainable Development defines the term as follows:

> Corporate Social Responsibility is the continuing commitment by business to contribute to economic development while improving the quality of life of the workforce and their families as well as of the community and society at large.
>
> (**www.wbcsd.org**)

TABLE 9.1 Definitions of Corporate Social Responsibility

Author	Definition
Bowen (1953)	Corporate social responsibility refers to the obligation of businessmen to pursue those policies, to make those decisions, or to follow those lines of action that are desirable in terms of the objectives and values of our society.
Frederick (1960)	Social responsibility in the final analysis implies a public posture toward society's economic and human resources and a willingness to see that those resources are used for broad social ends and not simply for the narrowly circumscribed interests of private persons and firms.
Friedman (1962)	There is one and only one social responsibility of business – to use its resources and engage in activities designed to increase its profits so long as it stays within the rules of the game, which is to say, engages in open and free competition without deception or fraud.
Davis and Blomstrom (1966)	Social responsibility ... refers to a person's obligation to consider the effects of his decisions and actions on the whole social system.
Sethi (1975)	Social responsibility implies bringing corporate behaviour up to a level where it is congruent with the prevailing social norms, values, and expectations of performance.
Carroll (1979)	The social responsibility of business encompasses the economic, legal, ethical and discretionary expectations that society has of organizations at a given point in time.
Jones (1980)	Corporate social responsibility is the notion that corporations have an obligation to constituent groups in society other than stockholders and beyond that prescribed by law and union contract.
Wood (1990)	The basic idea of corporate social responsibility is that business and society are interwoven rather than distinct entities.
Baker (2003)	Corporate social responsibility is about how companies manage the business processes to produce an overall positive impact on society.

SOURCE: Kakabadse, Rozuel and Lee, 2005, p 281

These two definitions emphasize that businesses do have a wider responsibility towards society in terms of being ethically, socially, economically and environmentally responsible and form the basic understanding of what is implied by the term Corporate Social Responsibility.

The next section moves on from the definitions of Corporate Social Responsibility to its link to corporate governance.

What is corporate governance?

As stated previously, corporate governance is the system by which organizations are directed and controlled. Companies have historically been managed to meet shareholders' best interests, but it is the importance of other stakeholders as well as the need for companies to behave in a more ethical manner in order for society to be happy that are driving businesses to consider being socially responsible.

The concepts that corporate governance covers such as accountability, transparency, ethical approaches and stakeholder perspective imply that businesses need to focus on doing 'what is right' and what is expected by society from organizations, not just what is right from an economic and legal viewpoint. The underlying principles of corporate governance imply that Corporate Social Responsibility has a direct linkage to a company having good corporate governance procedures and is therefore an important part of how a company operates if it is to adhere to suitable corporate governance policies.

However, without a legal framework to enforce companies to behave in a socially responsible manner, how can other stakeholder needs be safely protected and considered when a business undertakes its activities?

What is Corporate Social Responsibility and how does it link to corporate governance?

Corporate Social Responsibility refers to organizations considering and managing their impact on a variety of stakeholders. Organizations are not simply independent units operating in isolation to make money for shareholders and achieve their overall objectives. Companies employ people who rely on them for their income to support their families. Suppliers need businesses to purchase goods from them and pay for them promptly. Customers purchase goods and services from businesses in order to meet their needs. The local community is affected by an organization in terms of who it employs, how they spend their income and how businesses carry out their production activities. How products are made is having a big impact on society in general, in terms of pollution and employment levels and the impact that these methods have on the environment in which we all live.

Corporate governance is all about how an organization is governed in pursuit of its objectives.

Corporate Social Responsibility is all about how a company will manage the impact of their operations on the economy, society and the environment, over and above the requirements imposed by regulation.

The sections so far have provided an insight into the growth in emphasis on CSR, its definitions and links to corporate governance. The following section delves into the history of its development in more detail.

Historical perspective of Corporate Social Responsibility

An important area to review is how the term Corporate Social Responsibility came into existence. As far back as the nineteenth century, social problems such as poverty and poor conduct of businesses (Wood, 1990) developed the idea of firms needing to behave in a socially responsible manner but it was not until the term came into wider use from the 1960s that the concept became more accepted.

> CSR is not a new concept. As long as business has existed, we have also had expectations from governments, stakeholders, NGO's and individuals concerning voluntary obligation to society.
>
> (Van Der Laan Smith, Adhikari and Tondkar, 2005, p 2)

A generally accepted view should be that a good business is also a good citizen. Corporate Social Responsibility started with the actions of businessmen like Joseph Rowntree carrying out genuinely philanthropic activities such as providing good housing for his workers (**www.jrf.org.uk**). Richard and George Cadbury developed Bournville Village because they wanted their factory to operate in a 'green' environment and to provide a good quality of life for their employees by providing a village community for them to live and work in. In 1895, they purchased 120 acres near their factory to build affordable housing for their employees, which resulted in Bournville Almshouses being set up in 1897. There is still a charitable trust that exists today, the aim of which is housing reform in the UK. However, in today's society CSR activities are usually carried out in the hope that some kind of return will be there for the business in the future, such as an improvement in its reputation winning it more customers in the future, unlike the more genuine activities of the Rowntrees and Cadburys, who were more concerned about their employees well-being (**www.bvt.org.uk**).

According to Carroll (1999) the issue of CSR can be traced back centuries but from an academic point of view the concept of CSR is really a phenomenon of the twentieth century and can be traced back to Howard Bowen and his book *Social Responsibilities of the Businessman*. Due to his early and influential work Carroll regarded Howard Bowen as the 'Father of Corporate Social Responsibility' (Carroll, 1999).

The modern era for the subject of Corporate Social Responsibility can be said to have developed from the 1950s, as stated by Carroll and Buchholtz (2006) who said that the CSR concept has 'gained considerable acceptance and broadening of meaning' (p 33). This view has also been supported by Griseri and Seppala (2010) who said that the modern era for the subject of CSR can be traced back as early as the 1930s but it only became an area of general concern for businesses in the 1960s.

Since the 1950s the concept of Corporate Social Responsibility has been an area of high interest and research by academics and corporations. The shareholder model introduced by the ideas of Friedman was expanded in the 1950s to introduce the idea that businesses were there to serve society as well as to try to seek profits. In the 1960s and 1970s academics started to show interest in CSR and began to research the concept, leading to the development of a number of models and theories. In the 1980s stakeholder models and corporate social performance concepts were introduced such that by the 1990s a broadening out of the ideas behind CSR and challenges to its understanding had been researched.

Further similar insights and overviews into the historical development of Corporate Social Responsibility are worth considering, such as those by Lee and Carroll. According to Lee (2008) the CSR concept has gone through several stages of development: social responsibilities of businessmen in the 1950s–1960s; enlightened self-interest in the 1970s; corporate social performance models in the 1980s; and strategic management in the 1990s. Carroll (1999) defines stages differently:

- the 1950s: the modern era of social responsibility begins;
- the 1960s: CSR literature expands;

- the 1970s: definitions of CSR proliferate;
- the 1980s: fewer definitions, more research, and alternative themes;
- the 1990s: CSR further yields to alternative themes (Carroll, 1999, pp 269, 270, 273, 284, 288).

Whichever historical perspective is most relevant and accurate, the general consensus is that considerable development and change has happened over the period from the 1950s to the 2000s, emphasizing the growing interest and research into Corporate Social Responsibility.

Therefore this section highlights that the CSR concept has been around for a long while and has gathered more momentum and interest in the last 50 years, with the focus and emphasis of the research changing and developing decade by decade.

The next section goes on to discuss the CSR reality.

The reality of Corporate Social Responsibility

Most markets judge a business's performance by its financial performance. Socially responsible actions by a business may invariably have an impact on its reputation but it would be very difficult to show them having a direct impact on its profitability and share price.

If all companies are to follow ethically and socially responsible principles the financial markets would need to be seen to reward such activities, and accounting systems would need to be altered to ensure that financial statements are not just 'financial' but also include other indicators covering environmental and social factors. The bottom line needs to be expanded to cover not just 'financial' profits but Corporate Social Responsibility. John Elkington has written a book all about the 'triple bottom line', in other words, a bottom line that measures financial, social and environmental performance (Frankental, 2010).

The key is to audit companies based on financial, ethical and social performance so that a company acting in a way that is not socially desirable, for example, has this highlighted in their accounts and sees its share price drop as a consequence. If this was the case, all companies would take Corporate Social Responsibility seriously when they were carrying out their activities and decision-making (Elkington, 1998).

In the meantime, some companies may act in a socially responsible manner but others will not and those that do probably see it as a way of getting free publicity that will boost its profitability.

One reason why changing to the 'triple bottom line' or something similar is not that easy is that finances are more concrete and specific to measure and therefore can be reported on. A lot of Corporate Social Responsibility actions are more subjective and therefore more difficult to report on accurately, which could cause a lot of problems for auditors and businesses to provide a 'true and fair view' of such activities.

Therefore Corporate Social Responsibility needs to be very clearly defined and understood. It needs a specific definition that is suitable for the variety of businesses that exist. Measurable processes and auditing procedures then need to be introduced.

The following section highlights developments towards triple bottom line reporting and the broadening out of auditing from merely financial performance.

Getting to the bottom of the triple bottom line

The aim behind the triple bottom line concept is that a business's success or health can and should be judged not only by the traditional financial bottom line, but also by its social, ethical and environmental performance (Elkington, 1998).

Businesses and institutional investors in the United Kingdom are paying greater attention to issues of long-term social and environmental risk. Corporate Social Responsibility is being paid more attention in the UK than the US because British society is developing an increased concern about ethics. More awareness and publicity has heightened the importance of the concept of risk and risk management and there has also been growth in the media exposure of concerns to do with Corporate Social Responsibility (Elkington, 1998).

If triple bottom line reporting is to take place, though, auditing techniques will need to adapt accordingly.

Auditors and Corporate Social Responsibility

The aim of an assurance engagement is for a professionally qualified accountant to assess a subject matter that is the responsibility of another party against identified criteria. The accountant then draws a conclusion to provide a level of assurance about that subject matter.

Carrying out an audit of the financial statements enables the auditor to form an opinion as to whether the financial statements are produced, in all material respects, in adherence to the financial reporting framework. The auditor ascertains whether the financial statements 'give a true and fair view' or 'present fairly, in all material respects' the proper financial position of the business. A similar aim applies not only to the audit of financial information but also to any other information produced in accordance with appropriate criteria. Auditing utilizes accounting, auditing and investigative skills when conducting an investigation and can be applied to ensure that an organization is carrying out its Corporate Social Responsibility activities appropriately.

In producing the audit opinion, the auditor obtains enough suitable evidence to be able to formulate conclusions on which to base that opinion.

The auditor's opinion provides credibility to the financial statements by giving a reasonable, but not absolute, level of assurance. Absolute assurance from an audit is not possible due to factors such as the need for judgement, the fact that testing is used, the inherent restrictions of any accounting and internal control systems plus the fact that the majority of the evidence provided to the auditor is persuasive, rather than conclusive, in nature.

Audit-linked services comprise reviews, agreed upon procedures and compilations of any aspects of a business required by a client. Audits and reviews are aimed at enabling the auditor to produce reasonable and limited assurance respectively, these terms being provided to illustrate their comparative ranking. Assignments to carry out audit-related services such as negotiated procedures and compilations are aimed at enabling the auditor to be able to provide assurance. Presently, guidance in this area is derived mainly from International Auditing and Assurance Standard Board pronouncements.

Although it is considered that management are primarily responsible for the detection of error and fraud, auditors are also required to consider the likelihood of fraud in the conduct of an audit. An annual audit may act as a deterrent to the occurrence of fraud.

An auditor must be a member of a recognized professional body and be suitable under the rules of that body. Traditionally, the auditor carries out his task because of legal obligations imposed upon companies to have an audit. As a consequence of this it is reasonable for the law to frame statutes and regulations within which the auditor must work. Governments, have required auditors to express opinions on financial statements, through various Companies Acts.

Audit standard-setting bodies include the International Auditing and Assurance Standard Board based in New York, which issues International Standards on Auditing, and the Approved Practices Board based in London, which issues standards for use in the UK and Ireland.

The mission of the International Auditing and Assurance Standard Board is to develop high-quality auditing, assurance and quality control and related services standards and to enhance the consistency of practice by professional accountants throughout the world. This will therefore strengthen public confidence in the global auditing profession and serve the public interest appropriately.

Auditors have different responsibilities for different parts of a company's annual report. These include:

- auditing the financial statements;
- reviewing the company's compliance with certain areas of the Code of Corporate Governance; and
- reading all the information in the report that is not subject to any other requirement.

The company is required to disclose, in a narrative statement in the annual report and accounts, how they have applied the Code principles. The auditor is required to read this. The company has to make a statement in the annual report and accounts as to whether or not they have complied throughout the accounting period with the provisions of the Combined Code. The auditor needs to gain enough appropriate evidence to support the compliance statement made by the company.

Social and environmental audits

Environmental matters can lead to misstatement in the financial statements and so are of direct concern to the auditor. Also, environmental and social reporting are very much in vogue in some industries and present new opportunities to accounting firms.

Issues to consider include; the fact that social and environmental issues may have an impact on some sets of financial statements; auditors may be called upon to produce environmental or social reports; and auditors may be called upon to attest to social or environmental reports produced by others, such as directors.

Global warming, pollution, the effects of industrial activities etc have, due to public awareness, led to the development of legislation in this area. Public opinion and legislation have forced many companies to improve their environmental performance. Some accounting regulations and auditing standards impact upon environmental issues, including Financial Reporting Standards 11: Impairment of Fixed Assets and Goodwill, Financial Reporting Standards 12, International Standards on Auditing 540, 315, 330, 250A and International Auditing Practice Statement 1010.

Fixed assets can be impaired by environmental factors such as pollution and contamination, asbestos in buildings can affect their value etc.

When an auditor realizes that his client may have environmental issues that could have an effect on the financial statements he must take a number of steps to gain appropriate audit evidence.

It may be possible to carry out an audit of purely environmental matters. This can be conducted by firms of accountants but some consider it better done by firms with specific expertise. An environmental audit is a tool used by management that consists of a systematic, documented, periodic and objective evaluation of how effectively organizations, management and equipment are doing, with the objective of contributing to the safeguarding of the environment by allowing management control of environmental practices and assessing whether company policies comply. This includes adhering to regulatory requirements and standards where applicable.

In its widest sense, an environmental audit should involve examining all aspects concerned with how an organization impacts on its environment.

The European Union has established a voluntary community that carries out an environmental auditing scheme, called the Eco-Audit Scheme. It is designed for organizations carrying out industrial activities.

Social matters

Companies are concerned with social matters. It is good business to have an acceptable social policy and to deliver this policy. Many companies now publish social and environmental reports but few attach audit reports to these statements. It is possible to conduct an audit on social, environmental or health and safety matters and to attest to the report to add assurance to its authenticity. Poor social activities carried out by businesses may create risks for them; for example, financing arrangements may not be renewed because of the influence of an ethical investment policy.

The Carbon Disclosure Project is the world's biggest register of corporate greenhouse gas emissions. Climate change is an issue for investors and companies, but most of all for consumers. Since 2002, the Carbon Disclosure Project has been writing annually on behalf of an ever-growing mass of financial muscle to the heads of the *Financial Times* top 500 companies, asking how big a risk climate change poses to their businesses and what they are doing to reduce emissions. Their website summarizes what large companies emit (**www.cdproject.net**).

The following sections cover some specific schemes and standards that exist to provide structure and performance indicators for Corporate Social Responsibility activities.

The European Union Eco-Management and Audit Scheme

The European Union Eco-Management and Audit Scheme (EMAS) is a tool for companies and organisations to use so that they can assess, report on and develop improvements in their environmental performance (**www.iema.net**). The scheme has been open for companies to participate in since 1995 and at first was limited to companies in industrial sectors.

Since 2001, the scheme has been available for all economic sectors covering both the public and private sectors and was further improved by the integration of Environmental Management Systems and the International Organisation for Standardisations accreditation (EN/ISO 14001) as the environmental management system required by the EMAS. Being part of the scheme is not compulsory and covers both public and private enterprises operating in the European Union and the European Union Economic Area. It aims to highlight and benefit enterprises that go further than the minimum legal compliance and regularly develop and improve their environmental performance.

Organizations registered with EMAS are legally compliant, carry out an environment management system and document their environmental performance in an independently verified statement. They can be recognized by the EMAS logo, which reinforces the reliability of the information provided.

To be able to register with the EMAS an enterprise must carry out the following activities: one, carry out an environmental review covering all environmental aspects of the enterprise's activities, both its products and services, its systems to assess them, the regulatory framework and current environmental management practices and procedures. Two, based on the results of the review, the organization must develop an effective environmental management system designed to achieve the organization's environmental targets as determined by the management of the business. The 'management system' is required to set objectives, operational procedures, training needs, monitoring and communication systems. Three, the organization must conduct an environmental audit reviewing the management system's position and consistency with the organization's policy and objectives as well as adherence to appropriate environmental regulatory requirements. Four, it must produce a statement of its environmental performance that states what the company has achieved against its environmental objectives and the steps that will be taken in the future in order to continually develop the organization's environmental performance.

The environmental review, environmental management systems, audit procedure and the environmental statement must be by an accredited EMAS verifier and the validated statement needs to be sent to the Eco-Management and Audit Scheme body for registration and made publicly available before an organization can use the Scheme logo.

The Eco-Management and Audit Scheme gives guidance on what performance indicators to use to enable environmental performance to be evaluated and reported on and produces sample reports and indicators to cover the wide range of areas that may be relevant to businesses.

ICLEI – Local Governments for Sustainability

ICLEI – Local Governments for Sustainability is an international association of local governments and national and regional local government organizations that have joined together to make a commitment to sustainable development.

ICLEI was set up in 1990 as the International Council for Local Environmental Initiatives. The council was set up when in excess of 200 local governments from 43 countries met at its inaugural conference, the World

Congress of Local Governments for a Sustainable Future, at the United Nations in New York.

More than 550 counties, towns and cities plus their associations world-wide make up ICLEI's growing membership. The International Council of Local Environmental Initiatives acts alongside these organizations and hundreds of other local governments through international results-oriented, performance-based campaigns and programmes. The initiative offers train-ing, technical consulting and information services to share knowledge, build capacity and support local government in the introduction of sustainable development at the local level. The organization's basic aim is that locally created programmes can produce an effective and cost-efficient way to attain local, national and global sustainability objectives (**www.iclei.org**).

Global Reporting Initiative: Sustainability Reporting Guidelines

Sustainable development is a procedure that attends to the requirements of the current generation without compromising the future generation's ability to meet their own needs.

The Global Reporting Initiative (GRI) guidelines are a framework that helps an organization to report and monitor on its economic, environmental and social performance. The guidelines provide a structure for the content, quality, standard disclosures and key performance indicators to include in this area (**www.globalreporting.org**).

The objective of the Global Reporting Initiative is to develop a world-wide shared framework of concepts, consistent language and metrics about sustainability. GRI's mission is to fulfil this need by 'providing a trusted and credible framework for sustainability reporting that can be used by organ-isations of any size, sector or location'.

The Global Reporting Initiative has been dependent on the contribution of a large number of experts from a broad variety of stakeholder groups to improve the Reporting Framework from when it was founded in 1997.

The purpose of a sustainability report is to measure, disclose and be accountable to internal and external stakeholders for the performance of an organization towards the aim of sustainable development. 'Sustainability reporting' is a broad term that can be applied to cover reporting on environ-mental, social and economic impacts (also known as the triple bottom line, corporate responsibility reporting, etc).

Sustainability reports using the Global Reporting Initiative Reporting Framework as their basis highlight areas and achievements that were made within the reporting period in line with the organization's strategy, commitments and management approach.

The GRI Reporting Framework follows a procedure that aims at consistency through discussions with stakeholders from businesses, workers, organizations that lend money, society in general, accountants, the academic community and others. All Reporting Framework documents are the subject of testing and continuous improvement. They are aimed at providing a widely accepted framework to enable an organization to report on its environmental, economic and social performance. The framework is set out in such a way that it can be used by enterprises of any sector, size or location. It tries to incorporate the practical factors that a diverse range of organizations face, from small businesses to those with wide-ranging and geographically-dispersed activities. The framework covers general factors and content specific to certain sectors that has been approved by a diverse range of stakeholders throughout the world and is thought to be generally acceptable for reporting on the sustainability performance of an organization.

The Sustainability Reporting Guidelines cover areas to be included in the report and systems to use to ensure the quality of the data. They also provide Standard Disclosures consisting of performance indicators and other areas of disclosure, plus guidance on certain technical topics to cover in the report. The guidelines cover how to report, principles and guidance, protocols and what to report, standard disclosures and sector supplements.

Indicator protocols are provided for every performance indicator contained in the guidelines, covering definitions, compliance advice and other useful information to help those producing the report ensure consistency in how the performance indicators are interpreted.

Sector supplements exist on how to apply the guidelines to a given sector, including sector-specific performance indicators.

Technical protocols have been created to provide guidance on issues in reporting, such as setting the report boundaries. These are to be incorporated with the guidelines and sector supplements and cover issues that face most organizations during the reporting process.

Ethical Trading Initiative

The Ethical Trading Initiative (**www.eti-ten.org**) is an amalgamation of non-governmental organizations, trade union organizations and companies, all of whom have the aim of working together to seek out, improve and publicize what is seen to be good practice in corporate codes of practice that cover supply chain working conditions. The UK government's Department for International Development and the Department for Trade and Industry support this initiative. The initiative's aim is to make significant improvements to the lives of less well-off working people throughout the world by producing and encouraging a set of standards to be used in trade. Its key objective is to make sure that the conditions that workers operate in when producing items for the UK market are up to or exceed international labour standards. It was set up in 1998 when organizations providing clothing and food to consumers in the UK were being targeted with increasing pressure from consumers, non-governmental organizations and trade unions to provide an adequate working environment for the people employed to make the goods they sell. The response by these companies was to adopt a code of practice that stated the expected minimum labour standards they wanted their suppliers to adhere to.

The Ethical Trading Initiative's (ETI) Base Code was developed from International Labour Organization conventions. It consists of nine areas covering freedom of association, choice of employment and the right to collective bargaining. It also covers child labour, safe and hygienic working conditions, working hours, a living wage, non-discrimination, the absence of harsh or inhumane treatment and the provision of regular employment. Members of the ETI are expected to incorporate or adopt the Code. They must all demand, as a precondition for continuing business, that the suppliers they use adhere to agreed standards and have their performance measured.

The ETI, through a rigorous annual reporting and review process, monitors on a regular basis the progression of its members in introducing the Code.

The non-governmental organizations, corporate members and trade unions operate together to try to establish what comprises 'good practice' in the implementation of the Code and then share and promote this good practice. Through experimental projects and research shared through seminars, publications, conferences and the website, good practice is developed. Companies are encouraged to join the ETI, adopt the Base Code and incorporate it into their supply chains. All members must produce and submit progress reports annually on the implementation of activities connected with the Code. Through these reports, it can be seen that significant activity implementing the Code has taken place and that the suppliers used by members are making substantial improvements to their labour practices. Organizations that fail to meet the requirements are asked to leave the

Initiative. Guidelines exist on the format and content of the annual report required, which cover company information, management indicators, assessment, performance input, improvement actions, key performance indicators and comment.

This section emphasizes that a number of standards and initiatives exist but are all quite separate and have different regulations and requirements. No attempt has been made to integrate the standards into the financial statements, so activities in this area carried out by businesses are quite fragmented and inconsistent. Until methods for reporting company performance are amended to include Corporate Social Responsibility activities, businesses will carry out their CSR policies in a way that is thought to be desirable and appropriate at the time, but not necessarily followed through and given serious consideration because it does not have a direct linkage to share prices and ultimately stock market performance. Some businesses, such as Tesco, are trying to link their CSR indicators to remuneration packages, which is at least a start in terms of trying to ensure that organizations and the people who work within them are given the right incentives to carry out these activities effectively.

However, with the growing level of interest and importance placed on CSR activities and with firms like PUMA starting to produce their own environmental profit and loss account it is hopefully only a matter of time before financial statements move towards a more 'triple bottom line' approach. The next chapter looks at the measurement, models and theories of CSR in more detail.

CASE STUDY

A company manufactures chemicals used in the dyeing of fabric at its factory based in a small rural town in North Yorkshire. It employs 350 people and is the largest employer within a 50 mile radius.

The factory is located near a popular tourist location and is surrounded by open countryside.

Discuss

Discuss the social responsibilities of this business.

Bibliography

Baker, M (2003) Doing it small, *Ethical Corporation Magazine*, 20 August

Bowen, H (1953) *Social Responsibilities of the Businessman*, Harper, London

Carroll, AB (1979) A three-dimensional conceptual model of corporate performance', *Academy of Management Review*, **4**, pp 497–505

Carroll, AB (1981) *Business and Society: Managing corporate social performance*, Little Brown and Company, Boston

Carroll, AB (1991) The pyramid of Corporate Social Responsibility: Toward the moral management of organisational stakeholders, *Business Horizons*, July–August

Carroll, AB (1999) Corporate Social Responsibility: Evolution of a definitional construct, *Business and Society*, **38** (3) September, pp 268–295

Carroll, AB and Buchholtz, AK (2006) *Business and Society: Ethics and stakeholders management*, 6th edition, South-Western, Mason, OH

Carroll, AB and Shabana, KM (2010) The business case for Corporate Social Responsibility: A review of concepts, research and practice, *International Journal of Management Reviews*, **12** (1), pp 85–105

CIMA (2011) *Financial Management*, July/August

Davis, K and Blomstrom, RL (1966) *Business and its Environment*, McGraw Hill, New York

Elkington, J (1994) Toward the sustainable corporation: Win-win-win business strategies for sustainable development, *California Management Review*, **36** (2), pp 90–100

Elkington, J (1998) *Cannibals with Forks: The triple bottom line of 21st century business*, Capstone, Mankato, MN

Elkins, A (1977) Toward a positive theory of corporate social involvement, *Academy of Management Review*, **2**, pp 128–133

EU (2001) Promoting a European Framework for Corporate Social Responsibility, Green Paper, 18 July

European Multi-stakeholder Forum on Corporate Social Responsibility (2004) Final Results and Recommendations, available at: Europa.eu.int/com/enterprise/Corporate Social Responsibility/index_forum.htm

Frankental, P (2001) Corporate Social Responsibility: A PR invention?, *Corporate Communications: An International Journal*, **6** (1), pp 18–23

Frederick, W (1960) The growing concern over business responsibility, *California Management Review*, **2** (4), pp 54–61

Frederick, WC, Post, JE and Davis, K (1992) *Business and Society: Corporate strategy, public policy, ethics*, 7th edition, McGraw Hill, Maidenhead

Freeman, RE and Reed, DL (1983) Stockholders and stakeholders: A new perspective on corporate governance, *California Management Review*, **25** (Spring)

Friedman, M (1962) *Capitalism and Freedom*, University of Chicago Press, Chicago

Friedman, M (1970) The social responsibility of business is to increase its profits, *The New York Times Magazine*, 13 September, pp 1–6

Friedman, M (1982) *Capitalism and Freedom*, 2nd edition, University of Chicago Press, Chicago

GRI (nd) Sustainability Guidelines Version 3 [Online] https://www.globalreporting.org/resourcelibrary/G3-Sustainability-Reporting-Guidelines.pdf

Griseri, P and Seppala, N (2010) *Business Ethics and Corporate Social Responsibility*, Cengage Learning EMEA, Hampshire

Jones, TM (1980) Corporate Social Responsibility revisited, redefined, *California Management Review*, pp 59–67

Kakabadse, NK, Rozuel, L and Lee, DL (2005) Corporate Social Responsibility and stakeholder approach: A conceptual review, *International Journal of Business Governance and Ethics*, 1 (4), pp 207–301

KPMG (2005) *International Survey of Corporate Responsibility Reporting 2005*, KPMG

KPMG (2008) *International Survey of Corporate Responsibility Reporting 2008*, KPMG

KPMG (2011) *International Survey of Corporate Responsibility Reporting 2011*, KPMG

Lee, AS (1991) Integrating positivist and interpretive approaches to organisational research, *Organisation Science*, 2 (4) November, pp 342–365

Lee, MP (2008) A review of the theories of Corporate Social Responsibility: Its evolutionary path and the road ahead, *International Journal of Management Reviews* doi: 10.1111/j.1468-2370.2007.00226.x

Rizk, R, Dixon, R and Woodhead, A (2008) Corporate social and environmental reporting: A survey of disclosure practices in Egypt, *Social Responsibility Journal*, 4 (3), pp 306–323

Sethi, S. (1975) Dimensions of corporate social performance: An analytical famework, *California Management Review*, 17 (3) spring, pp 58–64

Smith, NC (2003) Corporate Social Responsibility: Whether or how?, *California Management Review*, 45 (4), pp 52–76

Van Der Laan Smith, J, Adhikari, A and Tondkar, RH (2005) Exploring differences in social disclosures internally: A stakeholder perspective, *Journal of Accounting and Public Policy*, 24, pp 123–151

White, AL (2006) Business brief: Intangibles and Corporate Social Responsibility, *Business for Social Responsibility*, February

Wood, DJ (1990) *Business and Society*, Scott, Foresman/Little, Brown Higher Education, Glenview, IL

World Bank (nd) *Corporate Environmental Responsibility: Is a common Corporate Social Responsibility framework possible?* Poitr Mazurkiewicz, DevComm-SDO

Websites

www.bsr.org
www.bvt.org.uk
www.eti-ten.org
www.globalreporting.org
www.iclei.org
www.iema.net/ems/emas
www.jrf.org.uk
www.kpmg.co.uk
www.wbcsd.org

Corporate Social Responsibility, its measurement, theories and models

10

LEARNING OBJECTIVES

The material in this chapter covers:

- CSR measurement
- CSR theories:
  - stakeholder theory;
  - legitimacy theory;
  - political economy theory.
- CSR models:
  - three concentric circles;
  - corporate social performance;
  - pyramid of social responsibility;
  - triple bottom line;
  - United Nations Global Compact, ISO Series, SA8000, Accountability 1000;
  - Global Reporting Initiative.

Introduction

The previous chapter introduced the concept of CSR, its importance, link to corporate governance, definition and history. This chapter discusses methods of measuring it and some of the models and theories surrounding it.

Corporate Social Responsibility measurement

The measurement of Corporate Social Responsibility has numerous standards – the Global Reporting Initiative, AA 1000, ISO 14001, OHSAS 18001, Dow Jones Sustainability Index, the Domini Social Index 400 to name but a few (World Bank, nd: 6).

In 2000, PricewaterhouseCoopers developed a 'reputational assurance framework' that 'enables companies to identify, measure and manage their corporate responsibility and accountability processes' (PwC 2010).

Some of the standards and initiatives that exist, such as the Global Reporting Initiative, ISO 14001 and the Ethical Trading Initiative (as discussed in the previous chapter), provide guidelines to organizations on how to act in a socially responsible manner and how they can report on their activities in this area. This leads to being able to research how companies report on their Corporate Social Responsibility activities and being able to measure this using an appropriate framework as a reference point (**www.globalreporting.org, www.british-accreditation.co.uk, www.eti-ten.org**).

Many companies have been forced by public opinion or legislation to improve their environmental performance. There have been a number of professional pronouncements in this area. For example, in May 1995 the International Federation of Accountants (IFAC) issued a discussion paper, 'The audit profession and the environment'. In 1998 they issued an 'International Auditing Practice Statement (IAPS) 1010: The consideration of environmental matters in the audit of financial statements'. In 2000 the UK's Institute of Chartered Accountants in England and Wales issued a discussion paper, 'Environmental issues in the audit of financial statements'. In February 2006 IFAC issued 'Assurance aspects of G3 – The Global Reporting Initiatives 2006 draft sustainability reporting guidelines' (**www.globalreporting.org**).

These tools can be used to measure and report on Corporate Social Responsibility activities and they have arisen from the theories and models devised by academics that have helped to develop the concept of Corporate Social Responsibility, which are discussed below.

Corporate Social Responsibility theories

The following theories attempt to explain the practice and motivation of companies to produce CSR disclosures.

Stakeholder theory

Stakeholder theory plays an important role in understanding the relationship that exists between business and society. Gray, Owen and Adams define a stakeholder as:

> Any human agency that can be influenced by, or can itself influence,
> the activities of the organisation in question.
>
> (Gray, Owen and Adams, 1996: 45)

Two types of stakeholders can be identified from the definition above – primary and secondary stakeholders. Primary stakeholders can have a direct impact on the business and its activities. They are driven by the market (employees, competitors, customers, suppliers, stockholders, creditors). Secondary stakeholders are those groups of stakeholders who are directly or indirectly influenced by the secondary impact and involvement of a company's activities (local communities, media, public) (Post *et al*, 1996).

This theory highlights that an organization can have many different stakeholders, such as employees, customers, the government, communities, suppliers, competitors, shareholders etc. It also emphasizes the point that the financial performance of an organization depends on good stakeholder management rather than just focusing on the shareholders of the company. The concept that businesses have responsibility towards a wider group of stakeholders completely contradicts the viewpoint of Friedman (1970) who argued that the firm's only responsibility was towards its shareholders, ie the owners of the company.

Stakeholder theory provides a system-based view of an organization and its environment that makes a distinction between two variants. The first variant looks at the complex relationship that exists between business and society and how business and society interact with each other by considering the responsibility and accountability of the business towards its stakeholders. The second variant is linked with 'empirical accountability' where stakeholders are identified by the organisation itself rather than society as suggested by the accountability framework. Therefore according to this variant the kind of relationship that exists between the organization and its stakeholders depends on the self-interest of the organization. More effort will be exerted in managing the relationship with stakeholders who are considered to be more important for the success of the organization. Within the managerial perspective of this theory, information is an important component, whether it relates to accounting information or CSR information that can be employed by the company to either manage or manipulate its stakeholders to gain their approval and support (Gray, Owen and Adams, 1996). However, there is often conflict of interest between different stakeholder groups. For example, employees would be interested in a safe working environment, which is an extra cost, whereas shareholders would be interested in profit maximization, which expects reduction in costs, so it can be clearly seen that the interests of these two groups contradict each other. If a company is faced with this kind of situation then it is up to the company to decide which stakeholder group would take priority.

Legitimacy theory

Legitimacy theory is a development on the second variant of the stakeholder theory. Many companies use this theory as a motivation to report on their social and environmental activities. According to this theory an organization can only continue to exist if the society in which it operates scrutinizes that it is behaving adequately according to the values that society holds (Gray, Owen and Adams, 1996). Empirically the results about this legitimacy perspective are mixed. A number of studies such as by Deegan, Rankin and Tobin (2002) support this legitimacy perspective, whereas some believe that legitimacy is not sufficient enough in explaining the levels of CSR disclosures by companies (Guthrie and Parker, 1989). Despite being widely used within literature, Suchman argued that this theory has rarely been defined. In an overview of the literature he defined it as:

> Legitimacy is a generalized perception or assumption that the actions of an entity are desirable, proper, or appropriate within some socially constructed system of norms, values, beliefs, and definitions.
>
> (Suchman, 1995: 574)

Like stakeholder theory, legitimacy theory also has two variants. The first variant looks at the legitimacy of the individual organization. The second variant involves the organization as a whole and is known as institutional legitimacy. An organization can face many threats to their legitimization. To avoid these threats Lindblom (1994) suggested four strategies that organizations can adopt. First, show its stakeholders the changes the organization has made to its activities to improve its current performance. Second, attempt to change the perception of the public about certain events without actually changing the performance of the organization. Third, attempt to manipulate perception by moving attention away from the issue of concern to something else. Fourth, attempt to change external perception about their performance.

Political economy theory

Political economy theory is another important theory that is used by companies as a motivational tool to report on their Corporate Social Responsibility activities. According to Gray, Owen and Adams:

> The political economy is the social, political and economic framework within which human life takes place.
>
> (Gray, Owen and Adams, 1996: 47)

This theory also consists of two variants – the 'classical' variant and the 'bourgeois'. The classical variant provides a direct insight into the mandatory disclosure rules that are imposed by the government and enables stakeholders to understand general trends in CSR. According to Gray, Owen and Adams (1996) the bourgeois variant is more helpful in understanding why companies would not disclose information about their CSR activities. The main difference between the two variants as highlighted by Gray, Owen and Adams (1996) is that classical political economy includes structural conflict, inequality and the role of the government in the analysis, whereas bourgeois political economy takes such things as given and excludes them from the issue.

As evidenced above, there are numerous reasons why companies would disclose information about their CSR activities, as suggested by Deegan, Rankin and Tobin – 'there could be a variety of motivations for managers to voluntarily undertake certain activities' (2002: 312) – but it is really down to what individual companies want to gain from making such disclosures. Whatever the reason may be, companies do not have to disclose information on their Corporate Social Responsibility activities but might be able to gain many benefits from doing so, such as build sales, develop the workforce, boost innovation and enthusiasm, enhance trust, attract and retain staff and increase reputation (**www.hse.gov.uk**).

Although there are benefits associated with Corporate Social Responsibility reporting it does not necessarily mean that they will actually happen, which means it can be difficult to motivate companies to disclose such information. Many companies are still unsure about what should and should not be included in their CSR reports to gain the most benefit.

Corporate Social Responsibility models

There are numerous indices used as a proxy for corporate social performance, such as KLD (Kinder, Lyndenberg and Domini) evaluation, Fortune Reputation Rating (Margolis and Walsh 2003), Dow Jones Sustainability Index (DJSI), Dow Jones Sustainability Global Index (DJSGI), the Living Planet Index (LPI), Ecological Footprint (EF), City Development Index (CDI), Human Development Index (HDI), Environmental Sustainability Index (ESI), Environmental Performance Index (EPI) (Böhringer, 2007) and many others. There are also a number of sustainability reporting frameworks such as the Global Reporting Initiative (GRI), ISO 14031 Standard, World Business Council for Sustainable Development (WBCSD), the Global Environmental Management Initiative (GEMI), and the Coalition for Environmentally Responsible Economies (CERES) (Hussey, Kirsop and Meissen, 2001), which can be used both for reporting and evaluation of corporate social performance.

Hussey, Kirsop and Meissen (2001) evaluated companies' reports prepared under the frameworks mentioned above for sustainable development. This study showed that:

> measuring companies against principles of sustainable development such as those of CERES or GEMI is an inadequate method for differentiating companies' performance. These principles are too high-level and too general to provide the detail necessary for adequate measurement.
>
> (Hussey, Kirsop and Meissen, 2001: 17)

They also concluded that the Global Reporting Initiative is in fact the best available framework for reporting all aspects of sustainable development.

As Corporate Social Responsibility has been subject to heavy research since the 1950s this has led to the creation and development of various CSR models.

Three concentric circles

One of the early models was proposed by the Committee of Economic Development (1971), which viewed the Corporate Social Responsibility process as having 'three concentric circles', with each circle demonstrating different levels of commitment by the corporations. The inner circle covered economic functions, the very basic responsibilities of the business being provision of jobs, production of goods and contribution to the economic growth, and were classified necessary for it to carry out its economic function efficiently. The intermediate circle represented that the responsibility of the business was to accomplish this economic function and at the same time have an awareness of its environment and social values. The outer circle represented what can still be called emerging responsibilities of the business, which are to be actively involved in the betterment of social environment (Carroll, 1991).

Corporate social performance

During the 1970s there was a move towards finding a more specific definition of the term Corporate Social Responsibility. Over a period of time CSR was represented in many different contexts by academics such that Sethi (1975: 58) argued that the phrase Corporate Social Responsibility has lost its meaning and 'it has come to mean all things to all people'. He stated that there was a need for a structured framework that provides a stable classification and meaning of corporate social activities so that comparisons can be made over time and across industries and nations. To achieve this objective he introduced a model to describe various different elements of CSR that could be applicable to all industries and institutions. He labelled this model 'corporate social performance' and explained that corporate behaviour can be defined in three phrases as social obligation, social responsibility and social responsiveness.

First, he looked at corporate behaviour as a social obligation, which suggests that corporations must adhere to standard compliance rules imposed by the social system within which it operates. Second, he looked at corporate behaviour as social responsibility and stated that social responsibilities of corporations are to go beyond the minimum legal requirements and achieve a level that is expected of them in accordance with 'social norms, values and expectations of performance' (Sethi, 1975). Finally, he viewed corporate behaviour as social responsiveness according to which corporations adopt changes in their own behaviour and actions in line with social concerns raised by their own activities within the market place. Carroll (1979) built on from Sethi's model and introduced a four-part model of Corporate Social Responsibility in the form of a pyramid.

Pyramid of social responsibility

Carroll (1991) characterized the firm's Corporate Social Responsibility in ways that might be useful to executives who wish to reconcile their obligations to their shareholders with those to other competing groups claiming legitimacy. He devised a pyramid with four categories, namely economic, legal, ethical and philanthropic responsibilities (Carroll, 1991).

According to Carroll the first and foremost responsibility of business is to produce and sell goods and services that society wants, and to generate profits out of them. This is the economic responsibility of business. The second responsibility of business is to obey the law; according to this rule society expects that business should achieve its economic goals within the legal framework laid down by the society's legal system. The third responsibility represented by Carroll is 'ethical responsibility', which expects business to go beyond its legal responsibilities and adopt those norms and behaviours that are expected by society but are not required by law. The fourth responsibility discussed by Carroll is the philanthropic responsibility, such as making charitable contributions, making contributions to society and community welfare. Such responsibilities are voluntary in nature, meaning that they are carried out as a desire of the business to be involved in such activities rather than being mandatory, legally required or being part of ethical expectations. Thus he represented four different components of CSR, which when taken together make up the whole of Corporate Social Responsibility.

Carroll's model has been the most durable and widely cited in the literature because it is simple, easy to understand and has an intuitively appealing logic. Over the 25 years since Carroll first proposed the model it has frequently been reproduced in top management and Corporate Social Responsibility journals, mostly by Carroll himself. The model has been cited over 1,320 times and as recently as 1 March 2011 in *Business and Society* (**www.bas.sagepub.com**). Carroll has sought to assimilate various competing themes into his model, eg corporate citizenship and stakeholders. The model has been empirically tested and largely supported by the findings. The model incorporates and gives top priority to the economic dimension as an aspect of Corporate Social Responsibility, which may endear business scholars and practitioners.

Triple bottom line

Following on from models such as those developed by Carroll, 1991, the triple bottom line (abbreviated as TBL or 3BL, and also known as 'people, planet, profit') captures an expanded spectrum of values and criteria for measuring organizational (and societal) success: economic, ecological and social. With the ratification of the United Nations and ICLEI TBL standard for urban and community accounting in early 2007, this became the dominant approach to public sector full cost accounting. Similar UN standards apply to natural capital and human capital measurement to assist in measurements required by TBL, eg the ecoBudget standard for reporting ecological footprint (**www.iclei.org**).

In the private sector, a commitment to Corporate Social Responsibility implies a commitment to some form of TBL reporting. This is distinct from the more limited changes required to deal only with ecological issues.

In practical terms, triple bottom line accounting means expanding the traditional reporting framework to take into account ecological and social performance in addition to financial performance.

The phrase 'triple bottom line' was coined by John Elkington in 1994. It was later expanded and articulated in his 1998 book *Cannibals with Forks: the Triple Bottom Line of 21st Century Business*. Sustainability itself was first defined by the Brundtland Commission of the United Nations in 1987 (**www.iclei.org**).

The concept of TBL demands that a company's responsibility be to stakeholders rather than shareholders. In this case, 'stakeholders' refers to anyone who is influenced, either directly or indirectly, by the actions of the firm. According to the stakeholder theory, the business entity should be used as a vehicle for coordinating stakeholder interests, instead of maximizing shareholder (owner) profit (Elkington, 1994).

UN Global Compact

In recent years, questions relating to Corporate Social Responsibility have developed into a global policy issue. This gave rise to the establishment of the United Nations Global Compact (UNGC). The aim of the UNGC is to ensure minimum standards of 'good corporate conduct' are implemented and the socio-economic development of poorer countries are protected (Fritsch, 2008). United Nations Secretary General Kofi Annan introduced the Global Compact in the 1990s as a voluntary corporate citizenship initiative. Firms are asked to commit publicly to it, making the Global Compact and its principles part of the strategy, culture and day-to-day operations of their company. They must also undertake to make a clear statement of this commitment both to their employees, clients, partners and the public (Kilgour, 2007). It is the world's largest CSR initiative and is designed to advance responsible corporate citizenship with voluntary participation. By 2008 there were over 3,000 participating companies and stakeholders from more than 100 countries around the world (Orbie and Babarinde, 2008).

The Global Compact represents an ambitious initiative between UN, business and civil society actors to address the widely perceived dark sides of economic globalization (Fritsch, 2008). It is a strategic policy initiative for businesses that are committed to aligning their operations and strategies with ten universally accepted principles in the areas of human rights, labour, environment and anti-corruption (Williams, 2004; Runhaar and Lafferty, 2008; UN Global Compact, 2011; Gilbert, Rasche and Waddock, 2011). According to Ovum (2010), the Global Compact represents a global frame of reference for what Corporate Social Responsibility implies for the business community. It is a voluntary initiative, and by joining, an enterprise signals that it is striving to improve in relevant fields.

Following on from the Global Compact, several tools and documents have been generated to reinforce complementary initiatives and a learning environment on business social responsibility (Ashley, 2011). The Global Compact is a pact between the United Nations and global businesses on corporate behaviour (Clapp, 2005). The main objectives of the Global Compact are to 'mainstream' environmental and social issues into operations of business, and to encourage business to take action in support of the UN goals.

However, as it is a voluntary initiative, the Global Compact has been widely criticized by non-governmental organizations as being inadequate to bring about sufficient change in business practice (Clapp, 2005). Critics also contend that the principles of the UN Global Compact remain too vague and, without external verification mechanisms, allow companies too easily to claim compliance (Hartman and Painter-Morland, 2007).

The UN Global Compact is also part of the first category of international accountability standards referred to as principle-based standards. According to Gilbert, Rasche and Waddock (2011), these sets of principles aim at helping to shape corporate behaviours by providing a baseline or floor of foundational values and principles that responsible companies can attempt to live by. Voluntary CSR initiatives such as the UN Global Compact represent a set of efforts that achieves new global reach for national governments, the business community, and the international public sector (Arevalo and Fallon, 2008).

ISO series

The International Organization for Standardization (ISO) issued the 14000 series (1997), modified (2002), as an Environmental Management System (EMS) standard. The aim of this was to introduce consistency in reporting, enabling external parties to make judgements and assess trends. With the implementation of this standard there is a shift from compliance and end-of-pipe command and control approaches, to one of prevention and continual improvement with the focus on the company (Mathews and Reynolds, 2000). The EMS model includes requirements for management commitment to an environmental policy, including specifications for organizational responsibility and personnel, programme implementation, control procedures, emergency preparedness, verification and review, documentation and communications (Reynolds and Yuthas, 2008).

The ISO 14000 family of standards establishes a reference model for the implementation of company environmental management systems, defined as those parts of global management systems that describe the organizational structure, planning activities, responsibilities, practices, procedures, processes and resources for preparing, applying, reviewing and maintaining company environmental policies (Casadesus, Marimon and Heras, 2008). As noted by Mathews and Reynolds (2000), ISO 14000 is a specification standard and provides requirements against which an organization can be measured.

The ISO series, according to Hartman and Painter-Morland (2007), includes a number of standards; those that deal directly with external reporting include the ISO 14001 (which is the model adopted by organizations for their environmental management system), the ISO 14004 (which extends the definition of environmental management systems to include a general framework for external auditing); and ISO 14031 (a process by which companies can assess and report on their environmental behaviour).

In recent years, the number of available management system standards (MSSs) with an international and universally applicable character has increased substantially (Bernado, Casadesus and Heras, 2009). It is widely known that these standards began with the creation of the ISO 9000 family for quality management in 1987 and continued with the ISO 14000 series for environmental management in 1996 (Bernado, Casadesus and Heras, 2009).

Following a growing interest in Corporate Social Responsibility, the ISO announced plans for development of the ISO 26000 – guidance standard for social responsibility (Castka and Balzarova, 2008). The ISO 26000 was published in November 2010 and is the result of a five-year global discussion involving multi-stakeholder committees from more than 90 countries in the working group (Ashley, 2011). The ISO 26000 standard was based on seven core subjects, namely organizational governance, human rights, labour practices, the environment, fair operating practices, consumer issues and community involvement and development (Valmohammadi, 2011). Despite initial signals that ISO 26000 will be built on the intellectual and practical infrastructure of ISO 9000 and ISO 14000, the Advisory Group on Social Responsibility set a different direction: a guidance standard and not a specification standard against which conformity can be assessed (Castka and Balzarova, 2008). In Europe, for instance, fields that it covered in order to promote CSR practices include codes of conduct, management standards, Corporate Social Responsibility measurement and reporting (using the Global Reporting Initiative), labels such as eco-label and fair trade, and socially responsible investment (Gorban, Johnson, and Preissler, 2009).

It is in this light that the ISO 26000 guidelines were introduced, with the aim of assisting organizations and their network in addressing their social responsibilities and providing practical guidance related to operationalizing social responsibility, identifying and engaging with stakeholders and enhancing credibility of reports and claims made about social responsibility (Castka and Balzarova, 2008). However, in identifying one of the weaknesses of ISO 26000, Veleva (2010) noted that while ISO 26000 defines what social responsibility is, it does not provide specific guidance for companies in different sectors, which is critical for identifying key impacts and sustainable strategies.

SA8000

The SA8000 is the first international certification on social responsibility (Puri and Singh, 2007). It was created in 1997 by the Social Accountability Institute (SAI) which is a not-for-profit, non-governmental organization. Social Accountability 8000 (SA8000) is a uniform and auditable standard based on a commitment to establishing a cross-industry standard for workplace conditions and independent verification (Hartman and Painter-Morland, 2007). Its main objective is to guarantee workers' rights in such a way that everyone involved wins: companies, workers, trade unions, government (Puri and Singh, 2007).

The SA8000 is a global social accounting standard based on the universal Declaration of Human Rights Convention on the Rights of the Child and the various International Labour Organization Conventions (Dagiliene and Gokiene, 2011). The standard requirement, SA8000, is a management system that can be implemented in each country and sector (Juscius and Snieska, 2008). SA8000 standard has a change in focus and is concerned with fair labour practices worldwide. According to Reynolds and Yuthas (2008), the SA8000 is divided into purpose and scope, normative elements and their interpretation, definitions, and social accountability requirements.

Accountability 1000

The Accountability 1000 series, developed in 1999, concentrates on improving the accountability and overall performance of organizations by way of increasing the quality of social and ethical accounting, auditing and reporting (Hartman and Painter-Morland, 2007). The AA1000 standard provides both a framework that organizations can use to understand and improve their ethical performance and a means to judge the validity of ethical claims made. It offers a methodological framework to link new demands for accountability and transparency by stakeholders through consultation and measurement in order to build new understanding of sustainability in organizational performance (Juscius and Snieska, 2008). It helps organizations build their accountability and social responsibility through quality social and ethical accounting, auditing and reporting (Srivastava and Sahay, 2007). The AA1000 comprises principles and a set of process standards covering planning, accounting, auditing and reporting, embedding, and stakeholder engagement (Mathews and Reynolds, 2000).

The focus of the AA1000 is on improving overall performance through measurement, quality management, recruitment and retention of employees, external stakeholder engagement, partnership, risk management, investors, governance, government and regulatory relations and training (Reynolds and Yuthas, 2008). The AA1000 Assurance Standard complements the Global Reporting Initiative in that it provides an outline for independent third parties to assure and audit sustainability reporting (Hartman and Painter-Morland, 2007).

Global Reporting Initiative

The Global Reporting Initiative guidelines are a more comprehensive framework that helps an organization to report and monitor on its economic, environmental and social performance. The guidelines provide a structure for the content, quality, standard disclosures and key performance indicators to include in this area as discussed in the previous chapter (**www.globalreporting.org**).

Clearly a large number of companies are taking Corporate Social Responsibility activities more seriously and investing money and resources into introducing CSR policies and measuring CSR performance. The data established by KPMG's international survey on Corporate Social Responsibility and the fact that PUMA has taken steps to measure its own environmental impact highlight the fact that businesses are investing more time and effort into CSR issues and that social responsibility is on most businesses' agendas today. Some of the Corporate Social Responsibility activity may well be legitimate; however, a lot of it can be contradicted by stories in the media highlighting activities that are contrary to the bold statements and promises produced.

As evidenced above there is a large increase in corporate social reporting by companies but a key question is: what motivates companies to generate such reports despite it being mostly voluntary in nature? There could be many reasons behind this, such as maintaining a good reputation, increased profitability, peer pressure, to keep government at arm's length etc, but as yet there is no definite answer.

A lot of research has been conducted to investigate the motivation behind companies making such disclosures. Thien, Tregida and Kearins (2009) carried out research on financial services institutions in New Zealand to find out what motivates them to report on their CSR activities and concluded that there was a high rationale between Corporate Social Responsibility and the business case as compared with other motivations.

However, Ven and Graafland (2006) argued that 'the profit motive is not the only reason to contribute to Corporate Social Responsibility' and carried out research on 111 Dutch companies to find out what motive is more important for these companies: a strategic motive, which is linked with long-term financial success of the company, or a moral motive, which sees Corporate Social Responsibility as a moral obligation. They concluded that there is a positive correlation in both dimensions. They also found out that there was a weak relationship between the strategic motive behind CSR and actual efforts performed by the companies.

Gamerschlag, Moller and Veerbeten concluded from their research that the main motive behind companies making Corporate Social Responsibility disclosures is to 'reduce potential regulation and taxation' (Gamerschlag, Moller and Veerbeten, 2010: 24) and they also highlighted that the type of CSR disclosures made by companies are also affected by the company size and the industry they operate in. For example, companies from consumer and energy industries will disclose more information about their CSR activities as compared with companies from service industries.

A survey carried out by KPMG highlighted that the main driver for companies to report on their CSR activities was to improve their internal processes (KPMG, 2011).

Currently all such activities are voluntary with a view that they will have some impact on financial performance but not something which is specifically and directly measurable. Until methods for reporting company performance are amended to include Corporate Social Responsibility activities, businesses will carry out their CSR policies in a way that is thought to be desirable and appropriate at the time, but not necessarily followed through and given serious consideration because it does not have a direct linkage to share prices and ultimately stock market performance. If shareholders and share price performance are affected by a decision this will clearly take priority over Corporate Social Responsibility activities.

A useful statement to highlight the growth and importance of Corporate Social Responsibility policies is:

> In today's market where only twenty-five percent of FTSE 100 value is backed by tangible assets, maximising value for shareholders means managing and building reputation, as well as minimising reputation risk. Understanding and relating to stakeholders is a key part of that reputation management. Corporate Social Responsibility, then, is more than a 'nice to have,' more than a public relations exercise – it's part of running a modern business effectively.
>
> (Hoskins, 2005)

Businesses are beginning to recognize this but until more weight and legal emphasis is given to this area, it will not be given the priority and importance it deserves to protect the environment, resources and individuals affected by company's activities.

CASE STUDY

Discuss

- Suggest ways in which a haulage company could reduce its environmental footprint.

Triple bottom line accounting (TBL) implies that businesses should consider the full cost of their activities on the environment and community that they operate in whilst at the same time considering their contribution to sustainability.

- Consider whether the growth in a haulage business is sustainable in terms of TBL accounting in areas of:
  - economic sustainability;
  - environmental sustainability;
  - social sustainability.

Bibliography

Arevalo, J and Fallon, F (2008) Assessing corporate responsibility as a contribution to global governance: The case of the UN Global Compact, *Corporate Governance*, 8 (4), pp 456–470

Ashley, PA (2011) The master model on multi-actor and multilevel social responsibilities: A conceptual framework for policies and governance on stakeholders' social responsibilities, Working Paper 512, International Institute of Social Studies

Beavis, S [accessed 21 September 2012] Puma: business and the environment – counting the cost, *The Guardian* [Online] http://www.guardian.co.uk/sustainable-business/best-practice-exchange/puma-impact-environment-counting-cost

Bernado, M, Casadesus, M and Heras, I (2009) Management systems integrated audits: An empirical study, 3rd International Conference on Industrial Engineering and Industrial Management, Barcelona, September

Böhringer, C and Jochem, PE (2007) Measuring the immeasurable: A survey of sustainability indices, *Ecological Economics*, **63**, pp 1–8

Carroll, AB (1979) A three-dimensional conceptual model of corporate performance, *Academy of Management Review*, **4**, pp 497–505

Carroll, AB (1981) *Business and Society: Managing corporate social performance*, Little Brown and Company, Boston

Carroll, AB (1991) The pyramid of Corporate Social Responsibility: Toward the moral management of organisational stakeholders, *Business Horizons*, July–August

Carroll, AB (1999) Corporate Social Responsibility: Evolution of a definitional construct, *Business and Society*, **38** (3) September, pp 268–295

Carroll, AB and Buchholtz, AK (2006) *Business and Society: Ethics and stakeholders management*, 6th edition, South-Western, Mason, OH

Carroll, AB and Shabana, KM (2010) The business case for Corporate Social Responsibility: A review of concepts, research and practice, *International Journal of Management Reviews*, **12** (1), pp 85–105

Casadesus, M, Marimon, F and Heras, I (2008) ISO 14001 diffusion after the success of the ISO 9001 Model, *Journal of Cleaner Production*, **16**, pp 1741–1754

Castka, P and Balzarova, M (2008) ISO 26000 and supply chains: On the diffusion of the social responsibility standard, *International Journal of Production Economics*, **III**, pp 274–286

CIMA (2011) *Financial Management*, July/August

Clapp, J (2005) Global environmental governance for corporate responsibility, *Global Governance Politics*, **5** (3), August

Dagiliene, L and Gokiene, R (2011) Valuation of Corporate Social Responsibility reports, *Economics and Management*, 16, pp 21–27

Deegan, C, Rankin, M and Tobin, J (2002) An examination of the corporate social and environmental disclosures of BHP from 1983–1997: A test of legitimacy theory, *Accounting, Auditing and Accountability Journal*, **15** (3), pp 312–343

Economist Survey (2005) The Good Company, *The Economist*, 20 January

Elkington, J (1994) Toward the sustainable corporation: Win-win-win business strategies for sustainable development, *California Management Review*, **36** (2), pp 90–100

Elkington, J (1998) *Cannibals with Forks: The triple bottom line of 21st century business*, New Society Publishers, Gabriola Island, BC, Canada

European Union (EU) (2001) Promoting a European framework for Corporate Social Responsibility, Green Paper, 18 July

European Multi-stakeholder Forum on Corporate Social Responsibility (2004) Final results and recommendations, European Commission, Brussels

Frankental, P (2001) Corporate Social Responsibility: A PR invention?, *Corporate Communications: An International Journal*, **6** (1), pp 18–23

Frederick, WC, Post, JE and Davis, K (1992) *Business and Society: Corporate strategy, public policy, ethics*, 7th edition, McGraw Hill, Maidenhead

Friedman, M (1970) The social responsibility of business is to increase its profits, *New York Times Magazine*, 13 September, pp 1–6

Friedman, M (1982) *Capitalism and Freedom*, 2nd edition, University of Chicago Press, Chicago

Fritsch, S (2008) The UN Global Compact and the Global governance of CSR: Complex multilateralism for a more human globalization, *Global Society*, **22** (1), pp 1–26

Gamerschlag, R, Moller, K and Veerbeten, R (2010) Determinants of voluntary Corporate Social Responsibility disclosure: Empirical evidence from Germany, *Review of Managerial Science*, **4** (2–3)

Gilbert, D, Rasche, A and Waddock, S (2011) Accountability in a global economy: The emergence of international accountability standards, *Business Ethics Quarterly*, **21** (1)

Global Environmental Management Initiative [accessed 21 September 2012] *What is GEMI?* [Online] http://www.gemi.org/AboutGEMI.aspx

Gorban, M, Johnson, M and Preissler, S (2009) EU Communication on Corporate Social Responsibility and the effects on national and corporate sustainability agendas, *Economic and Environmental Studies*, **9** (1) December, pp 75–92

Gray, R, Owen, D and Adams, C (1996) *Accounting and Accountability: Changes and challenges in corporate social and environmental reporting*, Prentice Hall Europe, Hertfordshire

Gray, SJ (2005) Towards a theory of cultural influence on the development of accounting systems internationally, *ABACUS*, **24** (1)

GRI (nd) Sustainability Guidelines Version 3 [Online] https://www.globalreporting.org/resourcelibrary/G3-Sustainability-Reporting-Guidelines.pdf

Griseri, P and Seppala, N (2010) *Business Ethics and Corporate Social Responsibility*, Cengage Learning EMEA, Hampshire

Guthrie, J and Parker, D (1989) Corporate social reporting: A rebuttal of legitimacy theory, *Accounting and Business Research*, **19** (76), pp 343–352

Guthrie, J and Parker, LD (1990) Corporate social disclosure practice: A competitive international analysis, *Advances in Public Interest Accounting*, **3**, pp 21–45

Hartman, L and Painter-Morland, M (2007) Exploring the Global Reporting Initiative (GRI) guidelines as a model for triple bottom-line reporting, *African Journal of Business Ethics*, **2** (1)

Hopkins, M (1991) The Planetary Bargain: Corporate Social Responsibility matters, Earthscan, Abingdon

Hopkins, M (2006) What is corporate responsibility all about?, *Journal of Public Affairs*, Aug–Nov, pp 298–306, doi 10.1102/pa.238

Hoskins, T (2005) Corporate Social Responsibility, *Chartered Secretary's Magazine*, August 2005

Human Development Reports [accessed 21 September 2012] Human Development Index and its components [Online] http://hdr.undp.org/en/media/HDR_2011_EN_Table1.pdf

Hussey, J and Hussey, R (1997) *Business Research: A practical guide for undergraduate and postgraduate students*, Macmillan, London

Hussey, DM, Kirsop, PL and Meissen, RE (2001) Global reporting initiative guidelines: An evaluation of sustainable development metrics for industry, *Environment Quality Management*, **11**, pp 1–20

Institute of Chartered Accountants in England and Wales (2000) *Environmental issues in the audit of financial statements*, ICAEW, London

International Federation of Accountants (1995) *The audit profession and the environment*, IFAC, London

International Federation of Accountants (1998) *International Auditing Practice Statement (IAPS) 1010: The consideration of environmental matters in the audit of financial statements*, IFAC, London

International Federation of Accountants (2006) *Assurance aspects of G3 – The Global Reporting Initiatives 2006 draft sustainability reporting guidelines*, IFAC, London

Juscius, V and Snieska, V (2008) Influence of Corporate Social Responsibility on competitive abilities of corporations, *Engineering Economics*, **3** (58), pp 34–44

Kilgour, M (2007) The UN Global Compact and substantive equality for women: Revealing a well hidden mandate, *Third World Quarterly*, **28** (4), pp 751–773

KLD [accessed 21 September 2012] *Domini 400 Social Index* [Online] http://www.ftse.com/chinese/Indices/FTSE_KLD_Index_Series/

KPMG (2005) *International Survey of Corporate Responsibility Reporting 2005*, KPMG, London

KPMG (2008) *International Survey of Corporate Responsibility Reporting 2008*, KPMG, London

KPMG (2011) *International Survey of Corporate Responsibility Reporting 2011*, KPMG, London

Lindblom, CK (1994) The implications of organizational legitimacy for corporate social performance and disclosure, paper presented at the Critical Perspectives on Accounting conference, New York

Margolis, JD and Walsh, JP (2003) Misery loves companies: Rethinking social initiatives by business, *Administrative Science Quarterly*, 48 (2), p 268

Mathews, M and Reynolds, M (2000) One way forward: Non-traditional accounting disclosures in the 21st century, paper presented at the Eco-Management and Auditing Conference, Nijmegen School of Management, June 2001

Neu, D, Warsame, H and Pedwell, K (1998) Managing public impressions: Environmental disclosures in annual reports, *Accounting, Organisations and Society*, 23 (3) April, pp 265–282

Orbie, J and Babarinde, O (2008) Corporate Social Responsibility, *European Integration*, 30 (3), pp 459–477

Ovam (2010) [Online] www.ovam.be

Post, JE, Frederick, CW, Lawrence, AT and Weber, J (1996) *Business and Society: Corporate strategy, public policy, ethics*, 8th edition, McGraw-Hill, Maidenhead

Puri, SK and Singh, G (2007) Social accountability (SA8000) certification: A tool for discharging CSR, paper presented at First International Conference on MSECCMI, New Delhi, India

PwC (2010) Corporate Social Responsibility trends: Stacking up the results [Online] http://www.pwc.com/ca/en/sustainability/publications/csr-trends-2010-09.pdf

Reynolds, M and Yuthas, K (2008) Moral discourse and Corporate Social Responsibility reporting, *Journal of Business Ethics*, 78, pp 47–64

Runhaar, H and Lafferty, H (2008) Governing Corporate Social Responsibility: An assessment of the contribution of the UN Global compact to CSR strategies in the telecommunications industry, *Journal of Business Ethics*, 84, pp 419–495

SAM [accessed 21 September 2012] *Dow Jones Sustainability Index* [Online] www.sustainability-index.com

Sethi, S (1975) Dimensions of corporate social performance: An analytical framework, *California Management Review*, 17 (3) spring, pp 58–64

Socioeconomic Data and Applications Center [accessed 21 September 2012] *Environmental Sustainability Index* [Online] http://sedac.ciesin.columbia.edu/data/collection/esi/

Srivastava and Sahay (2007) The evolutionary journey of CSR, CJCS Invest Service

Suchman, MC (1995) Managing legitimacy: Strategic and institutional approaches, *Academy of Management Review*, 20, pp 571–610

Thien, G, Tregida, H and Kearins, K (2009) Corporate Social Responsibility reporting by New Zealand financial services institutions: Analysing understandings and motivations, paper reviewed and accepted for the 8th Australasian Conference on Social and Environment Accounting Research (CSEAR 2009) 6–8 December

UNEP News Centre (2011) UBEP Ogoniland oil assessment reveals extent of environmental contamination and threats to human health [Online] http:www.unep.org/newscentre/default.aspx

UN Global Compact (2011) UN Global Compact participants [Online] http://www.unglobalcompact.org/participantsandstakeholders/index.html

UN Habitat [accessed 21 September 2012] City Development Index, *UN Habitat* [Online] http://www.unchs.org/categories.asp?catid=9

UNIDO (nd) Issue paper on the state of Corporate Social Responsibility reporting in Central and Eastern Europe [Online] www.unido.org

Valmohammadi, C (2011) Investigating Corporate Social Responsibility practices in Iranian organizations: An ISO 26000 perspective, *Business Strategy Series*, **12** (5), pp 257–263

Veleva, V (2010) The new ISO26000 Social Responsibility Standard is launched, Center for Corporate Citizenship, Boston College Carroll School of Management

Ven, B and Graafland, J (2006) Strategic and moral motivation for Corporate Social Responsibility, *JCC*, **22**, Summer

Williams, OF (2004) The UN Global Compact: The challenge and the promise, *Business Ethics Quarterly*, **14** (4), pp 755–774

World Bank (nd) Corporate environmental responsibility: Is a common Corporate Social Responsibility framework possible? Poitr Mazurkiewicz, DevComm-SDO

World Wildlife Fund [accessed 21 September 2012] *Calculating the LPI* [Online] http://wwf.panda.org/about_our_earth/all_publications/living_planet_report/health_of_our_planet/lpi_how_calculated/

World Wildlife Fund [accessed 21 September 2012] *Ecological Footprint Index* [Online] http://assets.panda.org/custom/lpr/ecofootprint.html

Websites

www.bas.sagepub.com
www.british-accreditation.co.uk
www.eti-ten.org
www.globalreporting.org
www.hse.gov.uk
www.iclei.org
www.iema.net/ems/emas
www.kpmg.co.uk
www.ovam.be
www.pwc.com/gx/en/corporate-responsibility
www.unfccc.int/kyoto_protocol
www.wbcsd.org

Small companies, charities and other not-for-profit organizations

11

LEARNING OBJECTIVES

This chapter will enable you to:

- understand the different forms of organization including a small company, a charity and a social enterprise;

- appreciate the particular problems applicable to family-owned firms, including succession and conflicts of interest;

- evaluate how the growth and development of small businesses influence the development of corporate governance and the limitations that apply;

- understand how adopting good corporate governance principles benefits small companies and non-commercial organizations.

Introduction

Throughout this book we have looked at companies and organizations that have a form and structure. They have some form of management hierarchy which, no doubt, spends many hours discussing strategies, objectives and key performance indicators, they have policies and procedures, budgets and management information systems – in other words, they are big organizations with all the conventional management/workforce structures.

However, there is an enormously large tranche of organizations that have very little in the way of formal structures. These are small companies that may have some of the structure and formality of large companies but are either owner-managed or are family companies. Indeed, the family company is the most common form of ownership structure in the world.

Small companies, whether family businesses or not, together with charities and other not-for-profit organizations, present some governance and ethical situations that are very different from the corporate mainstream we have looked at so far. Indeed many small organizations effectively have no conventional corporate governance structures at all and see no need for them, whilst charities, which vary in size from behemoths such as Oxfam and the RNLI to tiny local charities set up for a specific purpose, have some rules unique to them but, generally, share many of the same characteristics of smaller private companies.

Forms of organization

Before we look at the particular aspects of these types of organization let us be sure that we understand the different forms they take, particularly in the charitable sector. In general terms a company is a company, no matter its size, and a small company, broadly, has the same objectives as a big one, ie to preserve itself, to generate profits and to grow the business. Charities are different, so let us be sure of our definitions.

Small companies

For the purposes of this book we will use the Companies Act 2006 definition of a small company; ie it:

- has turnover of less than £6.5m;
- has net assets of less than £3.26m;
- employs fewer than 50 people.

Now clearly a company with a £6m turnover is not exactly petite but adopting this definition helps us to include family companies with some structure and organization. Clearly companies that are, effectively, sole traders or that only employ two or three people, of which there are tens of thousands in the UK, are not really relevant for the purposes of this book, whatever the size of the contribution they make to the UK economy.

Charities and social enterprises

Charities are bodies registered, in England and Wales, with the Charities Commission. Charities established in Scotland are regulated by the Office of the Scottish Charity Regulator (OSCR). Charities must have aims that are for the public benefit; typically these include educational or religious objectives and aims including relief of poverty or the preservation of life but any potential charity that can demonstrate that its aims have a public benefit may be eligible to be registered. Consequently charities with aims such as the advancement of the arts, of amateur sport or of promoting animal welfare have been able to be registered. Accordingly charities must be outward facing and must not be formed in order to benefit those who take part in their activities.

Whilst large government or other public bodies, such as local authorities, hospitals or quangos do not carry on their activities with a view to making a profit, or more accurately a surplus, these are not what we are discussing here because they are not charities or community groups. What we are concerned with in this chapter are the smaller not-for-profit organizations such as community groups and voluntary organizations. Such bodies adopt various structures, including some corporate forms, which relate specifically to charitable or community-based objectives (Table 11.1). Included in the definition of not-for-profit organisations are industrial and provident societies – some of which can be very large indeed. These bodies include organizations such as:

- credit unions, which offer members savings and loan facilities;
- working men's clubs;
- friendly societies, which offer members investment, insurance, pensions and specialist annuities;
- the Co-operative Society, perhaps the biggest of all such bodies.

The essence of bodies such as friendly societies and credit unions is that it is members' savings that are lent out to borrowers and there are limits on how much can be borrowed. Such bodies do not indulge in financial speculations and their operations are carefully monitored as the organizations belong to their members.

TABLE 11.1 Forms of not-for-profit organization

Type of Organization	Features	Form or Legal Structure
Charities, Community Groups and Voluntary Organizations	Formed entirely for charitable objectives, often funded by voluntary donations or subscriptions, and includes both small local groups with community-based objectives and large international charities.	• unincorporated associations • charitable trusts • charitable incorporated organizations (CIO) • charitable companies
Social Enterprises	Social enterprises are involved in providing services or making goods. However, they have explicit social aims and social ownership with a structure based on participation by 'stakeholders' such as users, community groups and employees. Most aim to be viable trading concerns, making a surplus from trading alone which can then be applied for social purposes.	• partnership/limited liability partnerships • limited companies • community interest companies (CIC) • industrial and provident societies, divided into (a) bona fide co-operative societies (including credit unions); (b) societies for the benefit of the community

Most of the organizational forms and structures, such as limited companies, partnerships and limited liability partnerships, used in the not-for-profit sector will be familiar to readers but there are some more specialized entities that should be considered as each of them has special features that distinguish them from conventional businesses carried on with a view to profit.

Charitable incorporated organization (CIO)

This is a new form of entity and the rules for it have, at the time of writing, not been fully established. This is a limited company but one not incorporated under the Companies Act 2006. A CIO:

- is an incorporated form of charity that is not a company;
- only has to register with the Charity Commission and not with Companies House;
- is only created once it is registered by the Commission;
- can enter into contracts in its own right and its trustees will normally have limited or no liability for the debts of the CIO.

This provides the charity with the advantages of limited liability and the legal capacity of the organization to contract in its own right and will probably be less complex to administer than a charitable company but it will not be able to issue debentures as a company limited by guarantee is able to do. There is a Scottish version of the CIO, known as a Scottish Charitable Incorporated Association, with broadly the same features.

Charitable company

A 'charitable company' is an organization that has first become an incorporated organization and then has registered as a charity. An incorporated organization (usually referred to as a company) is recognized by law and has special functions, rights, duties and liabilities. There are several legal structures for a company, but the most common in the voluntary sector is a private company limited by guarantee. Members of private companies limited by guarantee make no contribution to the capital of the company when it is incorporated; instead, their liability is limited to a guaranteed amount payable when the company is wound up. Typically this is £1 but can, of course, be rather more. A charitable company must have entirely charitable objects and may only undertake work that is compatible with those objects. Any changes to the objects for which the company is formed have to be approved by the Charities Commission or the OSCR where the charity is established in Scotland.

Community interest company (CIC)

Community interest companies are limited companies, incorporated under the Companies Act and governed by the Community Interest Company Regulations 2005, with special additional features, created for the use of people who want to conduct a business or other activity for community benefit, and not purely for private advantage. This is achieved by a 'community interest test' and 'asset lock', which ensures that the CIC is established for community purposes and the assets and profits are dedicated to these purposes. The asset lock prevents distribution of profits and assets to members or investors. Registration of a company as a CIC has to be approved by the regulator who also has a continuing monitoring and enforcement role. The difference between this type of entity and a CIO is that a CIC has a business purpose, albeit for a charitable objective.

Industrial and provident society

An industrial and provident society is a corporate form of organization conducting an industry, business or trade, either as a co-operative or for the benefit of the community, and is registered under the Industrial and Provident Societies Act 1965. Co-operative societies are run for the mutual benefit of their members, with any surplus usually being ploughed back into the organization to provide better services and facilities.

Societies run for the benefit of the community provide services for people other than their members. There need to be special reasons why the society should not be registered as a company.

Reporting

Small companies have to file accounts with the Registrar of Companies but these may be heavily abbreviated and, in reality, are merely summaries of the financial statements. If they are to meet the statutory criteria for small companies they are not required to have a statutory audit. However, many do because an audit:

- adds credibility to reported results, which may aid relationships with suppliers or tax authorities;
- helps establish creditworthiness;
- may be a requirement of lenders to continue providing finance;
- helps enforce financial discipline in the organization through highlighting weaknesses in financial systems;
- may help to discourage or discover fraud.

Shareholders owning 10 per cent or more of the shares can require an audit be performed.

Charities have various reporting requirements. Organizations that are companies incorporated under the Companies Act 2006 must file accounts with the Registrar of Companies in the same way as must a trading company. In addition they must file documents with the relevant charities regulator.

In England and Wales charities with a gross income over £25,000 in the accounting year must file their trustees' report, which has a specified form and content, with the Charities Commission. Smaller charities must submit all or part of an annual return. The length of the report and the amount of detail included in it is in proportion to the charity's size. Charities' reports are public documents and are available on the internet from the Charity Commission.

In Scotland there were no reporting requirements for charities before 1 April 2006 except for the requirements to conform to company law. Since then the OSCR has progressively introduced a filing regime similar to that of the Charity Commissioners in England and Wales insofar as all charities must complete an annual return and, if income is in excess of £25,000, a supplementary monitoring return. The OSCR displays information concerning charities in summary form on its website but does not display the same depth of information as does the Charity Commission.

Family-owned firms

The term 'family business' conjures up the image of a small company started by mum and dad then passed on to son or daughter who comes into the business to carry on the family line. This is, undoubtedly, the situation in many businesses – the Institute for Family Business, in a report commissioned in 2008, estimated that there were approximately 3 million family businesses in the UK of which over half were sole traders with no employees – so they won't feature any further in our considerations! Of the remaining 1.4 million or so they estimate that over 1,000 had more than 250 employees. Some of the best-known names in the UK such as Warburtons, Timothy Taylors, JC Bamford and Specsavers are family businesses, as are Mars, WalMart, Samsung and Ikea; so the family business model is not necessarily a small one.

However, in this chapter we are looking primarily at the smaller business – one that does not have a multi-tiered management structure or a vast range of advisors, in other words the small enterprise that is dominated by related owner-managers. How then do we define what it is we are considering in this chapter?

One definition of a 'family business' is from the Family Entrepreneurship Working Group set up by the Finnish Ministry of Trade and Industry in 2004:

- The majority of votes are held by the person who established or acquired the firm or their spouses, parents, child or child's direct heirs.

- At least one representative of the family is involved in the management or administration of the firm.
- In the case of a listed company, the person who established or acquired the firm or their families possess 25 per cent of the right to vote through their share capital and there is at least one family member on the board of the company.

We have added our own size criteria above so what we are considering here is a small(ish) business that is predominantly owned by individuals who play an active part in the management of the enterprise.

Clearly where family companies are concerned many of the agency problems outlined in Chapter 1 experienced by non-family companies disappear as the agents are also, mostly, the principals so agency costs are minimal. Additionally, research has identified several advantages family firms have over firms managed solely by professional managers, which are summarised in Table 11.2.

The family firm is perceived to be a relatively tightly-knit unit where decisions are made quickly and which operates within a framework of common values. Family members tend to give a lot more time and effort to the business and are willing to carry out a variety of tasks within the business in order to get the job done. However, as several commentators have pointed out, there needs to be a separation between home and work, otherwise work becomes a dominant issue which can have adverse effects upon relationships with a consequent adverse knock-on effect on the business.

Most family firms have legends about the founder and how they worked night and day, made the stuff, drove the van, painted the shop, collected the money etc, and it is true that no successful business is built without considerable effort, care and attention to detail, and family firms tend to excel at this. Often owner-managers do instinctively what management grade employees have to go on expensive training courses to learn.

Owner-managers tend to:

- Appreciate that it is all too easy to fail, particularly in a competitive market place. They are very much aware of the consequences of failure to their family and they may have personally pledged their own wealth to secure borrowings so the price of failure is catastrophic. Employees tend to be more distant and blasé about the consequences of failure, particularly if they work for a profitable business, so feel they can afford to be somewhat less conscientious. Consequently owner-managers may be risk-averse, which may result in a reluctance to change even in the face of evidence of the need to do so.

TABLE 11.2 Special features of a family business

Commitment	Family managers have a commitment to success and a loyalty to each other.
Knowledge	Family members may develop special or unique ways of doing things or have developed special recipes or products that can be protected.
Flexibility in time, work and money	Family members tend to give more time to the business than would an employee and are prepared to work anti-social hours – sometimes to the detriment of family life.
Long-term planning	The family firm is seen as a long-term source of value to the family so where there is succession members may take a longer-term view of growth strategies – although this may be an informal rather than a formal process. If there is no succession family members will plan an exit strategy.
Stable culture	Relationships have developed over time. Family members will tend to share similar values and cultural norms and be less subject to outside influences.
Speedy decision-making	Family members have direct responsibilities and lines of communication are short. Decisions may be made quickly but may often be made without formal procedures and processes.
Reliability and pride	Successful family firms have solid, reliable structures and are conscious of the fragility of their businesses and the consequences of failure. They tend to work hard to establish good relationships with customers, suppliers and staff.

SOURCE: Leach, 1996

- Keep costs to a minimum. Owner-managers tend to understand the relationship between costs and revenues and how much has to be sold to cover costs so tend to be good at negotiating prices with suppliers and at keeping non-productive costs and waste to a minimum. Smaller family firms tend to be very good at instituting value-for-money practices even if they are not aware that they are doing so.

- Foster good relationships with customers and suppliers. Family businesses appreciate the value of regular creditworthy customers and of reliable suppliers and will work hard to maintain good relationships. In many cases customers and suppliers may also be family businesses so there is common ground.

- Network intensively. They will use both formal and informal networks to seek out business opportunities, discuss problems and keep abreast of legislation.

- Use advisors sparingly. They realize that advice generally costs so will buy in professional services only when required to do so. They may use their or other professionals informally, seeking free advice, but have no commitment to training or consultancy except for very specific purposes.

However, the structure and organisation of family firms has some drawbacks that can be a source of conflict. In a large organization a clash of values or cultures may lead to some disputes and management problems that professional managers will strive to overcome. Disputes within families, however, can lead to a sundering of relationships and splits which can, in extreme cases, become permanent.

There are two problem areas family companies have to overcome:

- conflicts between business values and family values;
- succession and generational conflicts.

Business vs family values

Table 11.3 contrasts the principal differences between the values that a family may espouse within itself and what are seen as key business attributes.

There may be problems where the interests of the family conflict with the interests of the business. These may manifest themselves in two ways:

1 Family members seeking a role for which they are not suited or not competent.

2 Family withdrawing more cash for personal benefits than the business is able to fund, or conflicts over the use of cash to build up the business instead of paying rewards to family.

TABLE 11.3 Business vs family values

Family Values	Business Values
emotional ties	unemotional
loyalty to family	self-interest
subjective	objective
shared decision-making	management structure, hierarchy
common values	perform or leave
care for individual members	perform or leave

SOURCE: Burns, 2011

One of the problems with family companies is the lack of formal processes and this brings us directly into the area of corporate governance. Many family businesses do not, as a matter of practice:

- hold regular formal board meetings that are properly minuted;
- separate the roles of chair of the board and chief executive – power tends to reside in the hands of a few individuals;
- carry out performance appraisals of directors' performance;
- appoint non-executive directors;
- match remuneration to performance;
- have formal accountability processes.

Many family firms are managed through what has been called 'negotiated paternalism'. Family members can often negotiate their roles depending upon the influence they have within the family and this can often lead to sub-optimal decision-making and reduced levels of business efficiency.

This lack of formal structure can, however, also make the business flexible and able to respond quickly to changes in business circumstances and, as we have seen, communications are better in family businesses than in more formal organizations, but this very informality can be a handicap where there is conflict that cannot be resolved through discussion. Consequently, where a family member seeks a role they have no capacity to deal with or, worse, actually attempts to carry out that role, the only resort the family has is informal pressure among relatives rather than objective measures. Families may be reluctant to involve outsiders so there may be an absence of experienced non-executive directors to add weight to the discussions.

Succession and generational conflicts

Succession can be a major problem for family companies. Clearly where there is no succession the owner-managers will devise an exit route which involves disposal of all or part of the business. It may be that the family wishes to retain an involvement but does not have any members with the capability or the interest to take on managing it. One option is either to hand the business over to professional managers and to adopt a purely passive role or to sell a controlling or major interest in the business, leaving a residual investment for the family.

A family member who is purely an owner may want to sell the business to maximize their return, but a family member who is an owner and also a manager may want to keep the company because it represents their career and they want their children to have the opportunity to work in the business.

Another source of conflict is often generational. If, for example, son wishes to come into the business in succession to father the process of handover can be fraught. Youth tends to be naturally rebellious and this may cause conflicts, particularly if father is reluctant to delegate any power even to a professional manager. The next generation may see the founder as outmoded, slow or risk-averse and may wish to institute policies the founder disagrees with. The founder may view his or her successor as brash, inexperienced and willing to take excessive risks. In the absence of formal processes conflict may ensue as the next generation is denied access to power or, having been granted it, is then heavily monitored by the outgoing generation.

Major disputes about succession or disputes within the family concerning, say, withdrawing cash from the business to create private wealth may leave the business traumatized and, in extreme circumstances, even force a break-up or early sale by the founders.

Non-family members

Research by the Institute for Family Business estimates that family businesses currently employ about 42 per cent of private sector employees, or around 9.5 million people. The difficulties employees face when working for family businesses centre around two issues:

- Decisions are ultimately made by the family who own or control the business. The absence of formal processes within the enterprise may mean that alternatives suggested by employees or criticisms of decisions made may not be recognized, leading to frustration.

- Opportunities for development and promotion are limited. It is unlikely that non-family members will be able to buy shares in the business and so will always remain on the outside. Non-family members may well become directors but the role of non-family director in a private family firm is very different to that role in, say, a larger plc or non-family firm. Often directorships are awarded in family firms for loyalty or long service rather than for the need of the owner-managers to have independent advice; consequently non-family directors can be marginalized and excluded from significant decision-making. Their role may be effectively delegated to that of minor management of the business and tactical decision-making to put into effect a strategy agreed between family members only.

Non-family employees may feel alienated if they see:

- cash being taken from the business to fund an extravagant lifestyle;
- poor, ineffectual decision-making designed to maintain the status quo rather than develop the business;
- an aversion to taking any form of risk, which results in missed opportunities for business development.

Consequently there is a danger that competent managers and staff leave, to be replaced by timeservers or toadies who reinforce the family's view of themselves. The absence of any form of self-appraisal will tend to reinforce the inclination of the firm to look inwards rather than outwards, which can lead to disaster.

Consequently family firms are encouraged to take on some of the key principles of good corporate governance and to document their plans and intentions in a form that they will adhere to so that succession issues and the principles of cash withdrawal are formally documented in a way that all family members can accept.

Charities and social enterprises

It may be a masterly statement of the blindingly obvious but charities and social enterprises are very different from commercial organizations. These differences relate not only to the most obvious point that one is carried on with a view to making a profit and rewarding participants in it and the other is not, but also extend to other, less obvious differentials (Table 11.4).

TABLE 11.4 Commercial ventures vs charities and social enterprises

Commercial Ventures	Charities and Social Enterprises
Objective is to create wealth for owners and provide income for managers and employees.	Objective is social or charitable purpose for the public good.
Financed by private capital or borrowings. Income generated by sales of goods and services.	Financed by subscriptions, donations and some level of trading activity. Some element of government or lottery funding in some circumstances can be available in the form of grants or loans.
Employees seen as having status in the community concomitant with role and size of enterprise.	Employees seen as lower status than working for a commercial venture.
Management is through acknowledgement of roles and status in organization.	Management is participative. Many employees may have social problems or disabilities and an inability to cope with formal structures. Managers tend to get involved with activities and roles and responsibilities may be rotated.
In general rewards and career paths may be extensive. Able individuals may be promoted or may move from job to job to enhance their income and status.	Incentives and career paths are limited. Pay is lower than in commercial organizations and management structures are flatter. There is little to distinguish individual organizations except for their objectives and activities; structures are remarkably similar and governed only by size.
Marketing is through conventional media and considerable resources may be devoted to promoting the enterprises' activities in order to attract customers.	Money available for marketing is generally limited and is used mainly for fundraising drives. General promotional activities tend to be through social networks or media reports about activities. Organizations may be promoted via local authorities or similar organizations if connections are present, eg the social enterprise is extensively funded through local authority grants.

Charities and social enterprises, whilst having many common features, are not the same so we will look at them separately.

Charities

All of the organizations dealt with in this chapter vary in size and charities are no exception. For example, figures available from the Charities Commission and the Office of the Scottish Charities Regulator show charities with income ranging from £742 (Dundee Indigent Sick Society) to £169 million (RNLI). Clearly, managing the resources of the RNLI is a rather different proposition to managing the Dundee Indigent Sick Society – but the objectives and principles are essentially the same:

- Both charities raise funds through donations, income from investments and, in the case of the RNLI, from a captive trading arm. Both have relatively little control over how much income they are able to generate.

- Both have to apply their funds for the purposes for which they were founded in accordance with their charter or stated objectives, which cannot, generally, be changed without resort to law or permission from regulators.

- Expenses may only be incurred legitimately in connection with running the charity. Salaries tend to be lower than commercial salaries for similar-sized organizations and there are few benefits or perks. Individuals working in charities tend to have a more societal-based ethos than those working in commercial organizations.

- Risk management is a key issue in charities. They cannot make commitments they are unable to fulfil and must manage their income and assets in such a way as to ensure commitments can be met.

As we have seen above, charities can be constituted in several ways, including some corporate forms but in every case they will have a board of trustees or directors who are charged with the governance of the enterprise. If the charity is formed as a company they may have responsibilities relating to that but here we will concentrate on the responsibilities of individuals charged with the governance of a charity. This does not require any particular skills, indeed the Charity Commission feels that 'most people have skills, knowledge or experience which they can bring to a charity'. However, they go on to say, and this is perhaps their most important attribute, that individuals actively involved, or wanting to become involved, with the governance of a charity should have a strong personal commitment to the charity's aims and objectives.

There is an overriding requirement that those charged with governance must act with integrity, and avoid any personal conflicts of interest or misuse of charity funds or assets. They must confirm, by reviewing the charity's charter, that there can be no possible conflict between the aims of the charity and any personal activity, particularly where they might receive some personal benefit.

Individuals charged with governance of the entity have a duty of care towards the organization. In particular:

- They must exercise reasonable care and skill as trustees, using personal knowledge and experience to ensure that the charity is well run and efficient.

- They should consider getting external professional advice on all matters where there may be material risk to the charity, or where the trustees may be in breach of their duties.

In particular individuals charged with governance of a charity must ensure that their charity complies with:

- Charity law, and the requirements of the Charity Commission or the OSCR as regulator; in particular they must ensure that the charity prepares reports on its work, and submits annual returns and accounts as required by law.

- The requirements or rules, and the charitable purpose and objects set out in the charity's own governing document. All individuals involved in governance should have a copy of this document, and be familiar with it.

- The requirements of other legislation and other regulators (if any) that govern the activities of the charity; these will vary according to the type of work the charity carries out, and whether it employs staff or volunteers.

They must ensure that the charity is and will remain solvent, which requires them to keep informed of the charity's activities and financial position. Their financial responsibilities are straightforward enough:

- To use charitable funds and assets wisely, and only to further the purposes and interests of the charity.

- To avoid undertaking activities that might place the charity's property, funds, assets or reputation at undue risk.

- To take special care when investing the funds of the charity, or borrowing funds for the charity to use.

So whilst the duties are not particularly onerous they do place considerable responsibilities on anyone who is involved with governance of a charity to make sure they are aware of the financial position of the charity to ensure it remains solvent, to monitor its activities and to ensure that a proper consideration of risks to the charity is undertaken.

These can present some problems from time to time, particularly in small charities where the number of full- or part-time staff is low and systems for monitoring and recording the actions of employees are weak or nonexistent. There are many unfortunate cases of charities being defrauded by unscrupulous workers who had access to all the financial records and who were not properly monitored by the trustees. If the charity is uninsured and the fraudster cannot make restitution the charity may well have to choose between curtailing its activities or closing on the one hand and trying to make a case against one or more trustees for negligence on the other, neither of which is an attractive prospect.

In terms of risk the biggest problems charities are likely to face are financial. Financial risks include:

- termination of funding from awarding bodies;
- decline in income from trading activities;
- drop in fundraising from the general public;
- decline in legacies and bequests;
- fluctuations in investment incomes and values;
- an unforeseen rise in demand for their services;
- frauds committed by unsupervised employees (eg bookkeepers or managers given unfettered authority).

Other risks that charities face include:

- compliance risks in respect of law and regulation; and
- reputation risk where some act by the charity or its employees brings the charity into disrepute with the result that income drops dramatically or regulators are called in to investigate, or, of course, both.

Clearly, individuals charged with governance must be alert and be involved with the activities of the charity and bring a strong ethical commitment and common sense into managing the charity's activities.

Social enterprises

A social enterprise is a business whose objectives are primarily social, and whose profits are reinvested back into its services or the community. With no financial commitments to shareholders or owners, social enterprises are free to use their surplus income to invest in their operations to make them as efficient and effective as possible.

Social enterprises come in many shapes and sizes, from small community-owned village shops to large organizations delivering public services; from individual social entrepreneurs to multi-million-pound global organizations. Well-known social enterprises include Turning Point, the Eden Project, the Big Issue, and Jamie Oliver's 'Fifteen' restaurant.

Social enterprises are distinctive from traditional charities or voluntary organizations in that they generate the majority, if not all, of their income through the trading of goods or services rather than through donations. This gives them a degree of self-reliance and independence, which puts them firmly in control of their own activities.

Social enterprises provide such things as:

- forms of health and care services for elderly or disabled individuals;
- recycling collection services;
- sale of new and recycled goods;
- community transport;
- community facilities;
- manufacture of goods using disabled employees;
- renewable energy provision;
- environmental construction services;
- social housing;
- access to broadband telecommunications.

These services are often combined with providing on-the-job training in a supportive environment for disadvantaged people, including people who have a disability or are long-term unemployed.

Social enterprises have multiple objectives – social and environmental as well as financial. They strive not only to ensure their continuity by making an operating surplus, but also to produce outputs that are not simple to translate into monetary terms, for instance in terms of the improved social welfare of their members, their customers and the local community. Methods of attributing monetary values to the costs and benefits of social enterprise are continually being improved; for example, their activity may reduce public spending on unemployment benefit, social security, health and policing services. Evaluating whether to support social enterprises and monitoring their performance requires special reporting, monitoring and evaluation techniques that take account of the social as well as the economic objectives.

Social enterprises can look like commercial activities so there are often comparisons between them which are fundamentally flawed as their objectives are very different. Key differences are:

- Social enterprises tend to suffer from low prestige as they have no commercial objectives so individuals working in them, at whatever level, will not be rewarded at the same level as they would be in a comparable role in a commercial enterprise.

- Incentives and career paths are sometimes limited, or perceived as such.

- Social and financial aims may clash, as may volunteer and paid employee mentalities.

- Social enterprises predominantly offer employment to people who have not gained formal qualifications or who have some form of disability or other handicap that may tend to disqualify them from obtaining work in the commercial sector (eg ex-prisoners).

As businesses, they must be well managed if they are to survive as they generally work on very tight margins and have little or no reserves. The specific nature of social enterprises means that they need specific skills and working in them demands flexibility rather than a commitment to fixed roles.

Social enterprises depend to a far greater extent on the motivation of their workers, which requires techniques of participative management to maintain. This means that, in many cases, individuals working in social enterprises decide the content of jobs and ways of improving results, rather than simply carrying out tasks as instructed. This relies on a keen appreciation of what it means to work in a team, and a commitment to a process of collective problem resolution and decision-making.

As we have seen, many people employed by social enterprises may be disabled or long-term unemployed, they may have social problems, be convicted offenders or have a range of social problems and personal issues that can intrude into their working lives, for example alcohol or drug misuse. This requires a very different approach to managing such individuals than in a commercial organization where, generally, individuals are motivated towards success and will be told what to do and how to do it. In social enterprises individuals may react badly to authoritarian approaches or may suffer from disabilities such that tasks have to be broken into multiple stages or for which extra time must be allowed for completion.

Positions of responsibility may be held in rotation over longer or shorter periods, and jobs may be shared. Working hours may be negotiated flexibly. To increase job quality, people may carry out a number of different roles in parallel or in succession. Strategic decisions will generally be reached through a process of consultation with all stakeholders. Feedback on achievements and results is to the annual general meeting of members, as well as to other stakeholders such as funding bodies or the public.

Governance of such enterprises requires those charged with governance to act in much the same way as they would with a charity, as described above. They must be aware of the activities of the entity and keep a careful watch on finances. Many social enterprises have a community aspect and their activities can be quite visible, which perhaps adds a small extra pressure on those charged with governance to ensure that what may be perceived as a valuable social service survives despite funding pressures and adverse economic circumstances.

The application of corporate governance to charities and small companies

Small companies often have structures that are inimical to classical corporate governance principles; however, charities and social enterprise companies often have to abide by the key principles of accountability and transparency as they raise money by subscription or from public funds and have to account for their activities and expenditure.

Charities and social enterprises are often governed in accordance with some sound principles. For instance:

- They have a governance structure almost entirely composed of non-executives.
- They must be transparent and accountable.
- They will take professional advice as required.
- Standards of behaviour are generally high owing to the ethos of such organizations.
- No one person has unfettered power over the activities of the charity, as this is prohibited.

Consequently, in this section we will look at small companies in particular and how corporate governance requirements change as the business grows and matures.

Corporate governance and growing businesses

The growth of a company is an evolutionary process – many never grow much beyond the initial founding stages and remain as small family businesses, but those which do grow may do so in steps:

- Initially the small company has simple structures and procedures dominated by the owner-managers who take all the decisions.
- The larger and more complex the entity grows, the more difficult it is for the solo entrepreneur to keep track of everything so they have to begin delegating powers and responsibility to others who may not be family members.
- These individuals have to have real authority to be effective so are appointed as directors, thus there has to be a formal board structure.
- As the company grows, the need for more independent advice becomes apparent and so non-executive directors start to be recruited.
- And so the company evolves, and the governance structures with it.

For the growing small company, adoption of the key principles of good corporate governance involves:

- delegation of authority away from one individual who is controlling shareholder, director and manager;
- institution of a system of checks and balances so no one person has unfettered control;
- professional decision-making based on reliable information supplied to a properly constituted and empowered board;
- accountability based on defined levels of responsibility;
- transparency regarding the firm's activities, to encourage high standards of behaviour.

All of these mark stages in the evolution of the company.

The creation of some sort of separate advisory board, without full appointment of NEDs, is another step – a recognition that the directors need the skills and experience of outsiders to help them manage their business. The beginnings of a limited separation of ownership from control, the institution of corporate governance processes and the delegation of control from one individual to a board is a key step in the maturing of the business.

This is a particular need if the firm wishes to shift away from dependence on the initial drive of the founding entrepreneur. Although the ability and dynamism of one individual may have been instrumental in establishing the enterprise this is unlikely to be sustainable over the longer term and, hopefully, the business will grow to be too large to be physically managed by one individual. As the enterprise grows in size and maturity – or outlives the interest or working life of the founder – governance processes must be established to ensure continuity and success beyond the efforts of one person. The interests of succeeding generations must be taken into account and a formal structure enables founders to introduce their successors into the decision-making process in a controlled way so that they do not immediately assume unfettered and unaccountable power.

The development of effective governance processes may:

- lift a significant burden from the founder;
- facilitate a swift succession; and
- allow access to a wider pool of expertise and know-how.

The result may be improved leadership, decision-making and strategic vision. Improved governance may also make it easier to monitor and manage the various risks to which the company is exposed, particularly as it grows in size and complexity.

Problems with adopting corporate governance principles

As we have seen, whilst unlisted companies are encouraged to abide by the key principles of good corporate governance as enshrined in the UK Corporate Governance Code, in practice many of these are difficult for owner-managers to accept and many of them regard these initiatives as bureaucratic and costly.

Research carried out in 2006 into the application of corporate governance principles to smaller listed companies found that most of them:

- recognized the value of appointing non-executive directors to the board but thought that two was enough;

- didn't feel that the split between the roles of chair and chief executive was appropriate as the chair needed to be close to the executive. This reinforced the need for a strong non-executive presence;

- did institute the various board committees as recommended, as these were seen as having value.

This is, remember, related to listed companies where adoption of corporate governance principles is virtually mandatory. Where companies are not listed adoption of these principles might best be described as patchy.

Surprisingly, there appears to be very little research in this area, whether because the unlisted sector isn't considered to be relevant or because of the difficulties in obtaining information. Anecdotal evidence and the authors' own experience indicates that the main reasons why smaller unlisted companies do not adopt corporate governance principles are:

- There may be no real difference between the roles of chair of the board and CEO – effectively an owner-manager doesn't see a distinction – they are 'in charge' so there is no separation of roles. They are not concerned about the relationship between management and external shareholders as there may be few shareholders not involved in managing the business.

- Advice is more often obtained from professional advisors, particularly accountants, informal networks of entrepreneurs and organizations such as Business Link than from non-executive directors.

- Non-executive directors would expect to be paid – this can be seen as a non-productive overhead by owner-managers.

- Committee structures don't fit the small company ethos.

- Non-participant family members may fulfil some of the role of non-executive directors to some extent, although they may lack business experience.

Institute of Directors' guidance

In November 2010 the Institute of Directors (IOD) issued a report called *Corporate Governance Guidance and Principles for Unlisted Companies in the UK*, specifically relating to good corporate governance for the smaller company. This recognizes the reality that much of the UK Corporate Governance Code really doesn't fit the smaller entity whilst at the same time acknowledging the part that good governance practices can play in establishing a sound basis for running the smaller business and building good relationships with stakeholders. It established 14 principles – nine of which relate to all companies and five of which relate to larger or more complex entities.

The guidance is designed to:

- ensure value is protected for shareholders, as there is often no ready market for shares in private companies;

- balance the interests of founder families with the success of the company; and

- promote long-term success and attract external investment.

Institute of Directors' proposals for good corporate governance in all unlisted companies

Principle 1: Shareholders should establish an appropriate constitutional and governance framework for the company through the Articles of Association or other agreement.

Principle 2: Every company should strive to establish an effective board, which is collectively responsible for the long-term success of the company, including the definition of the corporate strategy. However, an interim step on the road to an effective (and independent) board may be the creation of an advisory board.

Principle 3: The size and composition of the board should reflect the scale and complexity of the company's activities.

Principle 4: The board should meet sufficiently regularly to discharge its duties, and be supplied in a timely manner with appropriate information.

Principle 5: Levels of remuneration should be sufficient to attract, retain and motivate executives and non-executives of the quality required to run the company successfully.

Principle 6: The board is responsible for risk oversight and should maintain a sound system of internal control to safeguard shareholders' investment and the company's assets.

Principle 7: There should be a dialogue between the board and the shareholders based on a mutual understanding of objectives. The board as a whole has responsibility for ensuring that a satisfactory dialogue with shareholders takes place. The board should not forget that all shareholders have to be treated equally.

Principle 8: All directors should receive induction on joining the board and should regularly update and refresh their skills and knowledge.

Principle 9: Family-controlled companies should establish family governance mechanisms that promote coordination and mutual understanding amongst family members, as well as organize the relationship between family governance and corporate governance.

The first nine principles shown in the box are fairly straightforward, the only rather unusual one being the first where the IOD recommends that some sort of decision-making protocol is decided at the time the company is established. This requires founders to not simply accept the standard form of Articles found in the *Set Up Your Own Company Kit* but to modify them so that some decisions have to be made by shareholders, some can be made by directors and some delegated to managers. This requires some level of foresight, and indeed optimism, and is most likely to be ignored, but some form of agreement between, say, founding family members if they own shares but are not all involved in the day-to-day business is not a bad idea. For example, levels of dividend or remuneration may have to be decided by the shareholders collectively, not simply by the directors who then bully it through the AGM.

A carefully thought-through constitution can remedy shareholder and director disputes, generally preventing the situation where interested parties reach a deadlock.

Family councils and family assemblies

One area where the IOD differs significantly from the UK Corporate Governance Code is in respect of family-controlled companies. Research has shown that family-controlled companies rarely survive past three generations. The reason for this, according to the IOD, is the failure to distinguish between the interests of the company and those of the family. It is also natural that over time, as shares pass down generations, the number of family shareholders can quickly increase, which can lead to administrative difficulties and disagreements.

To address this problem the IOD suggests forming a family council and a family assembly. The family council would be a small body of family members, voted for by family members to represent them, which would liaise with the board and make decisions on behalf of the family. The family assembly consists of all family members and should meet twice a year to discuss their concerns with a view to pre-empting and preventing conflicts.

The IOD suggests formalizing this, drafting a family constitution that may take the form of a shareholders' agreement or nominee agreement. This should set out:

- the family's values, mission statement and vision;
- the role and powers of a family council and the family assembly to represent the interests of all family members;
- the role of the board of directors and its relationship with the family council;
- the process for establishing policies for important family issues, such as employing family members, restricting transfer of shares and succession planning for the chief executive; and nomination of family members to the board.

The intention of this is to balance the interests of the family and a strong independent board to promote the long-term success of the company.

The larger family business

As the business grows, matures and evolves there are certain events that have to be managed:

- Changes in the relationship between shareholders, the board and management. This may be triggered by the desire of the founder entrepreneur or family owners to withdraw from the day-to-day management of the company, and hand over executive responsibilities to professional managers. A special trigger of governance change may be the decision to nominate the first independent non-executive director on the board.
- Expansion of the shareholder base by attracting additional internal (family, group) shareholders. This may trigger important challenges for the sole owner (eg the founder).
- Change in the capital and shareholding structure, due to a desire to attract external financing. This will involve dilution in the ownership concentration of existing owners, and the entry into the company ownership of external shareholders.

● Increasing complexity in the firm's business portfolio, its business environment and its risk profile.

Once the business has reached a size when it can appoint NEDs and have formal structures the last five IOD recommendations (see box below) are designed to create a governance structure within it very similar to the UK Corporate Governance Code provisions required of listed companies.

Institute of Directors' proposals for good corporate governance for larger or more complex unlisted companies

Principle 10: There should be a clear division of responsibilities at the head of the company between the running of the board and the running of the company's business. No one individual should have unfettered powers of decision.

Principle 11: All boards should contain directors with a sufficient mix of competencies and experiences. No single person (or small group of individuals) should dominate the board's decision-making.

Principle 12: The board should establish appropriate board committees in order to allow a more effective discharge of its duties.

Principle 13: The board should undertake a periodic appraisal of its own performance and that of each individual director.

Principle 14: The board should present a balanced and understandable assessment of the company's position and prospects for external stakeholders, and establish a suitable programme of stakeholder engagement.

It is important to recognize that the approach is a step-by-step one – businesses, if they survive, evolve and the necessity for more complex structures such as formal boards and the introduction of non-executive directors, a key step, may come naturally. Alternatively they may be forced on a reluctant founder who has to bow to pressure, say, in order to obtain finance. In this case corporate governance processes will be perceived negatively as unnecessary bureaucracy and expense and the benefits will go unrecognized. The IOD claims that, in such cases, the business will never achieve its full potential as this will have become limited by the boundaries imposed by the founder reluctant to change or delegate power. This may well mean the company will not, in the long run, thrive and ultimately contains within it the seeds of its own destruction.

Governance and finance

Governance will become an increasing issue for unlisted companies as they develop new sources of finance. Initially, the primary source of funds is likely to be retained earnings or financing from internal networks, eg families or associated corporate groups. However, unlisted companies may also turn to banks, venture capitalists and private equity investors in order to finance their expansion and growth. A greater reliance on such external sources of finance will necessitate the implementation of a more explicit governance framework, as external financiers seek assurance that their investments will be well managed.

In particular, the involvement of additional owners in the company – even if the founder retains a controlling stake – will require governance mechanisms to resolve differences between shareholders with potentially diverging agendas. A governance structure that sustains the confidence of internal and external sources of finance – such as shareholders, banks and other creditors – will contribute to the long-term success of the firm by securing the commitment of capital partners. The reward to the company of such a governance structure will be more stable financing at lower cost than would otherwise be available.

The relevance of Corporate Social Responsibility to smaller organizations

The model of CSR that we have looked at throughout this book is one based on large organizations with the resources and ability to create champions to take the initiatives forward. In the small business and charity sector survival may be a more important priority than initiatives designed to benefit the environment or society.

This sector is diverse, with defined objectives mostly based upon the needs of the individuals involved with them and few CSR initiatives are tailored specifically for that sector – it is more usual to take CSR initiatives designed for larger organizations and shrink them to fit, which may not be at all appropriate.

Clearly there may be demonstrable benefits to adopting some CSR. Business advisors Business Link have outlined a case for the small business stating 'building a reputation as a responsible business sets you apart'.

They identify several advantages to business for adopting a CSR approach:

- Initiatives to reduce resource use, waste and emissions help the environment and reduce costs. Measures to cut utility bills and waste disposal costs can bring immediate cash benefits.
- A good reputation makes it easier to recruit employees.
- Employees may stay longer, reducing the costs and disruption of recruitment and retraining.
- Employees are better motivated and more productive.
- CSR helps ensure businesses comply with regulatory requirements.
- Activities such as involvement with the local community are ideal opportunities to generate positive press coverage.
- Good relationships with local authorities make doing business easier.
- Understanding the wider impact of the business can help in the development of new products and services.

One of the problems that small businesses face, however, is increased accountability and transparency. There is no escaping the fact that enhanced disclosure will increase costs, not only advisory costs in preparing reports but having to install systems to collect the data for the reports. Reports and exhortations cite the Co-operative as one organisation that produces comprehensive CSR reports, which indeed it does, but it is a very large organization with vast resources. It is difficult to contrast an organization such as that with, say, a building supplies company in Accrington and try to claim they should produce reports of the same depth and complexity.

There are undoubted business benefits but, as these can be quite difficult to measure, the SME sector remains reluctant to fully embrace the whole gamut of CSR and its possibilities.

Charities and social enterprises are, surprisingly, much closer to the principles of CSR than trading companies. By their very nature they are abstemious and spend as little as possible. Similarly, waste is frowned upon, as is excessive use of utilities and consumables. They already have to make quite comprehensive disclosures to their regulators and their activities are, quite frequently, open to public gaze and scrutiny by virtue of their activities.

Whilst they may not embrace CSR by name they may well be much further along the line of implementation than their commercial counterparts.

CASE STUDY

Roger Rundle has started a small business designing computer-based applications for Smartphones and computer games. He is co-owner with his cousin Harold Snapper of a small company called Roundabout Ltd.

Roger and Harold's software has been extremely successful – so successful in fact that they received commissions to design several more complex applications for a major software provider. This meant that they had to recruit staff and find larger premises. They did so and the new work proved so acceptable that several other companies also commissioned them to design software. Roger and Harold now spend little time on software design and most of their time is spent on managing the increasing number of employees, the financing of expensive new equipment and offices and quality control of the end product.

Neither of them have had any management training, they do not understand accounts and finance and are mostly concerned that the product they provide to their customers is of as good a quality as they can get it. They have appointed an accountant but rely heavily on their advisors and friends for advice.

They were approached by a rival business, Shark Software, to sell Roundabout and go back to being developers but they declined.

They now have to act to prevent the business spiralling out of their control and to reassure both the bank who have lent them money to finance the business growth and a potential new investor who wishes to invest in Roundabout that the business is being run effectively and that Roger and Harold have a clear vision and strategy for the future and are able to achieve it.

Discuss

- Is corporate governance important to a company such as Roundabout?

- Apart from financial accounting advice what other steps should Roger and Harold take to stabilize the management of the business and reassure stakeholders and potential investors?

- What impact would any actions they take have on the business in terms of Roger's and Harold's involvement in it? How might they come to terms with any loss of control?

- Is it likely that the cost of improved corporate governance to a small company is outweighed by the benefits that it might bring to the company?

Bibliography

Burns, P (2011) *Entrepreneurship and Small Business*, Palgrave Macmillan, Basingstoke

Family Entrepreneurship Working Group (2006) *Family Entrepreneurship: Family enterprises as the engines of continuity renewal and growth-intensiveness*, Ministry of Trade and Industry, Finland

Financial Reporting Council (2010) *UK Corporate Governance Code*, FRC, London

HMSO (1965) *Industrial and Provident Societies Act*, HMSO, London

HMSO (2006) *Companies Act 2006*, HMSO, London

Institute for Family Business (2008) *The UK Family Business Sector Report by Capital Economics*, Institute for Family Business, London

Institute of Directors (2010) *Corporate Governance Guidance and Principles for Unlisted Companies in the UK*, Institute of Directors, London

Leach, P (1996) *The BDO Stoy Hayward Guide to the Family Business*, Kogan Page, London

Ram, M and Holiday, R (1993) Relative merits: Family culture and kinship in small firms, *Sociology*, **27** (4)

Websites

www.businesslink.gov.uk

www.charitycommission.gov.uk.

www.co-operative.coop/corporate/sustainability/social-responsibility/

www.cciregulator.gov.uk.

www dh.ov.uk

www.fsa.gov.uk

www.ifb.org

www.iod.com

www.ocsr.org.uk

12 Emerging issues

'The world is becoming a smaller place,' is a term we are used to hearing. Through the internet, improved transport links and communication we can do business with companies operating on the other side of the world much more easily than ever before if it makes economic sense to do so.

As an individual travels to different countries, fewer differences are observed as the same shops, food outlets, banks and organizations operate in different countries using the same logos, brand names and procedures. Companies like McDonald's, HSBC etc appear on high streets in just about every country and every city visited throughout the world.

Barriers to trading between different countries are becoming easier in a number of areas around the world, such as the growth of trade areas (eg the European Union) that encourage the freeing up of trade and movement of individuals between countries.

Some global corporations have bigger financial clout than world banks and if they are allowed to grow unchecked they could have very detrimental impacts on the environment and economies in which they operate. With the growth of businesses worldwide and the impact of global brand names and businesses on employment levels, supply chains and customers affecting many countries, any failing of these large multinationals in a way observed with the likes of Enron and Arthur Andersen could be catastrophic.

In the United Kingdom, the Royal Bank of Scotland has already cost the British taxpayer £45bn to try to rescue the ailing bank due to the impact on so many individuals if it was allowed to fail. As companies become ever larger and more powerful the risk of failure and the need to control their activities becomes ever more important due to the effect it can have throughout so many different countries. But how do governments regulate companies that have bank balances larger than their own national banks?

One answer to this can be seen to be actions such as those taken by the European Union to standardize and regulate their members' activities. The European Union is considered as an example. It currently consists of 27 countries and has a population of nearly 500 million citizens (**www.eucountrylist.com**) with a growing list of candidate countries seeking to become full members. Of the 27 countries, 16 use the euro as their official currency, with a further five European Union countries also using the currency without formal agreements (**www.direct.gov.uk**). A number of International Accounting Standards (IAS) and International Financial Reporting Standards (IFRS) and related interpretations have been adopted by the European Union through the Commission Regulation (EC) No 1126/2008 of 3 November 2008, which adopts certain international accounting standards in accordance with regulation (EC) No 1606/2002 of the European Union Parliament and of the Council (**www.ec.europa.eu**), meaning that conventions to standardize accounting information in member countries exists.

Implications of things like the Lisbon Treaty also need to be considered. Signed by the Heads of State or Government of the 27 member states in Lisbon on 13 December 2007, it is designed to change the workings of the European Union and came into force on 1 December 2009. The aim of the Treaty is 'to complete the process started by the Treaty of Amsterdam (1997) and by the Treaty of Nice (2001) with a view to enhancing the efficiency and democratic legitimacy of the Union and to improving the coherence of its action'.

> The Treaty will provide the European Union with modern institutions and optimised working methods to tackle both efficiently and effectively today's challenges in today's world. In a rapidly changing world, Europeans look to the European Union to address issues such as globalisation, climatic and demographic changes, security and energy. The Treaty of Lisbon will reinforce democracy in the European Union and its capacity to promote the interests of its citizens on a day-to-day basis.
>
> (**www.europa.eu/lisbon_treaty**)

Agreements such as the Kyoto Protocol, which is an international agreement linked to the United Nations Framework Convention on Climate Change sets binding targets for 37 industrialized countries and the European Union community for reducing greenhouse gas emissions. Under the Protocol, countries' actual emissions have to be monitored and precise records have to be kept of the trades carried out. Reporting is done via the annual submission of inventories and national reports under the Protocol at regular intervals (**www.unfccc.int/kyoto_protocol**). International agreements like this linked to activities that feed into national measures that have to follow set formats can only put pressure on the need for more formalized and consistent means of reporting activities for businesses, as it should ensure national statistics are more efficiently and accurately reported and global businesses have reporting that can be understood in the majority of countries in which they operate.

However, how effective are examples such as these when the media is full of stories of corporate failure and inappropriate decision-making?

The excessive bonuses paid to directors of organizations are constantly making the headlines, with arguments of them not being linked to performance and setting poor examples of business conduct in today's ailing economies. The history and impact of corporate failures over the last 20 years, unchecked bonus payments, ever-increasing expectations of the need to continually review and improve auditing, reporting and disclosures and corporate governance procedures are commonplace and vital to protect economies and the communities living in them.

However, continual review and monitoring is essential and governments need to speed up their responses to ensure that they act responsibly to ensure that the ever-changing business world does not impact on our well-being and day-to-day lives in a detrimental way.

INDEX

(*italics* indicate a figure or table in the text)